A Hopeless Romantic

THE LIFE

ANONYMOUS

authorHOUSE®

AuthorHouse™ UK Ltd.
1663 Liberty Drive
Bloomington, IN 47403 USA
www.authorhouse.co.uk
Phone: 0800.197.4150

Published by AuthorHouse   04/10/2014

ISBN: 978-1-4969-7742-7 (sc)
ISBN: 978-1-4969-7741-0 (hc)
ISBN: 978-1-4969-7743-4 (e)

CONTENTS

A Hopeless Romantic, the life

I write this book at a time of deep depression in my life, having recently lost "my family".

I was rejected from the life to which I gave my whole, literally everything I had I've put into the last 11 months of my life, to be rejected, tossed aside and left suffering with severe depression dis-order.

My family was never my family, the woman, who I at this moment in time still love very deeply had a child from a previous relationship, I took this child into my life, with my whole.

My sibling tells me that I should just pull myself together and "get a grip". Well unfortunately I'm having difficulties doing that, so I feel the need to document my life, the reasons I am the way I am.

Why I'm left feeling so broken and hurt, pining for the love of my life to come back to me, that which I know she never will.

I mean no harm to anyone involved in these writings, they're merely me trying to come to terms with myself, my faults and my sorrows. I write this only as a way to express how truly messed up I am and how in me doing so, I hope to see my mistakes and be able to correct them.

I dedicate this book to the most amazing woman I've ever met, for her showing me a happy life, without my flaws, the woman I love with my whole. Unfortunately I couldn't see the love we had nor my faults and had to destroy the best thing that has ever happened to me, my love always, to you. I'm deeply sorry for the upset and hurt I've caused you, it was never my intentions, this is my way of explaining.

The Early Years— My earliest memories

The beginning of the life— How my life started

How to start, that's always a "writers" biggest problem . . .

Well I'm no author, writer, whatever you like really, I just have the overwhelming urge to write my thoughts out, to air my life. As I said in the preface, my sibling has told me that others have it far worse and I should just "get over it". Well this is my way of doing that.

Deep down I'm a hopeless romantic that just wants to love and be loved in return, I thought I had that until the 4th of January 2014, after some horrendous events my past finally caught up with me.

As a child, I had a very good life, I was born at home, moved when I was just 2 years old so have no memory of the first place I ever lived.

My parents provided for me, everything I wanted I had really, I lived in a very safe community, a small village in the Midlands, even the local news agents were accomodating towards the children, one of our "rituals" if you like was to go and buy penny sweets, they rarely checked the contents of the bag and "trusted" us to tell them how much we'd bought. So the challenge was to see how much we could get and say we only had "20p" or so, knowing full well had far more than that in the bag.

I think now, they tolerated that because it was such a small community, every knew everyone and life was good.

1

I also remember that I used to be able to ride up there and buy a pack of cigarettes for my Dad, at the age of just 6 or so, they knew they weren't for me and that I was going to take them home for my Dad.

I lived in a small Grove, there were only about 15 or so houses in the cul-de-sac where we lived, we knew almost everyone there, the odd house or two weren't too sociable but everyone got along extremely well.

The two houses prior to where I was, we got on extremely well with, we'd always be round each others places, having BBQs, all the "children" playing with each other, it was truly awesome.

I was constantly having a "girlfriend", we were always "on/off" but being so young it matters not, I tried to make her happy and we had some good times. We were the perfect childhood sweet hearts.

My sibling being 4 years my senior was friends with the elder children of the grove, however we always mixed together, never leaving anyone out. Playing lots of games, pool on either my Dads table, or a mates, ping pong at a mates, or just riding round the street or playing various games.

Sometimes we'd play dress up, round someone else's garage, one memory that amuses me now, I got told to dress up in a pink leotard—I must have looked quite the picture! I've never been a bulky person, quite the opposite, however it was all in good fun and even feeling very embarrassed, I still paraded myself wearing this quite ridiculous costume!

This chapter will be kind of brief, it is afterall from a very distant past, one that I've since covered several journeys, done much harm in my way but never intentionally. I'm as I said before currently in a state of severe depression, on medication which I've never really taken in my life (there will be mentions of when I have) and this book will be quite random, my thoughts are a bit all over the place but I shall do my best to keep in in chronological order.

THE EARLY YEARS—CONTINUING MY EARLY YEARS

As I've said, my early years are quite a distant memory for me, I've tried to eradicate many of the memories from my mind, to protect myself from the pain I suffered, there wasn't much pain—so my sibling tells me, it's all in my mind.

She had 4 years my senior, however I'm not there yet, we're still in the good years!

So my childhood, it was "perfect", our family was "perfect", my Dad had good jobs, worked for his Dad for some years, then for a French company, he always provided for us, there was nothing we didn't have.

All the neighbours were not jealous as such but in awe at what we had. My parents even tried to do their own business for a while, selling reflective wares, this was awesome!

I had loads of stickers to plaster all over my rucksack I used for school, the rucksack itself one of the wares, bright luminous pink! You couldn't miss me. Stickers everywhere, it was cool, no-one else had them.

So one of my earliest memories, having my bedroom re-decorated . . . I was a huge Thomas the Tank Engine fan, so what bed did I get . . . you guessed it, Thomas the freaking Tank Engine! I remember after going to pick one, that it would be awesome, I could lay "tracks" for it and have it take me round the house, to school, to my swimming, how my imagination used to run wild. The tracks in reality, were the wooden slats used to keep the mattress supported!

My bedroom was fully fitted, wardrobes, drawers, beside table, you name it I had it. I used to keep a small selection of stuffed toys on the headboard, one being a little hedgehog, another a bean stuffed frog,

I used to keep a "console" game device in my bedside cupboard, I say console because by todays standards, it would be laughable. It was given to me by a friend of my Dad, work mate, French guy, spent much time with him. It was enjoyable for me though, simple enough, just capture the butterflies, dual screened too, quite advanced for the time. I also kept in their the toys my Mums Dad gave to me, not electronic but little puzzle teasers, one being a pyramid with a spiral leading to the top. You had to rotate the "game" to get 3 metallic balls to slide up the spiral and get them in the hole at the top, I mastered this within days, could do it in 7 seconds on a good day.

Another was one of his "tricks" that being a box, containing a coin, you looked at the coin and I asked you to remember what it was, put the lid back on, took it off again and you were shocked that it wasn't the same coin! I say shocked, it was a cheap parlour trick, the original coin was hollow with a penny behind it, it was also metallic with the penny not so. As I slid the lid off for the first time, I slid it off, the second time, just pulled it straight off. not revealing the original coin stuck to it. That was fun for a while. Whilst my Mums parents obviously loved me, they never really showed this, yes the presents they gave me were awesome but going round there at weekends and such, they never expressed any emotion, sometimes maybe but this was something they'd done all their lives, they never really showed love to my Mum. To this end, I ended up having a preference to my Dads parents, they always lavished me with love and attention when I went round their, the grandmother always telling me what a "handsome boy you are, you'll make someone very happy one day".

So I'll now summarise the main events in my childhood years.

CHRISTMAS'—HOW GOOD ARE THEY!

So what child wouldn't remember their Christmas experiences!

Well they were always good! As I said my Dad had a good job, he worked hard, mostly away from home but he always made sure we had things we wanted.

I may be wrong in the ordering of these, it was a long time ago, however my Christmas presents that I most remember are as follows:

- A-Team "fortress"
- Go-Kart—self powered
- Optimus Prime!
- Black Chasis Technic Lego
- Mountain Bike—luminous pink no less!
- Another Technic lego—Red Race Car
- Stereo
- Atari Lynx

These are only the main presents from my parents, I may mention others . . .

Why do I remember just these ones, I don't know, they were awesome for me, the A-Team fortress had one let down with it though, the van I got for it didn't have the sliding door that the A-Team van did, oh well not to worry about that, I had a fortress to play with, lifts, rooms, the works, it was awesome! I remember playing in some kind of tent we had in the back garden, Jet our dog with me, I made a make shift lift and parachute for all the figures that came with it, truly awesome days. Being by myself playing with the things I loved, nothing was better. Jet being there was even better, he was a funny dog though!

He had his "pecking order", he was a rescue pup and never liked anyone with a bag, I remember coming back one day from some outing or other and he'd got out somehow—he was a bugger for that . . .

So he had the milkman, who petrified of dogs, pinned against the wall, soon as we turned up he stood his ground but took his orders to go in, not that he took orders often!

So his "pecking order" well me being the youngest, he always protected me first, then my sibling, the mother and finally the father, yet taking him for a walk, this order was reversed, he knew the hierarchy of the family but reversed it for protection, as I say a somewhat troubled dog but one that was very loyal none the less.

Sorry I digress, back to the Xmas presents.

The Go-Kart, was a Knight Rider themed one, how awesome was that! One problem though, Dad had got too pissed on Xmas eve and didn't manage to get it assembled correctly, I apparently stated, "Oh Santa must have had one too many and made a mistake here"—I don't recall making this comment but it appears it's had a profound effect on my life, this shall come later.

So I had a "Knight Rider" go-kart—after we finally fixed it up, was awesome, used to go the park and ride it down the "hill", that being a pile of dirt stacked under the slide to try and stop us hurting ourselves too much if we fell. I used that toy so much that it eventually broke, I was gutted that it couldn't be fixed . . . however shortly after that I got a present from the Dads parents, a motorized mini Rolls Royce!

My parents told me that I wasn't to let anyone else ride in it, so I didn't. I acted selfishly because they'd told me that anyone else could break it then it wouldn't be mine anymore, it would be junk.

I took this as anyone older than me, so used to let my friends of the same age have a go in it, it was awesome! Seeing them drive around in it, it having a "gearbox" and everything! Not sure if it did anything but it seemed to make a difference to "cruising speed". It wasn't to last though, it was constantly back for repair, the battery wouldn't hold its charge so the "garage" I kept it in, being the original packing, was constantly going back to repair. My Dads brother taking it most times since he had a Land Rover and space to carry it with.

So more digressions . . . I do apologise, things just come to me so I fill them out here, in my space, the internet (more on that later).

We get to Optimus Prime! How freakin' awesome was he, an Autobot, the saviour, one to look after all! I'd been collecting stickers for the "book", never did get it filled.

So I get Optimius Prime, it was all I'd wanted, turns out my Dad had literally driven all over the country to get one for me, it was the most desired present that year and he found one for me! Not only that but I got a load of other transformers, I could make pretend for hours on end now, content, the one thing I wanted most, I now had.

The Black Chasis, that makes me laugh, it took me nearly 2 months to learn how to pronounce the word, everyone asked me to say it "chasis" I couldn't. I would though and I did! It took me about a week to assemble it, it was very complex, I thoroughly enjoyed it though.

The gearbox was selectable and it changed the speed of the "pistons", it was truly wicked. I even got an electronic kit to go with it so I could hold the battery pack and make it move, couldn't steer it—that was another pack but it was good enough for me! I took it down and built it back up many times, each time getting faster.

So I've know grown up a bit, needing more activity and all my friends had mountain bikes . . .

This Xmas I get a pink 21 speed mountain bike!

I take it out the moment I get it and spend most the day cycling around, jumping off curbs, doing skids—much to the parents advice not to since it would wear the tires out! Did I care? No I was having fun! I shall return to this one later on.

The next year, I think, much the same as the Black Chasis, basically the same as but way more complex, this one took me nearly a month to build, I know had a nice collection of lego, lots of space themed ones, I had an entire moon base built, it was awesome, I spent my days playing with those.

4 years after my sister, I get a Sony stereo, it was awesome, lacked a CD player but what were CDs then, they'd only just come out, didn't need that, I rigged it up to a plug timer to wake me for school!

I had by this point also been given the "spare" room, again fully fitted, with my collection of ships, model toy cars in a display cabinet, those that I never opened, I was told they'd be more valuable if I just "appreciated them" so I didn't.

It always used to amuse me, after we'd finish opening our presents, Dad would immediately get the vacuum out to get all the bits off the floor, we could never just sit and relax until that was done, still new toys were there to be played with so what did I care what he was doing, he'd given me what I'd wanted.

So the Atari Lynx . . . well that needs to wait for one more filler.

THE XMAS BITS MISSING—MISSING BITS FROM THE XMAS LIST

Just to be complete with my depictions, I was never a patient child, the prime example of that was my sibling one year got me something that I couldn't work out what it was.

I've always had my brains about me and I couldn't figure this gift out, so one day I use a pen knife the father had given me to unwrap it, found out it was a diary and promptly sealed back up, without any trace, I was only about 8 at the time but I was still good enough then to make that happen.

This though made me feel terrible, I'd done something I shouldn't have, so come Xmas day I acted all surprised and I was truly grateful for the diary, I'd been meaning to write one for some time, it was again something my sibling did that I looked up to, wanted to do myself. Didn't really last though, I had nothing to write about really, playing games in the street, getting shouted at by the neighbours at the top of the street—that was a norm and we didn't go near them unless dared to, hell don't dare me, I've never turned one down in my life, it's simply not in me to do so!

So we have a nice Xmas, again the norm.

SWIMMING—THE LOVE TO HATE HOBBY

For most of my childhood, I participated in a swimming club, my first visit there still a vivid memory.

I dove into the pool and swam the whole length under water! Upon surfacing, the instructor asked me what kind of "stroke" was that? I'd used crawl style legs and breaststroke arms, oh well, I was here to learn how to do it properly.

Later in that session we tried diving again, I nose dived, splitting my nose open on the bottom of the pool, session over for me. I was prone to nose bleeds anyway, at one point it was considered to have it cauterized, thankfully that never happened. Many nights were spent though with a constant stream of blood flowing from it.

So I have this hobby, sometimes 6 times a week or more we'd go, me being born towards the end of the year, I was the youngest of the group, quite a change from school, where I was normally one of the eldest.

So over the years I complete all the awards I can, getting badges for my achievements, I still have those to this day. The greatest that you could complete in one session was the 5Km swim, I managed this at about the age of 10. It took me a lot longer than anyone else but I stuck to it, my Mum passing me much needed drinks, to stop the burning from the chlorine. My eyes red raw. They even had to close off one lane in the pool for me so they could open the rest of it to the public but I was damned if I was going to give up, there's just a few more lengths needed! I got there, absolutely exhausted, one of the few nights I slept well that night.

Every now and then the club would compete in galas, all over the county. I used to hate the thought of going to these—even going to the practises I used to protest but upon getting there I thoroughly enjoyed myself. In the galas I'd quite often end up competing against people 4 years my senior, I sometimes won, mostly coming in 3rd or so. I don't like to lose!

If my Mum wasn't able to take us, then we'd mostly not bother, since my Dad was never really interested in it, he'd go if we both insisted but we'd normally not bother with it.

I continued with this until about the age of 12, to this day I'm still a very competent swimmer, even in the sea with strong currents challenging me,

I have the greatest respect for the water, it can give much pleasure but also can be deadly.

One of the practises, after we'd finished we always used to have 10 minutes of play time. Big floats were given to us and the game was to see who could own the float. Flipping it over and conquering it was key. One time I got caught underneath the float, nothing I could do to escape it, every direction I went, it seemed to track me. I'm getting quite worried now, running out of air, how could I escape this? The only thing I could think of was to dive deeper and swam as fast as I could away from it, AIR! This small lesson, although it would have never ended with my drowning, taught me the respect that water deserves.

Because the private school I attended was very competitive, very big on sports, I used to get "asked" to compete for the school. We had sports afternoons on Wednesdays, I hated those, so I kinda struck an un-spoke deal, I'd do the swimming if I could be left alone on sports days, I did my homework instead. Even when I was practically forced to compete in the swimming events, because it was forced, I never tried my best, although I still normally won, it was against kids my own age and I had a huge advantage. So that kept the school happy with me at least.

So that's my swimming history, I made many friends through that, mostly girls, whom I usually fancied but never had the confidence to do anything about it, besides I had my sweetheart who I was always on and off with, come to think of it, I don't even think we kissed, just held hands, not even a peck . . . oh well it was fun at least.

BIKING—THE JOURNEYS ON WEEKENDS

So I had my lovely pink mountain bike, I also had a BMX, one that did "reverse pedal braking". That was awesome for doing skids on. Always needing to get new tyres for it since I'd wear them out . . . eventually I wore the bike out though, the handle bar mount welds became lose, it couldn't be fixed so it had to go.

Weekends we'd often go on a journey to another village, 15 miles away, 8 if we took the main road. An A road, maybe it was even a B road, it wasn't safe though, typical twisting narrow country road, so we mostly took the back roads.

We'd often do this, making a whole day of it, taking some food with us and enjoying messing around in the fields at the park there, there was also a pool there, where I used to swim, we'd sometimes go and have a dip and mess around in the pool.

I'd always make sure my bike was kept in pristine condition, constantly oiling the chain, tweaking the brakes to make sure they were almost touch sensitive, it was my pride and joy.

Sometimes we'd take a bike up to the old windmill, just to have a look around, or I'd often go to my grandparents (Dads side) and spend the afternoon with them, pouring them their scotch and soda, sometimes a gin and tonic. I'd usually be given a stones or two, it was awesome, they made me feel like a grown up.

Biking then was one of my main activities, even when I fell off it and nearly got ran over, it didn't stop me, I got back on it and rode home to tend to my injuries. I only fell because I was trying to be clever, riding with no hands, I tried to change the gear, not thinking the torque it would apply to the handlebars, causing me to career off into another biker, the car having to brake hard to avoid hitting us both.

Still, what doesn't kill you makes you stronger they say, straight back on it I was!

SUMMERS ABROAD—THE FUNS OF THE SUN

Most summers we'd go away on holiday for a fortnight, always a lavish affair, 4 or 5 star hotels. We usually went with friends who we met on a holiday one year, they became a fairly large part of our lives, coming round quite often.

So we'd go away on holiday, I was always responsible for "the booze bag", that which would be crammed with as much booze from the duty free as possible, we'd have a few drinks whilst awaiting to board, then continue to do so on the plane, me having a beer or sometimes a glass of wine or two.

The resorts we went to usually had many children the same ages, my sibling usually finding friends there instantly. I struggled to integrate, being so shy but usually got a friend or two, mostly girls, mostly who I developed crushes for. One in particular, a Scottish girl, I had a huge crush on, protecting her from the other boys by stopping them pushing her in the pool etc, I never had the courage to ask her out though, just "played it safe" by being friends.

I was constantly in the pool, wearing my hat and T-Shirt to stop me getting burnt. I was at home in the pool, confident, no-one else could match my swimming, well apart from my sibling, I was stronger though even though 4 years in junior.

We dined out most nights, rarely staying in the hotel, me sampling wide and varied foods, although I was a fussy eater. I'd pick something I liked and that would be all I'd eat, one year being kidneys and chips, my Mum having to ask for a bowl specially for me. Another year it was cucumbers, I did like my cucumbers! One time coming back from tesco, I was given one to hold on the way back, I ate the thing before we got home!

Lunch times we'd get coffee and donuts, I'd usually have a chocolate milkshake instead though. We travelled many places, Mallorca, Menorca, Malta, Hong Kong, France, Denmark, America just off the top of my head.

America was awesome, we went to Disney World, the Epoch centre and spent the rest of the time with friends. I'd spend most the time either in the pool or playing on the PC, the wheel of fortune being the most popular game.

Again we'd go out most evenings to dine, me sampling as much as I could, I was a bit older now and not having such a strict diet of the same thing. I tried such delights as snow crab, alligator tail amongst others.

Back at the home, we'd enjoy a drink in the evenings, me having a few lagers or glasses of wine.

SUMMERS AT HOME—HOME TIME PARTYING AT SUMMER TIME

Whilst not away, we'd always be doing something at home, usually BBQs if the weather permitted, even if it didn't—my Dad used to carry on regardless, huddling under a large umbrella.

Our BBQ was quite unique, it was made from the stump of an old oak tree. Lined with blast furnace lining to stop the wood from burning. My Dad never used to light it conventionally, he used petrol, liberally. One time I was playing with Jet and as he lit it, a jet of fire came out of one of the air holes and nearly burnt me, Mum was always going mad at him for doing this.

BBQs then were quite common, we'd have the neighbours round, friends of friends, it was always quite a big event. I'd be drinking Export 33 lagers, Dad used to bring them back from France when returning from work. There would always be a stack of them in the garage. After a BBQ one day, the holiday friends were round, so the kid and I asked if we could take some beers to the park with us, to play cricket. Since all the adults had had a skin full by this point, we were told to help ourselves, so we did.

Off to the park we went, pack of beer in tow, I remember this being the first time I got drunk, not even able to hit the cricket ball, I persisted though until the friend said enough was enough and we should head back, to bed for me!

Most times we'd all be in the cul-de-sac playing games and such, me and my sweetheart off and on. One summer she decided she was going to "go out" with the new kid that had moved in, we fell out over this, the boy and I, we almost had a fight but didn't, I've never fought in my life. I despise violence. To get my revenge though, one of the elder girls suggested I "date" one of their friends, a lovely fair haired girl, beautiful to look at. So she comes round and I greet her from the car, she gives me a kiss in front of my sweetheart, just a kiss on the lips, takes my hand and we go into my garden to chill for the afternoon. We carried this on for a few weeks, the jealousy obvious in my sweetheart so I called the whole charade off, to see my sweetheart again.

Her brother was 4 years our junior, however I think he looked up to me, he was always coming round asking if I could go out and play. This was quite annoying but he was a nice kid and we had some good times. One day we were helping my Dad defrost the garage "booze" fridge/freezer, we broke a huge chunk of ice out of the freezer part and decided to throw it in the air. I tossed it as high as I could manage, then ducked out the way. He stood their, transfixed on this block of ice, that came down to smash on his head! He ran back home crying for his Dad to then come and give me a bollocking. I explained it was an accident but none the less it was all my fault for being irresponsible. Oh well, we still remained friends.

One summer we had new neighbours move in, two beautiful girls for their daughters, I instantly took a shine to the elder one.

We'd play "spin the bottle" round one of the houses, I yearned for it to land on her, it did! So we vanish behind the garage to do "the kissing", I lost my bottle though so we just pretended we'd kissed, I never could find the courage to kiss anyone other than my sweetheart when we played that game, everyone knew there wasn't always going to be a kiss happening but it was exciting none the less. I always went out my way to try and help her, trying to gain her affections but always returned to my sweetheart.

So the summers were always fun, playing all sorts of games in the street, going for bike rides, having BBQs, watching videos late into the night, good times for everyone!

SCHOOL—THE JOYS OF SCHOOL

I attended a very good school from 3rd year juniors, got a part scholarship on entering the senior school.

I was promised I could build the go-kart I'd been designing for years if I got a full scholarship, I didn't get that, so instead I got an Atari ST 512, double dragon was with it! I'd spent many a time in the arcades playing the game, finally I could complete it.

The computer became the most prominent thing in my life from that moment, here was a gadget I could control and master, that which I did.

I did all my homework on it, well if I had any I could do on it. I didn't really participate much in lunch time breaks at school, instead preferring to get my homework done. Freeing up my evenings for gaming. I had it all planned out, even to the point of doing my homework on the lunch break just before it was due. I didn't struggle with any of it, well apart from the Latin and French, I've never been able to master a second language—spoken anyway, I've mastered a few programming languages.

School used to have a "prep book" that we were supposed to show our parents, who would then sign to say they'd seen our homework and it was done, I simply forged my Mums signature on it—they knew this but if they asked my Mum, she'd cover for me, I almost always did all my homework anyway, exceeding most the time.

I won an award for the neatest hand writing, something that would shock anyone who saw my writing now—I don't write, I type, I am a geek—this is what I do.

Still school was one of those love/hate things for me, I hated going but once there, I mostly enjoyed it. Those times were I didn't enjoy it, I'd go see the nurse with some "illness". This would always result in either me staying in the bed for the afternoon then going home, or more often than not, my Mum having to come and pick me up.

I generally kept my head down and just tried to do my best, trouble though it seems I have an affinity to and I'd sometimes end up with a detention, not often though. This wasn't actually a punishment for me though, it gave me time to do my homework.

When we did hockey on sports days, I was happy to participate in that. I had a stick to play with! That or basketball were the only ones I took part in, well gym days too, they were fun, playing with obstacles and rope climbing. I used to be able to scale the rope using just my arms, these were the fun parts of sport, rugby I didn't care for, nor football, those were the main things in sports days though.

I excelled at CDT, I love making things. We had to make a car one year, using plastic vacuum moulding. I put my best into making the chasis, the wooden template for the body to be formed with, it was pretty slick, stupid but I was proud of it. The teachers came round to inspect the work from time to time, they told me mine was excellent—how awesome! To then only be told it was a testament to how good their templates were to work from, I'd hardly followed any of the pre-designs, it was all my own work.

We made paper air planes using CAD and a etcher to mark the grooves, this was awesome, they flew for "miles". Key fobs was another we made, I made one with the Guinness symbol on it, I believe my mother still has that to this day.

Overall school was pretty good, I was always getting good grades, homework done in time, rarely in trouble. Had to get myself up and ready for the bus, 7:30 I had to be there for, never would I be hassled to get up and go, I'd always be ready in time. The odd times the bus wouldn't turn up, one of the parents would give us a lift. Getting home was a mission though, the bus didn't come back to the village, only about half way, so we used to have to get the train for the last leg. We were always pushing it to make the first train and often ended up running and jumping on as it was leaving, one time a friend had to literally drag me in, otherwise I'd have ended up falling and possibly getting ran over by the train.

The train station was a good mile away from home, so walking was needed, sometimes we'd get picked up but very rarely. All up hill too! We didn't mind though, we'd always have a laugh and a joke around, kept me fit anyway since I didn't participate in the sports.

DADS 40TH—THE 40TH AT HOME

My Dads 40th heads upon us, Halloween, we used to joke that he was evil because of this.

Naturally we're hosting a party for him, we're having it at home. Lots of friends and family come round, I'm barman for the evening, serving them all drinks from behind my Dads bar, the sign reading "I am the master of this house and I have my wives permission to say so".

This was cool, I was serving the adults the drinks, getting myself one every now and then. I was in charge of the music, so the selection was quite random.

Unbeknown to my Dad, they'd arranged a stripper—wow I thought as she came in. So she does a bit of a show, then sits on my Dads lap and tries to snog him. He didn't reciprocate though, later saying all he could think of was getting aids from her, even I knew you couldn't get aids like that, what a bigoted fool he can be at times.

The evening continues till late in the morning, everyone goes home, some stay over, it was an successful evening. The morning not so much fun though, everything to tidy up, so we all pitch in. House is put back in order quite promptly, my Dad not doing much since he has a hangover from hell. Still he gets the vacuum out, his prized possession and does his bit.

MUMS 40TH—THE BIRTHDAY PARTY!

It's coming up to my Mums 40th, obviously we've arranged a large party for her.

Friends from Hong Kong were over so I spend the evening with their son, him getting us pints of Old Speckled Hen. This was the second time I got drunk and drunk I got! I can't really remember much of the evening, just us sat talking, being stupid, as boys do.

I do remember the end of the evening though, suddenly I was in the toilets, throwing up! What was this I thought? Where had the last hours gone, back to the toilet again. My parents come to find me, laughing at me for being in such a state, saying "that'll teach you not to do that again!" How wrong could they be!

I wake the next day to feel like death warmed up, this was a new sensation for me, I drink lots of water, trying to rehydrate on the advice of my Dad. Later on he jokes asking if I want a beer, yes please! So I have a few beers with him watching TV, all a bit faded . . .

My first proper hangover after alcohol induced vomiting, this wasn't that bad, was it?

THE ATARI LYNX—WHERE IT ALL RUINED ME

So why does this one stick in my memory so much, it's the year that my life was destroyed.

All I'd known was this perfect life, happy parents, ok me and sibling argued but we always worked things out, she even had her own language with me when I was a child, I'd mumble and she'd know what I wanted, she "got" me.

One year after Xmas—she was addicted to chocolate, I charged her £1.50 for a minuscule bar of Dairy Milk, she paid cause she wanted it that bad . . . sorry off topic again.

So we're coming up to Xmas 1992, my parents have been arguing recently, something I'd never heard them do, I'm not entirely sure how to cope with this, we have the "perfect" family afterall.

My Mum comes to see me, I've re-arranged my room, I have my Atari 512 in prime position for late night gaming, that which I did so often with a mate. I only got the computer because I didn't get a 1ˢᵗ grade scholarship. If I had got that, I'd have been able to build my "own" Go-Kart! I failed there though so ended up with this computer instead. WOW, how much fun gaming could be, I'd spend hours with the neighbours children playing Double Dragon, Super Sprint, or more time with the family playing Tetris, or Arknoid, awesome times they were!

So here I am, with the old family TV in my room, taking prime space and Mum comes to talk to me, I'm already upset by this point because I've heard the argument, she tells me she's leaving but it's nothing to do with me, it's not my fault, she can't be with Dad any more.

My entire world is suddenly ripped away from me, she's going and doesn't know when she can come back to see me, if Dad will even allow that. Tears flow from me now recalling that memory. She leaves, I sob to myself, hysterically, how could this happen, everything we had was perfect. I can recall vividly the exact scenario.

My world has now ended my Mum has gone, as much as I know, forever.

My Dad comes to see me, tells me it's not his fault, nothing he could have done to prevent it but he still loves me, he leaves cause I can't talk.

I have to face school, I can't do that, everyone there knew the "good" life we had, how could I tell them it's all gone "Pete Tong" (sorry only learned that phrase some 3 years later).

So later on when I'm more "grown up" I learn this is because of his attitude, again I'll come back to this . . .

>Mum tells me she's left in March, I remember none of the months that passed, until Christmas<

So Christmas comes, Dad's there, Mum's not, my sister and I get up and go to see Dad, presents in sacks as they always were.

I've got my Atari Lynx, how awesome! It's lacking though, I've no mother there to see it, happiness soon replaced with sorrow.

I take my Dads advice to just enjoy the day, we'll get by, we've done so before—just him and I, I did afterall place a prank golf ball for him that vaporised when he hit it, he laughed at that. I'd also when we first started playing golf, clubbed him in the head with my 5 iron, I didn't mean to, he put the ball down for me and I just swung, him not telling me to wait until he'd moved out the way. 5 stitches he had to have, me being about 7 at the time, cementing my view on life not to harm anyone—I'd hurt my Dad, how could I do that?

Something I still hold to this day, I've never had a fight in my life, well apart from stupid things when I was very small, I couldn't even hurt a fly, or spider, spiders I'm particularly afraid off yet one night when I was 22, a mate saw one in my place and freaked out, I got over my fear that night, I picked up the spider and put it outside because her request was to kill it or remove it, just get it gone, I did that.

So that's a bit of my life, the first 12 years or so. Chapter one is now closed.

DESTRUCTION—THE BEGINNING OF THE DESTRUCTION—PART I

MY TURN TO DRINK—WHAT'S ULTIMATELY LEAD TO MY—HELL FUCK UPS

My parents split, I've just shared this, my "book" with my mum, "this" being the previous entries prior to this one. This is a new one for her too, I asked her for her thoughts, she's replied with "very good but my memory is out some".

No shit sherlock, I was 12! My Life was destroyed, everything I had **GONE**.

So what do I do, I follow the example I've seen from my Dad, he drank alot back then.

One night he goes to bed and tells me not to enter the room until the following morning, so I leave it at that an carry on watching TV.

My sister staying at her friends house, I forget the details, I just remember it being me and the father.

I feel something isn't right, so I go to investigate, I find a note, suicide! Not only is has my Mum gone from my life, my Dad's thinking to go for good. I ring the next but one neighbour, they come to console me and check on my Dad, he's OK it seems didn't take the pills he said he would. I'm crying my heart at out this point.

What do I next, hit the fridge and have a glass on wine, well a swig out the carton, that's what was there, my memories vivid . . .

So my Dad sits and tells me he wrote the note but after going to bed, couldn't carry it through, he couldn't hurt us that much.

By this point I'm really starting to slack off at school, my life is up and down, one moment my Dad's there, then he's off to work again, so Mum comes back to look after us, I didn't know whether I was coming or going. I couldn't face school so found any excuse to get sent home, as I've said, I'd become quite good at doing this.

So I decide I'm going to spend as much time with my Dad as I can, I go away with him to work for months, he'd let me drive around on the plant since it was private property, so by the time I was 13, I'd mastered the basics of driving.

I'd keep an eye out for the police when he was driving, using binoculars to scan ahead and behind us for them, so he could "put his foot down".

We'd eat either at the hotel or go out to a restaurant, me attending business meetings with him, always beer or wine, as much as I wanted. Someone complained to the hotel one day, I was too young to be drinking, well that didn't go down well. He was a regular there, so the staff just said to wait for her to go, my Dad didn't, he told her it was none of her business what we did.

The hotel even let me have drinks when I didn't go with my Dad to work, I'd sit and have a few beers, chatting away to the staff. Wow, I was actually chatting to people, me who's so shy. It didn't take me long to figure out that with a drink in, it me gave me Dutch courage.

So this starts to become the norm, we go out to work all day, come back and have something to eat and a few beers. I started a collection of different bottles, I was trying to sample them all. It dulled the pain of the parents splitting too. We go home one weekend, nothing particularly eventful had happened in all this time. Until we got home.

THINGS GET MESSY—
HOW QUICKLY THINGS TURN BAD

We're there one evening, Mum was round too, Dad had been drinking, I think I had joined in with him.

Things start to get heated between the two of them, Mums trying to walk out. I'm in bed at this point but the shouting is getting too much, I get up to tell them to pack it in. They're in the hallway.

Dad's stopping her from getting to the door to go, he threatens to punch her. I'm not having this, I dart between them and shout at him he's going to have to do me first, he won't get to her, I won't let it.

He backs down, Mum leaves, he glares at me. I stand my ground for once and tell him he was bang out of order, the one thing he's always told me is you never hit a woman. He starts to cry, telling me he didn't want to but he didn't want her leaving. He can't cope without her. We go into the lounge and have a few whiskeys, the TV as background noise. He pours his heart out to me telling me how it hurts, he just wants her back, will do anything she wants. I have no answers for him, I always have answers, why haven't I now I wonder? So I tell him to give her some space and give it time, things will work out.

We have another whiskey, he asks if I want a smoke? Hell no, that's disgusting, I'll have the drink though. We go to bed, both in tears.

CHANGES—EVERYTHING STARTS
TO CHANGE

The divorce is no imminent, no going back now. I don't know where my Mum's living, she comes round when she can, it's difficult though since Dad is still upset.

Mum tells me she'll let me know where she is when she's ready, my sibling knows, why can't I? Doesn't she trust me?

This goes on for sometime, eventually Mum picks me up one day after school and takes me to her lodgings, awesome I know where she is now, not 5 minutes walk from my school. The guy she's renting from is really nice, he welcomes me into his home and makes me feel like it's my home too.

For a brief period of time he was very active in my life, we went to a theme park with him and his niece/nephew, amongst other things, it was all very good. He made me laugh though—he kept an axe next to his seat in the car, "Just in case" he told me. Blimey I thought, don't want to mess with this guy—didn't strike me as the type though, he was always happy, had a very infectious laugh, it was awesome.

One day Mum comes to pick me up, she says she needs to talk to me about something. She's bee working two jobs now trying to make ends meet. She tells me she's met someone else, would I be prepared to meet him? What the hell is this, I thought there was still a chance our lives could be put back together. I'm not sure, I can tell she's obviously very fond of him. Where did you meet? At the pub she works at, he's a regular there, he asked her out a few times and she accepted.

I give it some time to think about it, ok why not, it's obvious things have changed for good now, let's see what this brings.

We go out for something to eat, a Ruby I believe, his son's there with his girlfriend. We have a good evening, this guy is really nice, he talks to me with respect, doesn't look down on me. We go home and they stay for a few drinks then leave. This was against the rules though, Dad had said no bringing anyone new back to the house, I had to keep quiet about that. I was asked though, I can't lie. Dad explodes at Mum, asking how she could do that, him drinking HIS whiskey. Shit times again.

I try to convince my Dad that he should move on, find someone else. I tell him to tell me if he has because that will make me feel happier that he has someone in his life again. He promises me that he will.

Weeks pass, still doing the same as usual, working with Dad, helping him out, doing his spreadsheets for him when I can. Then one weekend, he tells us that he's not going to be around so Mum can come over. By now the sibling is looking after me most of the time. Something isn't right though, we decide to go visit the grandparents, Dads side. We arrive in time for dinner. Who's this? A woman, with Dad?

Dad tries to explain it's just a friend, it's obvious she's not, why didn't he tell me, he promised me he would. So we sit and have a roast dinner, as the grandparents did mostly. The conversation turns to the new woman, she explains a bit about her, she has two children, one of which is slightly younger than myself and we'd make an ideal match, it turns to me. I glow red with embarrassment—how did this turn to me? So they all joke about how we'll end up being married, I've never even seen the girl, what the hell is going on here, I'm raging at the father still, he lied to me, he got caught out and now it's all on me, the standing joke.

The sibling and I leave, tell Mum that he's another woman in his life. Good she says, that should keep his attentions away from me, I'm happy with my new man.

The house is up for sale, there's not much interest in it though, my home, soon to be gone.

New families—A new life, new families

The house has been sold, the sibling and I go with Mum to look for a new one. Neither of us really like anything we see but we eventually settle on a terrace not far from where we were.

We'd decided that we wouldn't go far, to keep our friends. Mum's still working two jobs, I rarely see her. The sibling busy with her exams and friends, has no time for me. I see my friends as much as I can, them mostly coming over and us ordering pizza, we used to joke that we were the only ones keeping them in business, we ordered that often from them.

Mums new partner is round quite often, this is awesome, he's showing me how to do things, we fit the loft with boards, well he showed me how to do the first then left me to it. He's fitting a new bathroom, so I go over and help him, being trusted with the blow torch to join the copper piping.

He takes me clay pigeon shooting at the weekends, turns out my left eye is dominant so I have to shoot left handed, that would explain why I didn't do so well at it at school. We then have a lunch together and go home. He sees the problem with me drinking so stops himself, apart from when we go to the pub. I try to follow his example for a while but don't manage.

A friend rings me, there's a party going on, I should go, why not I figure. So off I go, meet my friend, have a chat with her parents as I always did, we got on nicely. We go to the party, lots of Scholl lager is there, the host being over 18 it wasn't a problem. I get stuck in.

There's several attractive ladies there but only one catches my eye, I see her making out with someone else so figure she's off limits. I need some Dutch courage first anyway, so get stuck in even harder. Someone I've never met before comes over to chat to me, he tells me he's feeling quite drunk, he's had 4 beers. Only 4 I reply, this is my 10th! He's 4 years my senior so takes that as a challenge and promptly drinks another 4 to try and catch up, then starts to look quite pale. He says he has to go see someone else, I find my girl friends. We have a laugh and a giggle, them telling me how many of the guys they've gotten off with. We joke about how it's difficult for blokes, given there's obvious signs to them being aroused, one of them tells me yeah, all it takes is a hand movement towards that area and disco! Something's awake!

I start talking to one of the other girls there, now it's obvious she was flirting with me but I didn't have the sight then, I just talked to her like I would normally, how foolish I was, she was lovely too!

The evening continues until it eventually has to come to an end, the parents have said 4o'clock is late enough. We walk the girls home, I always walked the girls home no matter what, after all, I'm a gentleman. We make sure all the girls are safely in their homes. We then go back, intending to keep the party going, just quietly so to keep the parents happy. Everyone is telling their stories of victory with the women, they ask me, "No-one" I reply. They all laugh. We carry on walking back until I find an opportunity to escape, home I head. How could I have not seen I had a chance with this lovely girl? Oh well, home at last, I stumble in, crawl up the stairs and put myself to bed.

NEW YEARS—A HAPPY NEW YEARS

The first new year in our new home, my sibling had plans to go out, Mum was working, so I invited the usual group of friends round, even though we'd only just all got together as a group, we bonded quite nicely. We get some beers in, order pizza as was the norm and listen to some music.

We have a good laugh for the evening, midnight comes, I have to ring Dad, I'm feeling quite drunk by now, I've mixed myself some cocktails, at a dare from the others and it was quite potent! So I'm on the phone to my Dad when I feel a familiar feeling rising in my throat, oh oh.

I try to make the conversation short, Dad though having more than a few drinks in him keeps on rambling on. I tell him I have to go. Shit, not going to make it, I raise my hand to cover my mouth, catching my tie in the process, damn it can't make it, tie ruined, well soiled at least.

The sibling returns with partner, they're laughing at me being in the toilet again, the partner cleans up my mess for me, muchas gracias! I then get upset, missing the life we had, I get told to pull myself together, the partner then picks me up and puts me outside, locking me out. Thanks.

They leave me for about 20 minutes, my friends have to leave so they let me back in, I go to bed, to wake with a hangover from hell the next day, easily solved, lots of water took in and I'm feeling almost normal again, starting to get the hang of this I think.

ENOUGH OF SCHOOL— I'M UNHAPPY WHERE I AM

I'm wanting to live with my Dad by this point, I've had some arguments with my Mum, I've not spoken to her for 6 months.

Although I've put a lot of work into decorating my room, I want to be with my Dad. I spent weeks preparing the room, I wanted to just have sky blue coloured walls, so had to pollyfill all the gaps, then meticulously sand it down to smooth surfaces. It took me two weeks.

School is now just something I have to do, a friend and I are dealing pornos to the other kids, another friend bought a gun in, he asked to put it in my locker since I had the strongest padlock there. We used it a couple of times to scare the prefixes when they were being power freaks with us. It was never loaded but it did the trick, how we didn't get reported for it, I'll never know.

I'm also making a nice earner out of my mate, he keeps on borrowing £1 from me, telling me he's going to pay me 50p interest each day, this is happening almost daily and once a week, he gets his allowance and pays me what he's promised me, happy days, snacks galore at the tuck shop for me and my mates!

Then one day, I just decided I couldn't face it any more. I'd had enough. I excused myself from my lesson, heading to the nurse. My mind was made up, I was going to live with my Dad.

I'd talked about this with Mum and she didn't think it was a good idea but if that's what I wanted to do then she'd back me. The nurse looks at me without surprise, "what today 'you'?". I can't even remember the excuse I gave her but it must have been good, next minute I was allowed to leave by myself to get the bus home, a massive weight felt like it had been lifted from my shoulders as I walked away from the school, to the bus stop. I knew I wasn't coming back here, ever.

I got the bus home, rang my Dad and told him of my decision. He was happy but said he didn't know if I could, since he didn't have a home and was lodging with new partner. He tells me he'll come back to talk with me.

We talk and it's agreed, his partner says that's fine, she's spoken with the school there and can get me into the same one as her children, at least I'll know some one there. I pack my things and go. Mum trying not to show her upset.

I now have 6 months before school starts, awesome times, new life, new beginnings.

NEW HOME—ANOTHER NEW HOME

As is the norm with me, my decision caused a lot of disturbances, I had to have the step brothers room, him sharing with his sister, the house was small but they were looking to get something bigger, to accommodate us all.

Things were good to start, got on with the step sister, she was hot, quite fancied her but knew that could never happen, she's a really kind caring person. The step brother was a bit more of a challenge, he used to bully me, even from the very starts, I guess trying to assert his domination, he tried it on with Dad a few times too, in jest to start . . .

School starts and I get the bus with the step siblings, I've heard a lot about a particular friend they have, one the step sister fancies to no end. I wonder who he is. I get directed to my class, the registered is called, no mention of this person yet I'm told he's in my class. Turns out his nickname was what they were using. We become friends.

School is ludicrously easy for me, I'm now in a state school, they put me in the bottom group for math, just to start to see what level I'm at. First lesson, work out the area of a rectangle . . . really, I'm used to doing algebra, quadratic equations, is this it, all they have to challenge me with?

I air my concerns after a week of this, I was doing this stuff 4 years earlier. It's decided I should be moved to the top set. Awesome, that means another lesson with a girl I've got my eye on.

Still the lessons aren't challenging me, a meeting is arranged and we speak with the headmistress and my teacher. They suggest I do my GCSE a year early then concentrate on A level math, since I'm obviously quite good at this math business. This is taken and we roll with it.

All my lessons are boring me, apart from the IT lessons and geography but everything I'm doing I've covered years before. I complete the entire 2 years of work for my geography in the first term. I have nothing to do so cause disruptions, when the teacher tells me off I retort with "well if you could give me some work to do, I'd do it". I'd do my other homeworks instead. All of it bar French was easy.

Geography was interesting given it wasn't based on knowledge or skill, this was just a group dumped into the room. I got teased by "The Lads" about if I was a virgin or not, I lied, making up a story about a friend from before, they were intrigued. They obviously were too but were lying also, it was the done thing. I let them linger on the thoughts for a few weeks until it was bought up again, I laughed in their faces telling them they'd fallen hook line and sinker for my scam!

The bullies tried it on with me, it never bothered me though, I used to turn what they'd say back on them, using my intelligence to make them look foolish in front of their friends, I did just enough to make the bully not understand me but his friends would. Worked wonders, kept me out of trouble. Well that was until one day the "lads" decided my bag was in need of "decorating", swear words galore were plastered all over it, I didn't mind though, they were at least accepting me into their circle.

It didn't take long before that got noticed, to the head mistress with me! Dad and partner in tow. For once my Dad proved to have something about him, he explained that surely this was a better way of me being accepted by the other kids than me having to fight them to gain that? She agreed and I was let off.

Things were looking up, the new house was coming soon . . .

MOVING—THE NEW HOUSE AND ITS TREASURE OF FUN

We finally move into our new home, a bungalow with loft conversion into two bedrooms, mine the furthest one but I had to go through the step brothers to get there.

We're moving in, everything's going nicely, I hear my Dad shout me so run to see what he needs, trying to jump over the double glazing runner for the patio door. What the hell's this, I see something bend in front of me, next thing I remember was being on the floor, everyone around me laughing at me. The door was closed and I'd bounced off it knocking myself out for a moment! Well that was funny, I chuckle but bugger me does my toe hurt, that took the brunt of the impact.

We start to decorate everywhere, it's coming on nicely, my room being a replica from the one I'd just moved from. I go out one night with some friends, have a few too many beers and decide it would be a good idea to finish off the painting, yeah right, that was wise, arse planted firmly in the paint tray! Oh well, these jeans were almost done with anyway, I crawl into bed and sleep it off.

The house is completed, all rooms as wanted, Dad has his little office, only accessible via a tiny door that you have to crawl through. I've extended the ring mains to include my room, so I have enough power for everything. Whilst doing that, I was deep in the crawl space, the step brother was supposed to be looking after the lunch, I hear shouting and get told to come here. The chip pan has caught on fire and the step brother is blaming me for it . . . I simply say I had no idea and I've been deep in the crawl space all morning, he gets another bollocking for lying.

Now the funs can begin! Dad has made it clear that if I ever have a party here whilst he's out, he'll turn a blind eye to it so long as there's no damage and his booze is left untouched—how freakin' awesome is that! We had up until that point been meeting at the shops and hiding out behind them to have a few beers.

I got introduced to some friends of my friend, they challenged me to a drinking contest—ok I say, where and when? We arrange a date, so I ask them what they'll be bringing. 6 cans they say. I laugh and tell them it's a joke and no way, I was contemplating 24 cans and a bottle of whiskey. They look ashamed at trying to challenge me. They didn't quite believe it until my mate said he could vouch I'd handle that much.

So the parties start, this was a great way to get popular at school, everyone wanted to party at the weekends, me again doing my homework at school so I had my time free at home. Everyone wanted an invite to my parties.

I had one the first year I was there, for my 15th. Plenty of booze was provided and given I was a big Pulp Fiction fan, the theme for me and my closest mates was a tux. I'd invited everyone I wanted to, things were going swimmingly. Then someone turned up who wasn't welcome, he was promptly ejected from the premises by my Dad, my mate was DJ'ing, he had the whole setup, it was an awesome night. It ended with me and my closest mates sharing a few bottles of red wine and some cheese. Them crashing out on my floor, the morning was fun—where's the water gone . . . .

CONTAINED—NOT ALLOWED TO VISIT MUM

We've moved and I've not seen my Mum for months now, I want to see her, I'm told I can't, I need to settle first.

I don't take this as a valid excuse, I argue back that a weekend won't harm, they're hearing none of it. So one night after we've been out for a meal, we sit and crack into the red wine and cheese, I ask again if I can go see my Mum, just before Christmas. I'm told again no.

I've had enough of this, I need to see my Mum, I left her in such a harsh way I need to see that she's ok and tell her I love her, I have no shoes on. Does that bother me, no. I storm out, in the rain intending to walk the 188 miles it was to her door. I decided instead to see a mate first and try and borrow a pair of trainers, my feet would have been a mess otherwise.

They let me in, the parents calling mine, they were friends with Dads partner beforehand so knew her. I get collected and bollocked once more. I explain how I'm feeling, that I just need to see my Mum to make sure she's ok, again my pleas rejected.

So there I am prisoned, not to worry though, things were about to start getting good!

PARTY TIME!—OH THE PARTIES I HELD

The parties, how fun they were, I had permission from my Dad so I took full advantage of it. He'd go out with his partner almost weekly, so every time he did, he'd let me know at least two days before and I handed out the invites, verbally of course.

The first one came and my mates and I are awaiting—wondering if anyone is going to come, sure enough they did, they did in droves! There was always a friends of friends welcome policy so most nights we'd end up with about 200 people in the house! They all respected me though, there was never any damage caused, no-one touched my Dads booze, they all bought their own, a lot of the time, there was left over to be added to the stock. I had a crawl space in my bedroom, that used to contain it all. We'd party hard all night, then I'd get a phone call from wherever the parental units were saying a taxi was ordered, everyone but my close mates would leave instantly and we'd break out the cleaning gear.

House was put back to normal in 15 minutes, everything spotless, we'd then be sat around the kitchen table when the units arrived home, them being allowed to smoke so did so, I still wasn't a smoker at this point.

We tried this tactic at another of my friends, however things never seemed to work right there, something always got broken or damaged, one thing that particularly stands out is their kitchen table, a very hot girl spilled her "White Lightning" on it, it stripped the lacquer off it! I swore from that day never to touch that shit!

So the parties continued on a weekly basis, some times the neighbours would come round and join in, it was awesome. Then one evening the step brother invites 4 of his friends, I tell them their not welcome, I'll call the police, he threatens to beat the shit out of me, so I relent.

They started drinking the untouched booze, opening bottles on the kitchen sides and causing no end of mayhem. The phone call came and we cleaned up the best we could, the damage was done though.

My uncle tried to hide the damage to the worktops in the kitchen but my Dad saw through him.

I got the bollocking of my life for it, 4 of his friends compared to over 200 of mine and they did more damage than anyone else combined. Still the parties were allowed to continue, my Dad cleared this with my away from his partner to make sure things were good with us.

VISIT ALLOWED!—
ALLOWED TO VISIT MY MUM

So finally they relent and say it's been long enough for me to go and see my Mum, she's now moved in with her partner.

So I hop on the train, anxious to see my Mum, get there and we enjoy a nice weekend, things were good, it stopped me feeling anxious and things were OK with us, she told me she understood why I wanted to be there, no longer was I having to cook, clean, do everything myself, like I had to when with her, only because she had to work so much to cover the costs but it wasn't my fault for wanting to be somewhere with "a full time mother".

That didn't bother me, the cooking, cleaning etc. It made me the person I am today, by the age of 13 I was fully independent, well as much as possible without being able to work. The choice I have is if I decide to look after myself, that which I tend to not do. I'm capable of it, hell my ex told me I missed my calling by not becoming a chef, there will be more on this later though.

So I see my Mum, all is good, everything is going well, parties are frequent, school is incredibly easy, I'm sitting back and just living life, enjoying every moment of it, what could possibly destroy this?

ARGUMENT CITY—THEY KEEP ON COMING

So things back at home with my Dad and partner aren't exactly peachy anymore, they argue it seems now constantly, they'll go out, come back and have some more drinks then start to argue.

Quite often I get dragged into this, one time the partner deciding that she was going to leave, I try to remain calm and act as impartial as I can, yet I can see the pain it's causing my Dad. She's now turned her attentions to me, so I ask her if she'd like to slap me, presenting my cheek for her to do so, she did, 5 times. I stepped back and told her well done, she'd let the anger out. She stormed off and slammed the door behind her, a glass door no-less. It shattered cutting her in several places on her face.

I had to applaud this, it was too comical. She storms off again and gets some things then drives off, leaving me and the Dad alone again.

We sit for hours talking, him asking me what he should do, drinks flowing freely, whatever I wanted, whiskey with milk I believe I was on at this point. The night has to come to an end though so we head to bed.

Water . . .

Cure the hangover, hey I'm getting good at this, I don't throw up anymore, I can cope with the hangovers, I can rid them quite easily. I have a confidence that I didn't have before with a drink, so what's the harm? I don't get nasty when I'm drunk, at least I hadn't up till now . . . . I shall explain more later on that. Things were awesome, ok, big fight but she'd come back, they'd made up so all was good again.

This routine happened probably on a monthly basis, sometimes I'd get more involved than I should, I was only trying to protect my Dad from being hurt, things were never happy there. I buried myself in whatever I could, usually involving my PC. My first PC, I got that before we moved, used all my savings to buy it, it was awesome. My Dad came home to have a look at it since I'd called him to say it had arrived, the look of horror on his face was amusing, see I'd pulled it all apart, I needed to find out how it functioned, so everything came out. I told him not to worry, I'd rebuild it, so I did, flawlessly.

KEEPING BUSY—THINGS TO KEEP MY MIND AWAY FROM THE TROUBLES

So I game, now though I'm less interested in the gaming side, I want it to do things for me, so I start looking into these "web page" things that are becoming quite popular. I use Front Page to design on visually, not that I have design skills but just so I could reverse engineer it.

I figure it out very easily, build a few mockup pages and leave it at that, although not for long . . .

Dad and I go to the supermarket where the step brother works, there's a guy there washing cars, so I ask if he needs any help, yes! Awesome! I've got my first job!

So my mates at school start taking the piss out of me because I'm washing cars on my weekends, till mid afternoon. They soon stopped laughing though when I showed them I was making up to £200 a weekend, £1.30 I used to get for each car, plus tips. "Like your car washing madam, soapy wash, rinse and leather down" was the phrase we used. It didn't take me long to master this either, within two weeks, I'd got it down to less than 3 minutes for an average sized car, spotless, everytime. Any complaints meant losing money and more importantly time wasted on something, so I made sure it was perfect.

So I'm spending my time at school doing my homework, coming home and playing around with things on my computer, the partner used to get me all sorts of software from work for me to try so I experimented around with it, deleting the windows registry one time, only to realise that was a huge mistake. I learned by making mistakes with it, to the point now, I'm a competent windows administrator, well up until that fiasco that is Windows 8. I'm doing my car washing at the weekends, making more money than I know what to do with. Partying hard and enjoying life, the arguments I'm ignoring and keeping out of.

I start to write a diary, the step brother is still constantly bullying me. I don't trust him, I install padlocks on my drawers but still don't feel that's enough, so I tear out each page of my diary and send it to my sister. I don't know if she read them, if she even kept them but I had to write my feelings down, as I am now doing again, this time though for the world to share.

The guys I wash cars with aren't exactly what you'd call the cream of the crop, they've had hard lives, bad areas they live in. Still they're good guys. I decide to ask him one day if he can get me a "tinth"—a bit of smoke, he agrees and comes over later that afternoon to give it to me, £15 it cost me. Friends and I go and get some rizla, I'm excited, something I've never done before, what's it going to do?

So we go back to mine, head upstairs to my room and try to work out how to roll a spliff . . . never done this before but how hard can it be? After several attempts I make something that somewhat resembles a spliff. We go out, to the fields to smoke it . . .

This is funny, I'm now finding everything very amusing, we all start giggling. We head back to mine. The parental units suspect something is up with us but dismiss it that we've had a drink.

I roll another before bed, smoke it out the window, I sleep for the first time I can remember.

SLEEP—ISSUES WITH SLEEPING

I've had problems with sleep from an early age, as a baby I'm told I used to be like clockwork, I'd wake every 4 hours for my feed but once I was put to bed, I'd sleep soundly, the opposite to my sibling.

My sibling always said there was no time for sleep, too much needed to be done, I however had no problems. Until about the age of 7 or 8. I then found my brain was too busy, thinking about the lessons at school, what more could I learn? I'd often stay up late at night, under my duvet with a torch reading the latest books from school. I even used to get all the coursework from WH-Smiths in advance and complete those, I'd be up until 5, then having to be out of bed by 06:30 at the latest. This continues to this day.

So I'd found this substance, that made me relaxed, happy, extremely giggly and most of all, it allowed me to sleep, that which I'd only otherwise managed with drink. It was nice, waking up without a hangover, I'd heard that mixing it with drink was bad and you'd "throw a whitey" so I avoided drinking with it. This didn't last long though, within a week, my Dad came up to my room, I'd just rolled myself the most perfect spliff to date, it was awesome! He enters so I hide it behind my back. He tells me to show him what it is I have, otherwise I'll burn my hand.

He was thinking it was just a cigarette, when I showed him, he was disgusted with me. Took my "supply" away and told me if he caught me again I'd be out the house.

No problem, I'd revert back to my drinking instead. Well at least when I knew there was a chance of being caught.

The parties continued, now though we had an extra ingredient to add to the mix, getting stoned! Sleep was becoming quite nice, I was dreaming again for the first time I could remember, nice dreams, of being happy. So I continued to smoke the weed, being extra careful to not get caught, I wasn't again.

My "boss" kept me supplied, I was earning more than enough, hell I was treating all my friends, if people didn't have any money for beer at the parties, I used to buy it for them, just trying to make sure we all had a good time. I didn't care for the money, it was just a means to enjoyment.

SUBSTANCE ABUSE—THE CONTINUATION OF ABUSING, NOW MORE!

So I now have another element to my arsenal of self abuse, substance abuse, this one though allowed me that which I sought so much—sleep. I found myself more suppliers, trying to expand on the range of the types I could get. Each one had different effects, sometimes the giggles, other times, just chilled out and relaxed, how different this was to the drink, I'd sit back and just relax, hours seemed to pass even though it was only minutes. I could think about things in peace.

So by now I'm rolling perfect spliffs, similar to the one pictured but I used to use small "skins" so needed three to make one, they were always perfect though. Never rolled a bad smoke, they were always smooth.

I smoked with my suppliers, mostly they'd ask me to roll up, since mine were much nicer smokes than theirs, something they'd done for years, something I'd only just started doing, yet I managed to do it so well.

So I tried a little test, how much could drink and smokes not mix, well for me it appears they could mix very well. I managed to remain in control no matter how much I drank or smoked, very, very rarely "throwing a whitey".

This then became a thing for me, how much could I push the limits of my body, my mind to remain in control. Friends used to question how I could do it, drinking so much, smoking so much, yet the next day, I'd be up ready and raring to go again! Mind over matter I told them, so long as my mind remained in control, I was capable of anything, this I did for about a year, always in control, the life of the party, hell most cases the host of the party, nothing could get me down, life was good.

I had my smokes, they helped the sleep, I had my beer, that gave me the confidence I sorely sought after, what more did I need, a girlfriend would be nice, that happened soon enough . . .

THE FIRST GIRLFRIEND—THE ONE I FIRST FELL IN LOVE WITH

I wanted a girlfriend, I had the reputation of being the mad one, always up for a party, never being sent down by anything, I was awesome. Nothing could stop me.

I find out my best mates sister is kinda interested in me, so I ask her out, at a party one night, booze induced confidence.

Things are a little messy around this stage of my life so the time frame might be wrong, it matters not though, just my thoughts are needed to be poured . . .

I'd fancied her from the moment I met her, she was and still is such a lovely person, very kind and compassionate, beautiful too! So we kiss for the first time, this being only my second kiss. My first being at Butlins a year previous, we went there for the step sisters dancing, I met random bird, we talked for hours before she finally asked me if I wanted to kiss her, me lacking the confidence to kiss her . . . I remember going back to the caravan we were staying in, doing the Dancing in the Rain, skip and clicking heals thing—I'd finally had a kiss, it was awesome!

So I now have a girlfriend, things are good, 15 and my first girlfriend that I'd actually kissed, she was a year younger than me though, who cares about that. I loved her.

We had a party one night at their house, the parental units turned up early, we didn't get our alert call, they went somewhere different. Something had to be done.

Everyone scrambled out the house, through the back patio doors, I confront the parents as they come through the door, they're suspicious—rightly so. So I ask if we can talk, they're taken aback by this. None the less though they entertain me and we head to the kitchen, me saying we have some beer in and I'd like to share that with them. Thus giving my friends time to clean up, so what could I say, something had to be said but what?

Being the hopeless romantic that I am, they know I'm dating their daughter, I tell them that I'm in love with her, they're shocked. I explain yes we're young but I really did see myself spending my life with her. Again they're speechless. The clean up process is almost complete by now.

I ask if they're ok with it and things are still going as they are, if they'd object to me marrying her, asking permission to. They again were shocked but they'd known me know for a year or two and liked me, they told me that would be fantastic.

Job done!

I never slept with this girl, things went pair shaped for us but nowhere near as bad as my life suddenly had to endure . . .

Devestation—
What killed a part of me

Part of me dying—How a little
part of me died, so very often

Things are all going great, I've a girlfriend, the sister of one of my best mates, what could be better, not a lot! My Dad was happy with his new partner, they were finally getting along, to a degree, my Mum was happy, they were going to get married, her asking me to give her away! Her Dad not being well enough to do it himself.

So I go to Scotland for my Mums wedding, kilt and all! It was awesome, obviously I didn't break tradition and went commando. Kilts are great, it gives the boys room to breath, I don't know why they never took off!

So we do the wedding, obviously lots of drink involved, I give my Mum away to her partner, one of the most awesome people I've ever known. Miss him dearly, he was the Dad I never had, now he was legally "My Dad". Freaking awesome!

How happy we all were, nothing could have been better, we went on a holiday to the Norfolk broads, sailing in a yacht, he taught me how to handle the boat, it was brilliant. We hit a road block though, a bridge! Well we managed to get the mast down to go under it but then getting the mast back up, that was a bugger, even with both of us trying, it wasn't happening. OK I'm not the beefiest person in the world but I can move things when I need to.

41

We had to call the rental agency, they sent a bloke out, within 30 seconds he's put the mast back up. How foolish did we feel. The holiday though was awesome, we used to stop where ever we were, find a pub and have some food, the husband and I would then play the fruit machines, we always won enough to cover the cost of the meal. He'd also sketch, I have one of those still, very dear to me. I don't display it though, I can't handle questions about it, it upsets me too much, I thought I was over that but it would appear not, my sessions with my therapist have revealed that, I've just had to have a little cry for him, this truly amazing person that was the Dad I never had, tried to show me the right way to do things, well a toast to you sir, you're awesome!

So you might have guessed, things didn't last.

I got woken one day, by the intercom, lazy Dad couldn't even be bothered to come up and see me in person, asking me to come down, there's a cup of tea waiting for me. I'm thinking this is a little odd, it's an hour earlier than usual but put my dressing gown on and head downstairs.

We sit at the table, them both looking very serious. I ask "What's up?"

They tell me mums partner has died, sudden heart attack last night. WTF I'm thinking, no I'm having a nightmare, I slap myself to make sure I'm awake.

I'm in a daze, this truly amazing person has gone, I have to see my Mum, she needs me. Dad tells me he's going to take me to the train station, he does but late, I almost miss my train. I don't get a ticket, this I'm used to by now since I was always late thanks to my Dad, it wasn't in his interest to get me there on time.

I board the train, without a valid ticket, something I'd done numerous times before. The last time I did this I was told I'd be fined, it was an "offence" to board without one. Well fuck you British Rail, I needed to be somewhere and you were the only way I could get there. I had the money in my pocket to pay for the ticket, just not enough time to purchase it. Thanks Dick!

So I'm sat on the train, wishing the conductor to come and see me, ask me for a ticket and reject my reasons for not having one. I wanted to release some anger, how could this have happened. I wanted for the first time in my life to hurt someone, I was feeling such a loss. I wanted him to come and see me, so I could smash his head through the window. I knew it would be hard to do, I'd tried before to put my fist through a windscreen, I failed, nearly broke my fingers, this time I wouldn't fail though, his head would be through that window.

Thankfully it didn't happen. I was picked up from the NEC train station and headed to mourn and mourn we did.

The funeral was quick in coming, a blur to me now, all I remember was afterwards, a friend coming to see if I was ok, I had no idea who it was, he was a friend of my sibling, I knew I did know him but couldn't recall who he was at the time. He gave me a hug, told me it would be OK. How could it, I'd just lost the only person that ever acted like a father to me?

I'd at this point only lost my great grandparents—never used to see them much anyway so what did it matter, I could cope with that, now though, my "new Dad" gone, rips me in pieces even now, he was only 54.

It couldn't get much worse than this surely? I'm just 15 now, my prime years to develop myself, suffering a great loss, I can get over it though, I'm awesome afterall, the life of the party, partyboy, mad 'you', I just have fun! Everyone loves me when I'm there, I listen to everyone, take on their problems and try and help them, this is afterall what I do, help others.

I'm now feeling very lost, I lost one of the only people that tried to help me, show me love for what it really was, without expectations, just take it as it comes, gone, wiped out my life. I shall return to this later on, Ouija board is what you need to look out for on that one.

IT GETS BETTER—HOW THE PAIN CONTINUED

Suffering the loss of my "Dad" I continued. My Mum rings me one day out the blue, asking if I'd mind her moving to Hong Kong, of course not, that would be awesome, free holidays to somewhere great!

She does so and rents the house to the afore mentioned friend, close friend, he's been great over the years.

So my Mums is off to Hong Kong, brilliant, went there as a baby but never remembered it, least I could now.

I do my GCSE in maths a year early as agreed and start studying for my A level math, this is getting quite hard now, it's new and I'd let my brain stagnate with everything else being so easy and covered years before.

The results come in, my step brother having sat all of his the same year.

I get an A*, whoot! I'm awesome, didn't even study for it. I ride home to tell the good news, I was late getting there, nervous at the result so I'd been out the night before, woke up with another hangover but that was fine, I was used to them now.

I walk in beaming, I've got a A* a year early, proud of my result. It's overshadowed though, my step brother having failed miserably at everything. I have to hide my excitement and glee. I continue seeing my girlfriend, having the party life, being "the bad boy". I was never nasty, always loving towards everyone, a lot of my male friends thought I was gay because of how loving I was towards everyone. I wasn't gay, just trying to be happy, giving love that I'd had taken so cruelly from me. I'd discussed this with my Mum before. A friend when I was growing up always acted very camp, that our parents used to joke about this, turned out later on he was, I asked if she ever thought that of me, no chance she tells me. Sure I love many of my friends who are male but I've never felt an attraction to them, not in that way. I've only ever felt for women, just unable to actually act out and be bold enough to talk to them in a way that could lead to something. Well I had a girlfriend now, that was awesome.

So this life continues, constant partying, I obtain some fake ID so we can get the lagers, wine, cider, anything we wanted. I was earning ~£200 a weekend, that would fund everyone, there was nothing anyone ever wanted that I couldn't provide for.

We get a phone call, my grandmother, Dads side is sick with cancer, heavy smoker all her life, no surprises there.

She's doing ok for a while then we get a phone call, doesn't look like she's going to make it the night. We decide to head there, Dad's had a drink, I've not at this point so I tell him I'll drive.

120mph, the Honda Accord he had at the time wouldn't do much more than that, I was going to make sure we saw her, at that speed, 188 miles would be done in 1 hour 34 minutes, there abouts, obviously I'd have to take into account speed cameras and such but fuck me, I'd get there the fastest way I could.

It was raining heavily, Dad fell asleep in the passenger seat, fuck this shit I think, need to get there for my Grandma. I put my foot down, tailgaiting, being very aggressive at driving.

I got my license just two months after my birthday of the 17th. I took my first test after just 28 days. I'd been driving for years anyway, I don't know why I failed the first, I shouldn't have, I drove flawlessly, the second, I even bounced the car over a curb and still passed, how does that work?

My first lesson was amusing, since I'd already been driving for 4 years now, I'd picked up my Dads bad habits, the instructor talked to my Dad afterwards, explaining this. I spent the entire first lesson with my arm resting on the window steering and the other on the gear stick. He told me that I'd be ready for my test within a month but thought we should cram 10 lessons in to get rid of my bad habits. I failed that and had to wait another month before trying again. It started raining, towards the end of this one, I'd never had rain so didn't remember where the wipers were, I knew we were heading back though, we pulled in just as it started to require wiper operations! I just passed, one more minor and I'd have failed, still a license at least!

It amused me that the instructor spoke to my Dad after my first lesson, he stated I had some bad habits, what did he mean?

I had my hand on the gear stick, the other arm resting on the window, cruising like a "rude boy". Hell I'd been doing this for 4 years, it was easy for me!

So I pass my test and now I'm hurtling down the M1 at 120+mph, screw the police, if they stop me I'll tell them I need to see my grandma before she dies. The rain is pouring down so heavily, I can barely see 10m in front of me, I let my instincts take over. I'm not even looking any longer, I don't see the road, I'm just driving, my Dads partner later tells me she almost shit her pants at the way I was driving. I was safe, I was in control. I had my instincts, they lead me through the rain.

I remember at one point I hit 130mph, the revs showing about 4.5K. The engine couldn't take much more of this. My Dad asleep next to me, his partner "shitting her pants" behind me and I. I might as well have had my eyes closed, the rain was heavy and relentless, visibility was virtually none existent. I trusted in myself though, I'd 4 years driving experience already, I knew the limits of the car, I tested my limits.

We arrive safely of course, otherwise I'd not be typing this now!

We go to see the grandmother, she's bad but the nurse is there, saying she'll be ok, awesome she's in my life still!

Things went downhill from here though she quickly went into deterioration passed within a few months.

No matter how I drove, I couldn't save her, she wasn't to be, **gone** another of my family gone, I still had my grandad and other grandparents though, I could cope!

I continue "studying" for my GCSE's, a friend used to come round, us telling my Dad that we were revising. Revision consisted of two bottles of red wine each and watching Pulp Fiction. I had the script for it too, we must have watched it hundreds of times, we knew the film inside out, the entire dialogue—everything about it.

I sit my GCSEs, knowing I've done pretty good in everything, it's decided that I'm continuing my maths and adding physics and chemistry to the list. ok sounds good, I like both of those.

THE STEP GRANDMA—
WELL ANOTHER ONE DOWN

Then after that, the new partners Mums passes, devastated again, we go for her wake, I eat duck, in memory of her, that's what she always ate, it was appreciated by the partner.

Another whom I loved deeply, ripped from my life.

MO—MY GRANDAD

So Mo, my Grandad is now the only person I have in my life that was precious, he was awesome.

We went to look at cars one day, he knew how to play the game, got his cheque book out on looking at a Ford Scorpio, the sale mans eye lit up, he had a sale, Mo was too good for that.

By now I'm smoking, I ferry my mates around in my car, me being the eldest and passing my test first, it's on me now, they all smoke in my car so I figure why not, gives me something to do whilst driving.

I've been smoking for a while whilst drinking with my mates, only when drink was involved though, I realise that yes I'm a smoker, time to buy my own—so I do. Fuck it. I'm a smoker now, 17 and I'm now a smoker, something I'd promised myself I would never do, oh well.

So Mo moves in with us, he's very ill, he lets me drive him everywhere, always treating me to lunch, dinner whatever, money was never a question for him, he loved me and I miss him so much, bless him, he's awesome! He gives me smokes when I'm broke, I'm never broke, I have a good job washing cars, he does the same for other step siblings, he's awesome, tears pour thinking about him.

He drove one day, realised he'd made a mistake so turned around, on a round-about! in the slip lane, he was truly self concerned, didn't give a shit, his family was all her cared about, I salute you Mo, you showed me a good way to go.

He lives with us for a few months, then the cancer takes over. I went to a few sessions with him, it was always bad news, he was doomed.

He stuck around though, long enough for me to get to University anyway, what a joy that was!

HONG KONG—ANOTHER VISIT TO MUM

I go to see my Mum in Hong Kong, we have a nice time, she treated me to everything, loads of new clothes, meals out at the top places, drinks everywhere, one place a small bottle of beer cost something like £8, still she had some money so it didn't matter, so long as we're happy.

I return home to find my girlfriend telling me she's got off with one of my mates whilst I was gone, she was laughing when she told me, my mate just grinning. She asked if I minded, well of course I did, that's it, we're over. I lose my mates for a while, isolating myself. Working every day over the holidays, earning stupid amounts!

I go out with the guys who I work with, turns out they spiked my drink with speed, wasn't happy about this, out to the town we go, I didn't have shoes on so wasn't allowed in the club, I asked sarcastically if I could take my trainers off and go in bare foot. I'm told to leave, my mates not realising that I'd been turned down, so I have to go home. They apologise the next day. Work continues to bring in more money, being spent as quick as I got it.

I start my A levels, these are trickier.

I've let my brain stagnate for the last year, chemistry isn't too bad but the math, that was proving hard to get my head around. Physics was just crazy, who uses this shit in the real world, I certainly couldn't see a use for it, oh well, I struggle through.

I have a big project to do, a whole week dedicated it, I get a call from my Mum, her Dad has passed. Another funeral to attend, I ask if I can delay my project for a week since I need some time to mourn, denied, just get on with it. Fine, I'll fail this one then.

I go out to see my Mum again in Hong Kong, I meet her work mates, how interesting there's a couple of very attractive young women there, they seem interested too . . .

We all go out for an evening, having my Dutch courage in me, I'm quite chatty with both of them, seems I have a choice this time, this is unreal! We're singing on the Karaoke, for once I'm actually sounding quite good, or at least that's what I'm thinking, a mate had given me some training and I was actually in harmony with this very lovely young woman.

We end up going out for drinks, just the two of us, we kiss, this is great. She comes back to the apartment with me, she tells me she doesn't trust herself, she wants to get to know me better. Me, virgin still tell her it's fine, I'll not get carried away, who was I kidding, myself. So we get carried away and she ends up jumping on top of me, this is going to happen I'm thinking, I must stop it, too late. Wow does this feel good. She stops, looking frustrated at me, telling me how I was supposed to stop her. I apologise and tell her I got carried away. We head into the bedroom to get some sleep. The next morning she tells me that she is ready, so we go at it again, being totally stupid and not having any protection but I didn't care, I was finding out what this sex business was all about. I think I might even be falling in love with this girl.

The following day, Mum confronts me, we'd been seen by the maid. Oops, an apology is in order there too then. That was embarrassing to do, had to be done though. She tells me it's ok, just be more discreet next time. Hah, how that wouldn't happen—not in that house though.

I get some money from Mum and get a taxi to go and meet her after work. We have a few drinks, mostly just walking round the town though, there were so many interesting places there, every turn you'd find something new.

She has to get the ferry home, so we walk to the harbour, there's a slightly secluded area although totally in plain site. We sit on the wall waiting for her ferry. We're kissing, all of a sudden my trousers are round my ankles, she's lifted her skirt and she's on top of me again, this is awesome.

Her ferry arrives but we continue, people are walking past and not even noticing, we weren't exactly quiet either. Hundreds of people walked past whilst we going at it, this was amazing. We finish up just in time for another ferry arriving.

We kiss passionately her telling me she might be falling for me as her last words. Off she goes, I'll see her tomorrow.

Creme are in town, I'm invited out with all the work mates, awesome, love Creme, have some albums back home. Mums mate sits me down to talk with me, she wants me to report back on her staff??? What they get up to, who drinks what, what drugs are taken, every little detail she wants to know about them. This is a bit out of order I'm thinking, they've been good enough to invite me out and I'm being to spy on them?? She then heads out for a holiday for her 40th, my step brother her new partner, from Mums second husband, my Dad that never was.

I turn up at one of their houses, 23:00, this is a bit late to start a night but it didn't matter, I was used to late nights. I've already had a few beers, I'm prepared. I'm offered a joint, I turn it down, I wasn't sure I could hide the signs from my Mum so didn't. That's one thing already that's going to be a strike against them, I can't do this. We go the club, it's awesome, the music is pumping, drinks are flowing, I'm dancing like an idiot but who cares, we're all having loads of fun.

One of the girls notices there's something bothering me so grabs my hand and takes me outside to talk. I can't hold it in any longer, I've never been good at lying, I can't lie, the only one I'd told was because I felt stupid and took my mates on a ride, I came clean though. So again I come clean, explain what I've been asked to do, assure her that nothing is going to be reported, I'll say I can't remember from drinking too much, this was always a valid excuse for me. That way I wouldn't really be lying.

It made no difference though, she went straight to her boss in rage.

It comes to 05:30, we leave the club and head to a bar for more drinks. We're all laughing and giggling, a truly awesome night. I'm starting to feel it though, I say I'm going to the toilet, then leave, getting a taxi home.

Mum wakes me the next morning asking me what the hell I've done, why did I blow the whistle on her mate. It wasn't fair to ask me that in the first place I explain. We argue for hours, I eventually leave, head to a local I know, get some smokes and sit drinking all night.

I return home, Mum still raging at me. I go to the balcony and light up a smoke. What am I doing? She asks. I tell her I've been smoking for a few months now and it's my life. She starts to rage again, I ignore her. I simply tell her it was not right, to ask me to spy on people showing me their hospitality, totally out of order. She ignores me.

The next day though, she asks if I want to go see Titanic, it was in the cinema. I figured this was her apology so we head out. The film was good, I excused myself half way though to have a crafty smoke. She asks me if I have, I ignore her.

The next few days pass, then the mate returns, furious with me. She lays into me, lashing me verbally how I've done something so stupid. I retort telling her it was not I who was stupid but she. She should never have placed me in that position and any reaction to it was her fault. She's almost steaming at this point. She hands me a letter and some money. There's a taxi outside, there's your plane ticket, go home.

How freakin' awesome is that, I've been ejected from a country! I'm not even allowed to say goodbye to my Mum. I ring her from the airport and tell her what's happened. She tells me she's not surprised, lots of love, see you soon.

I land and get a train, then taxi home. I ring a friend, too busy working, another, he's not in, can't get hold of anyone, finally I get hold of someone, we go the pub for a drink, I tell him about my experiences, we have a good laugh over it all.

Get home to a raging Dad, I've had enough of this, I was put in the wrong position and I'm getting blamed for my honesty? We argue for a bit then eventually calm down. He offers me a smoke, I look at him surprised, he tells me a mate has dropped me in but since he's a smoker, he can't be a hypocrite. So from now on, I'm allowed to smoke at home, this can't be so bad afterall.

Bed time comes, finish the drinks and off we go.

SUMMER JOBS—MORE MONEY

Friends come over to stay one whilst the parental units are away on a holiday. They run a local restaurant, ones who used to give me tip offs when the units were heading home. They ask me if I'd like to work there, it would be illegal since I wasn't yet 18 and would be needed to serve drinks but I agree. Besides the wife would do most the drink serving so I wouldn't have to do that, just waiting on the tables, washing up and such.

Can't refuse more work, it won't clash with my car washing, why not. This is fun, I find it hard asking people for their orders but it's got to be done, can't have a drink either since I have to drive. No Dutch courage here. I work here 3 or 4 week days and most weekends.

I get asked to do an afternoon, that's odd, we don't open during the days. Oh well off to work I go. They're having a one off meeting, a bunch of debt collectors need to discuss things. I was appalled at the conversation. They were telling tales of their "victories" with collections. One in particular was very proud how he'd taken away a small, 5 or 6 year olds playstation. They were despicable. One of them was my bosses father, he seemed just as sickened with these types of "victories".

I finish there for the day, cleaning up and head home, meet my mates and to the pub we go.

Having a BBQ one day, the boss rings me—he needs me tonight, crap I tell him, I've just had two pints, we're having a BBQ. I have to go. I try and refuse but he makes it clear, I have 2 hours. Now I'm stuck, lots of water. I drink water for 30 minutes, trying to flush the alcohol out of me. I knew it would be risky but 2 hours should just put me legal, fingers crossed.

I drive sensibly, observing all the rules of the road. Get there and it's fine. We have a good night, make a lot in tips, I diligently divide these at the end of the shift. I'm now pretty much running the show, the wife is pregnant so taking it easy. I'm managing the bar, doing all stock takes, washing the cutlery, waiting on tables, taking orders, bookings, meeting and greeting. Thankfully it was only a small place, 12 tables at most.

Some nights though we'd serve 100 heads or more. I could manage though, I got on well with the boss, we had a rhythm, we worked together. I sometimes had a chance to eat but it mostly was too busy to stop, soda water consumed by the bucket, had to keep hydrated, I was sweating lots. It was fun though, I was gaining more confidence with the customers. It no longer was such a hardship, it still took effort but I was getting there.

We'd often finish the night by getting a burger from the next door kebab shop, he didn't want to cook anymore, who could blame him. I got my mate a job there, we needed more help, the boss couldn't cope with the washing up any longer, so we took it in turns driving, although it was mostly me, I was still enjoying it and he didn't have his own car yet. This lasted for about 6 months, then I got a call, I was not needed that evening. Odd I thought, oh well I'll go tomorrow, again another call. How strange, oh well.

I'm back in with my old mates again, we've buried the past, my ex now dating my work mate from the restaurant. Happy days, we're all out at the night clubs most nights. One night we end in the town with the restaurant, me and mate decide to go and see them—see how they're doing.

I sit out the back with the boss, he's quiet tonight so doesn't have much to do, I ask him why he doesn't want me anymore. The wife saw me taking from the tip jar I was told! I'm stunned, how could they think that of me, I explain that the only thing I'd have been doing was getting change, the float was always low—if at all. He tells me he knows this but the wife is convinced of it so I can't work there. I'm deeply upset by this, I'm not a thief. We have a few drinks and I wish him well, the last to be seen of him.

A LEVELS YEAR 2—THE FINAL YEAR.

I finish the year, average results. This wasn't me but I was hurting, my heart wasn't in it anymore, those I loved and cared about were all done, only a few of them left now.

We go on holiday, as was now the custom again. This was a bit of a gamble though, Dad was beginning to get a bit tight with his cash, he had none he kept saying. Ok he's just bought a large house, can understand that, I don't need any from him anyway, I'm earning silly amounts and spending just as quick. So the gamble was we didn't know where we'd be staying.

We hit the jackpot! A friend of Dads was also there and he'd spent nearly 3 times for the same place. Good going Dad, we got a right deal!

We arrive and immediately I go and get some beer with my step brother, we spend the day looking around and drinking. We go back and get ready for the evening meal, we're both quite drunk at this point, we were actually getting on quite well for a change, it was nice.

We head out to the find parental units, they're having drinks with friends, so we approach. I attempt to stand but lose my footing and fall over, like a weeble, I bounced back up, straight away, well everyone thought this was hilarious, I vanished into the bush for a split second then was back. They couldn't stop laughing all evening about it. Least I could make them laugh.

Following day I spend in the pool, mostly paddling around on the li-lo, until I was kicked off it by the step brother, well he didn't learn that one quick enough, he had the advantage over me on land but not in the water, a few dunkings later and he was put in his place.

Few more drinks and out we go. Stop at a few places, there's always some kind of drinking game going on, we're game.

That's all we did, messed around in the pool, then went out in the evenings, I hooked up with someone one night, went back to her hotel and had some funs, I sneak out half way through the night, her mate had come in later on, now naked on the bed next to us. I'd managed a few hours of sleep at least.

The holiday ends, home we go and a final year of A levels to do, least the summer was good.

Dad has now setup business with the car washing guy, we have a unit to do valeting, this is great. I can now do a full valet in 40 minutes—at a push. I still work the car parks mostly though, more money to be had there.

I'm doing my studies, any free periods I have, I chip in at the unit, I've a car now, purchased from my sister, well Dad went halves, I had to find the other half, should have been easy but I spent everything as soon as I had it, Mo sneaked me the other half since the sibling was given the car and he thought it was wrong I had to buy it.

My heart really isn't into the studies, Chemistry is the only thing I'm enjoying, get on great with the teacher, he's a bit green but he's funny and has a passion for his work and the "kids" young adults now really. He'll come and find me and a couple of mates if we're late, he knows we're either in the pub or in my car having a smoke.

The first term finishes and I'm again just scraping by.

18TH—LEGALLY ALLOWED!

My 18th arrives, finally I'm legal to buy the booze!

We go out for a nice meal, a place we frequented and knew the staff there. Red wine was the order of the day, duck in honour of the step grandma. We finish there all having a good time, I compliment all the staff, including the chefs, you walked past there to get to the toilets, the food was, as always superb.

We're going out clubbing, the taxi takes us there, they don't let me in, saying I'm not old enough, well I have no ID, do they really think I'd have all these silly streamers hanging off me, a huge 18th badge if it really wasn't, I wasn't that desperate to go clubbing, I'd been doing it since I was 14 at the local club, they were quite lax so we managed to get in without troubles.

No worries then, we try the next, denied again. I'm quite frustrated by now, eventually we find one, my sister again decides to have a dig at me, telling me to slow down. It's MY birthday I retort, I can do what I want, she rages on me for a while, I just walk away, flag down a taxi and pull out my mobile.

I locate my mates with ease, they're at one of the uncles, brilliant, he's always a good laugh. I turn up, welcomed by everyone, they hadn't come with us earlier since it was a family event. Ah the whiskey comes out, just what I need. I tell them about my sibling, I ring and rage, quite nastily, the whiskey has kicked in now and I'm feeling angry. They're laughing at me, I calm down and we have a nice evening. I go back to one of my mates to stay, the exs place, have to crawl up the stairs, my legs have gone.

Morning comes, my word what a headache I've got, I can't move. I've heard nothing from my family so I ignore them, I'm more than welcome to stay here as long as I want I'm told by the family I'm staying with. The DTs kick in, I decide to ride these ones rather than having another drink, it had caused me to act totally out of character and I wasn't doing that again. I eventually ride the wave through and watch a film, Dazed and Confused, it was one we'd watched years before whilst getting stoned, happy times return to me. I barely sleep and get up the next morning, shower, thank them for their hospitality and head off for the walk of shame home.

I return, offering my apologies, I'm forgiven, not without a lecture though, no my apologies were never good enough without being lectured on. We have a few drinks whilst watching Bond on TV, preparing for the new year.

NEW YEARS II—ANOTHER NEW YEARS

We're having a huge party for new years, all my friends are coming, all the family friends are coming—friends of friends again, we had quite the reputation for our parties by now, the neighbours, even the ones we rarely spoke to were coming.

Dad having gotten a gas BBQ for Christmas decides he's going to cook using it. It's freezing outside but that doesn't stop us, preparations begin early in the day, so does the lager.

The guests all arrive, everything starts to come together. I'm behind the bar, my friends scattered around the house, it's all good. Everyone's happy.

Most of my mates from school turn up, including the girl who I'd fancied from day one. I'm wondering where my best mate is—something funny had just happened so off I go to find him. Located, in my Dads office, ontop of the girl he knew I had a massive crush on, not the first time he'd done this. Oh well I knew she fancied him, she'd told me previously, leave them to it, they've not noticed you.

The evening continues, eventually having to come to an end, I walk the girls home and return home, have a few whiskeys with my Dad, some smokes and we go to bed, drinking lots of water just before sleeping, I'd worked out this eased with the hangovers.

Anonymous

A LEVELS, LAST TWO TERMS—
THE FINAL TERMS OF COLLEGE

I continue with my studies, my work is still going well, I have money to do whatever I want, always helping my mates out when they had none. I'm preparing for my final exams now, I'm not feeling confident, I know I'll get a pass but will it be good enough for the University I want to go to?

I hear Nottingham has a 4:1 ratio of women to men, I've looked at a few but this one seemed good, for some reason, Chemical engineering was my chosen subject, I figured this would be lots of chemistry and building things, no-one gave me any advice on what to take. My chemistry teacher telling me this was a tough subject but he thought I had it in me to do well.

The exams come, I now know I've not done well enough, possibly just enough to get in but nothing like I should have, my "party life" had consumed too much of me, letting my brain stagnate, shit happens though and only myself to blame.

This time of my life is very cloudy, there's a few other things that have happened which impacted my life, here's a good a place as ever to put them.

I've another job—working at a conference and banqueting place, I got all my mates jobs there, found some good friends there and was basically in charge of all of them, that and a girl I worked with, she was a good mate, one I didn't have any issues with.

I'm also working at the pub next to the college, 3 jobs now, possibly 2, at some point around this stage in my life, Dad fell out with the car washing guy so that all went tits up. Either way I'm working as much as I can, to feed the supplies of booze and smokes. Treating my mates when they're short, they were always short.

At the conference place, I had full rein, I was getting good at this waiting business but my best place was behind the bar, I had a flow behind there, I'd hear the order and work out the best way to get it done, Guinness first but finished last, putting a 3 leaf clover in the head, if something is going to be done, I might as well do it right I told myself.

Me and the girl I befriended there would always flirt with each other, we knew nothing would ever happen but we both enjoyed it, it was good for my confidence but I knew it was fake, it never really sank in. We'd often sneak off for a few hours and sit in the cellar, helping ourselves to the booze, if I wasn't driving. I used to keep a pair of shoes in my car, couldn't drive in those so did so in my trainers. They stayed there though so I could just jump into my car at any notice and know I'd be prepared for work.

The pub I was working in was also helping boost my confidence, first night there as was tradition, I had to call last orders, my first attempt my boss laughed his head off at me, it was pathetic and he didn't even hear me, so I tried again. Since it was obvious I was so shy, the regulars used to pick on me—in a fun way though, my nick name being "wing nut", I didn't get it. After weeks the guy who started it told me, my ears! Well they are rather large, so I countered with, "they need to be so large to hear all your back stabbing ;-)" that got a good reception.

The partying is going strong, when I'm not working, life is pretty good, I'm never short of cash, if that does arise, I clean the house top to bottom, wash the cars, mow the lawns, whatever needed doing. I did this anyway, was the least I could do, my Dad worked away a lot and the step Mum worked long hours, I didn't expect anything back but it had become routine that me doing these things would end up in cash rewards! Bonus. I'm still mourning the losses though, I don't quite know how to get over them. I go see a tarot card reader, she tells me all sorts, it almost eases the pain. I knen my Dad had also seen her, so didn't quite trust her "readings", most of what she told me could have been gleaned from the father.

I got taken to the doctors, this was actually when I was about 15 or so, after just being caught with my joint. The Dad telling me it was for my acne. True I was suffering and did get some tablets, not to be mixed with alcohol! That thankfully saved me from being scared badly, this was at the insistence of my Mum, my Dad though wanted a blood test. Well I'm not stupid, he was checking to see if I was still smoking the weed. I also knew the doctor couldn't tell him anything, I made sure he knew I was aware of this and if the father was told anything, I'd take action. Nothing ever came from it, just my tablets, not to be mixed with alcohol—yeah right.

My step brother one night attacked my Dad, pulling his cigarette from his mouth telling him "I treated you like a father—how could you do this to me" then head butting him. A big fight then ensued. Me, upstairs in bed hearing a row, I wanted to go down and see what was up but didn't, not until I'd heard the door slam. My Dad bruised and bleeding, good job I hadn't come down, I think then I may have been capable of hitting someone, my step brother. He hurt my Dad and I'd have got revenge.

He's then forced to move out, they get him a place a few miles up the road, not far but far enough. I had to take him home one night. My two best mates in tow, we dropped him off and started the journey home, the intentions of heading to the pub, what else would we do? Driving back, I know the road quite well by now, I know there's a nasty bend coming up so I ease off the throttle. It's night time, full beams are on, another car is approaching so I switch to dipped, for a split second, I'm in total darkness.

I feel the wheel jolt. We've hit the curb, control is now lost, I know there's nothing I can do. I tell my friends to brace themselves. I push myself deep into the seat and put my other hand on the roof, forcing me in place. A tree is approaching fast, we impact, the car rolls and flips, air bags going off everywhere. We're on an angle, I can't get my door to open, the passenger side being lower than me, my mate gets out the passenger seat, I release my seatbelt and drop out the car. I release the seat and help my mate out.

We've landed on a rock, petrol tank first, I tell them both to run, fearing the car is going to explode. We reach the roadside and there's already someone there, an off duty police officer, she's already rang it in.

The police arrive and take details, I get breathalysed. I pass of course, green light, I don't drink and drive.

We get loaded into the "meat wagon", we're not criminals but it's the only place for us. Back to my place, I pour a whiskey to calm my nerves and then have to call the parental units, the police man needs to speak with them. I ring my Dad at the restaurant where I know he is, asking to speak with him.

He asks me what's wrong, so I tell him "Well I have some good news and some bad news, the good news is the airbags on the car work, the bad news, the car no longer does!" He thinks I'm joking, he's seen me drive, he knows I have full control of the vehicle. I pass the phone to the policeman, he's on his way home.

I wait for them, step mum comes in first and rages on me, I'd just written off her new car—was just two months old, oh thanks for asking if I'm ok, yeah I'm fine thanks, just have some burns on my arms where I got friction burns from the air bags. My Dad insists I get back in the car, so I'm not scared. We drive to where it happened, a little slower than usual but my confidence still there, I wasn't that shaken by it. We pass the scene, car now removed.

Turn around and show me what happened. I replay the incident, dictating what's going through my mind the previous time how "Now I dipped the lights". This time though, his headlights didn't have a split second of darkness. Home we go, whiskeys all round, it's been an eventful night, the officer who was off duty had explained we were lucky to have come out without more than a few scratches each, by rights we should have been dead. I always insisted seat belts were worn though, I'd even pulled over and stopped because I noticed someone had taken one off before now. I wasn't getting fined for one but also safety first!

There was also a birthday I went to with best mate number 2. His work mates 18th. They fixed me up with her as a joke on me, she was a lovely girl, just not someone I'd find attractive—sorry but I do have some levels . . .

Well they get me well plastered and arrange the fix, I'm all up for it now, we end up back at her house, talking with all the family, we go to bed and have fun, I sober up halfway through though thinking "what am I doing??" stop and say I'm tired. Sleep prevails for a few hours.

We get up the next day, best mate 2 is also there, on the floor, we didn't care much in those days! We know we need to escape, so make our excuses, work mostly and off we head, first stop, the pub, raging hangovers require another beer to fix.

Unbeknown to us we landed ourselves in the roughest pub in the area. We enter and get ourselves a drink. The landlord decides to play a little joke on us, gives us a raw saveloy each, I try to politely turn it down but I see from his look that I have to eat this. My friend happily gorges this raw meat down, I take one bite and have to run to the toilet, to vomit. I return and the whole pub is laughing happily at me. Oh well things aren't so bad, another few beers and we'll ring and get picked up.

He rings his parents, they come and collect us, furious that we hadn't let them know we were staying out and it was now mid afternoon, they were ready to call the police and report us as missing. We'd told them we were going out and might not be back until the following day. Oh well.

We get back to his, my parents there already. Step mum again rages on me, telling me how irresponsible I was. I tell her the same, we were going out and you knew we might not be coming home. They then go on about the pub we were in, how it wasn't safe there. I didn't feel frightened in there, I never start trouble so what did it matter. She rages more, I offer to drive since I'm drunk and she can have me arrested if I'm that much trouble for her. I get a slap, several again in return. My car is there so Dad tells me to get in it, we're going home, I'm "grounded". Yeah right, that won't last long.

The short journey home he was ranting and raving at me, belittling me about how I was in danger, I wasn't, there was no fear, ok the pub might have the reputation but I believe good in people and there wasn't trouble if we didn't start it. I take my seat belt off as we approach the house, open the door and tell him "You're not my father, you don't understand me" and jump out the car, roll to counter the speed we were doing, pick myself and run.

I take a route not drivable to my friends house from the conferencing place. She welcomes me in, I check to make sure I've not been followed. I have my bank card at least so can pay for my lodgings, she's more than happy to have me there as long as I want. This I know to be risky given her ex was the violent and jealous type, I could risk this though, I needed a few days to clear my head. We had a good laugh for a few days, we always did get on like a house on fire.

I realise it's time to face the units. Thank her and give her some money, she refuses to take it, telling me I'm more than welcome anytime. The walk home takes longer than I remember it taking me to get there, even though I took the direct route. I get home to be told I'm not welcome, they won't even let me in, they take me to stay with my step brother for a while. He of course loves this since I'm now in the same boat as him, I'd not head butted or hit anyone though, I never have.

They leave me festering for a few days, then I'm told I can come back. Ok forgiveness took a while this time. It did come though, I didn't want to cause them pain, my Dad telling me that me saying that after my visits to Hong Kong made him think that he really wasn't my Dad, I told him no, I was just angry with him for being so harsh on me, yes I made a small mistake but it really was trivial in the big picture of things.

Things are back to normal for a while, then I hold another party. Dad knows I'm doing this and tells me explicitly that if the step brother shows up, I'm to call the police instantly, he's not welcome at the house and he doesn't trust him.

So the party is in full swing, I have a hundred or so guests around, mate DJ'ing on his decks, he'd had them around mine for a while. The step brother shows up, I tell him he's not welcome, Fuck off! I ask him again to leave, otherwise I have to take action that's not good, Fuck off! Well I gave him a chance. The police are called. I await them outside. Word gets to him that they're on their way, he comes outside looking for, charges at me and tries to hit me, I grab his arm and twist him onto the ground, arm behind back and sit on him, my leg pressing into his neck, ensuring he can't move. I explain to him quite calmly I'm not going to fight him, I didn't want to call the police but I'm under orders, he'd hurt my Dad and I wasn't happy with him. His mate standing by. I tell him that I'm not trying to harm him but protect him, that's why I've not hit back (not that I wanted to anyway) and that the police were on their way and how would it look if we were brawling. I at this point shoot his mate a challenging look, did he want to have a go to, he'd tried in the past, was he willing to now? His mate says they should just leave—quickly. I ask the step brother if that's what he's going to do, leave quietly and I'll dismiss the police when they arrive, stating that you left quietly after you understood why you couldn't be there. He agrees, I release him. They run, to the fields, fearing being spotted by the police no doubt.

The police arrive, I give my report, I apologise for having to waste their time, he left when he realised but it took that action for him to leave. I don't like calling the police, I don't really have much trust for them but it had to be done.

LAST SUMMER AT HOME—
THE LAST OF LIVING AT HOME

So summer is upon me, I've passed my A levels, just 2 C's and 2 D's. Not my proudest achievements but good enough, I'm in to my University of choice. Nottingham, just a few more months and I'll be there.

There was never a question of if I wanted to go to University, it was just expected of me, so that's what I was doing.

I got another job, working for a monitor maker, in the factory. This was fun, the first few weeks there, I was asked to get all sorts of things, a left handed screw driver was the first, I was going to bite this one in the bud straight away!

I asked sure, I'll go get you one, would you like some sky hooks with that too, how about some tartan paint, left handed hammer too you must need, a whole load of the usual pranks. The lads realised that they weren't going to get one over on me that easy and accepted me. I wasn't too bothered about those though, this was only a time filler before University. I instead got in with the managers, sitting with them on lunch breaks, trying to learn from them. I didn't say much, just listened.

The pub I'm working at is getting a refurb, damn that's that job gone, oh well not long and I'll not be around here much longer. We have a final night, I'm working as was expected of me, the managers told me they loved me like a son, I'd always been their favourite worker since I joined, I finish my shift. A lock-in ensues, well since the beer was going to be thrown away—we tried to drink the lot, we all had a good laugh and joke, a very nice evening, a few tears were shed, they were moving miles away now, to try and turn another pub around, that which they did so well. I have a taxi called at 06:00, I have to be up for 06:30 for the factory job, to pick up my other mates since they don't have cars. This is one of the only times I knew I shouldn't have driven but did, I had layed off the drink hours previously, I knew I had to drive, 30 minutes of sleep though, I wasn't feeling good, mates picked up, we head to the monitor factory.

I got an easy job that day, as I did most days, unpacking the packaging! All I was required to do was open the container of Styrofoam packaging. Easy enough, split the plastic it was wrapped in with my knife and stack them on the loading rollers, ready for the guy to slap them either side of the monitor when it was raised, to be fed into the boxing machine, we worked out a method that worked for us both. We had it refined so much that I could quite often go and have a coffee whilst he worked with the stock pile of packing I'd present to him. Happy days, I hadn't had time to remedy my hangover so to the water cooler for me, stop the raging in the head.

It was a Friday so we only worked half the day. Thank god for that! I collect my mates, we sign out for the day and our usual ritual continued, to the pub! Food was ordered, large breakfasts all round, pints for all. Best mate number 2 did his usual, took all his pay out and promptly loaded up the slot machine with winnings for someone else. Every week he'd do this, we'd have a few pints there, then head home, sometimes I'd not drink but sometimes I would, leaving my car there until the next day. We'd then go home and get ready and hit the town, some night club or other, we were all 18 now so ID wasn't a problem.

Best mate 2 and I had another ritual, we always arrived at the clubs early, about 22:30, way before anyone else, so we'd hit the bar. Few whiskey chasers later and the club would be filling up, no-one would be dancing though, so we'd down the last of our pint when enough people were there, slam it on the bar, turn to look at each other, nod and hit the dance floor.

We were always the first there, we'd quite sternly walk into the middle of the dance floor, turn to face each other and again give a nod, then we let rip! Neither of us had any rhythm—we didn't care though, it did the job.

Within minutes the dance floor would be filled, we'd look around, nod again that the job was done and go find a table to sit at. Often times we'd get a bottle of champagne, all at my cost, he'd just filled the fruit machine up afterall and had no money for another week. We'd go and have a little dance once in a while but mostly just sat and drank. We were usually at the same place in each venue, people would come looking for us, knowing there would be an endless supply of drinks.

It was nice, having people come and find you in a club, they'd talk to us all evening, having a good laugh, it was happy times, me using as it an escape from the reality of the pain I was suffering. I had replacements now, no-one could replace those I'd lost though, I tried to lie to myself, succeeded for a while but it would always come back to bite me in the ass, always at the worst possible times too. Instead of facing my fears, I covered them with the "good life" the "bad boy", "party boy" anything to make people happy and want to be around me.

LEAVING HOME—TIME TO GO TO UNIVERSITY!

So it's coming up time to go to Uni . . . this is awesome, I'd been to see my sibling there a few times, how they liked to party!

I should have mentioned these times earlier, however now is a good a time as any. My plan to keep this structured by time has failed anyway, yet it's probably for the best it comes as it does, otherwise I'll leave things out . . .

So I visit my sibling a few times whilst they're at Uni, I always went prepared! I obtained the best weed I could from my car wash boss, more than enough to last me a month but I was intending on using the lot on just this weekend.

I'd arrive by train usually, picked up and taken to the dorms, stopping of course at the off license to get supplies, I had some already, mostly I'd smoke a few on the train down but now beer was needed. I'd get enough to last myself the night, I wasn't providing everything—hell I'd spent enough on the weed already.

It would usually just be a couple of nights, we'd go out for something to eat, then back to party, not always but they're the parts I remember.

The music would always be awesome, I'd find myself a comfy position for the night and constantly roll joints, I was fucking good at rolling by now, have a few puffs myself then pass it on, my sibling always giving me her sad look and shaking her head, as if to say what am I doing . . . I didn't care though, there were always people there that appreciated it, I'd constantly have someone to talk to.

I'd always have a beer in hand and if not a joint then a cigarette, I was unstoppable, as I've mentioned before the two don't usually mix but for me—I was in control of it.

I've always looked for approval from my sibling, very rarely obtained, this certainly didn't help but her peers appeared to be grateful, why would they not be, I was a machine . . . churning out joint after joint, drinking pint after pint. It was rare now for me to "throw a whitey". It happened a few times here though, I covered it well, slinking off to the bathroom, puking, drinking some water then focusing my mind, getting myself back in control. Once achieved back to the same, more punishment to myself, hiding away, being in control but not, forcing myself into states so I didn't have to think about the pain I was feeling still.

I could go on more about those visits but that's about the crux of them, always me, people commented lots how I was always doing "something" being smoking, spliff of cig, drinking, how could I keep on doing it. This just enforced my view I'm in control, no-one else can do what I'm doing, so pushed myself further, seeing if that control could be lost, very rare, not with others anyway, only when I got another girlfriend did my ugly side come out again, the Father in me.

Things are awesome though, I'm off to Uni! One small problem though, my Dad nor step Mum had bothered to ask me about sorting out accommodation, I assumed that was automatic, no-one had told me otherwise.

Two weeks before I'm due to start my term, it's realised I have no-where to stay, an emergency journey is in order. We head there that weekend, buy a load of newspapers and scan through, the Uni telling us everything they had was taken. There's nothing much that's within the budget, one place though looks promising, we go to visit.

It's above a shop, the shop keeper the owner, he tells us that we'll need to talk with the other flat mates, we go up to see about arranging that. They say they need to "interview" me and me alone, ok no problem, the parental units go for a coffee.

So they interview me, one of the first questions was "how do you feel about drugs?" Well that answer is quite obvious but I didn't want to let them know that straight away, so I told them it's a none issue for me, what people do to themselves is their choice and none of my business, I'm not a grass and believe it's wrong for people to not have the freedom to do what they wanted. Bingo, I'm in. Turns out most of them enjoy a spliff themselves, awesome!

So I move in the following weekend, packing all my stuff into my little Fiat Uno, I had to keep the choke open most the journey just to keep at 70mph on the motorway, the old little engine struggling, used nearly all the tank of petrol but I got there. My first place, ok shared but my first place I could call my own!

University year—The year—almost at Uni

Moving in—The start of my new home

So I arrive, get given my keys and start to unpack my stuff, I'm given the middle bedroom, it's big enough, carpet's a bit shit but I don't care, I've loads of new stuff, I can cover the damaged parts and it'll be cool!

First priority, get my new computer setup, I'd managed to convince my Dad I needed a new one for my studies, I truly did, my old one was showing its age now and wouldn't cope.

My new flat mates give me a hand moving some of my stuff into the house, they were so kind! They were at all stages, some in their 2nd year, some in their 3rd. They seemed cool though, one of the girls was particularly cool, very hippie and spaced out all the time, took a strong liking to her—as a friend.

So I get my room setup, big blowup chair covered with a blanket—had to prevent it getting rock burns and getting it a puncture—surprisingly that lasted years!

My computer on, I get some music from the other flat mates, Dj Shadow, Lamb, loads of stuff I'd never heard of but it was all awesome, exciting times faced me. I thanked my flat mates and got us all some drinks in appreciation, we had a good evening relaxing, I asked for a spliff and my request was granted, most of us got stoned, this was going to be happy years, I could find myself here I thought.

I go to the Uni the Monday to register, there were so many people, all so "green", not having a clue, I at least had the experiences of my past to take this in my stride, I registered, got a new bank account, even a credit card, I'd save that for emergencies I thought. I had an overdraft, just £250 for the first year, £600 for the second, then £1,600 for the final year, if I did a 4th year, it could be discussed and maybe upped to £2,500. WOW, ok all done, I have my ID card, registered, what's next?

I explore the campus for a while, check of my faculty, it looks interesting enough, lots of pipes, machines, equipment, a computer lab this is going to be cool.

It's getting on now so I do as my flat mates suggested, hit the student bar to find some friends, it was an unwritten rule that anyone who wasn't new wouldn't go there this night. So I go and have a few drinks, meet some people that are on the same course as me, we appear to get on, how cool is this! I'm starting to think though the drink isn't agreeing with me, I've hardly had anything compared to what I normally would, time to go, it's late now anyway, could do with a good sleep for a nice fresh start in the morning, my first day.

I walk home, not quite certain of where I need to be going, I'll find it though, I'm good with directions, I know roughly where I came from. That feeling I've not felt for some time emerges, hmm not good, I carry on walking, I tilt my head, whilst still walking and foam spews forth, the beer it seems wasn't right, they'd upped the gas, a cheap trick to sell more for less, how naughty. Still it doesn't phase me, the security guard asks if I'm ok, "Sure, no worries, just one too many" I banter back with him, smiling.

I get back to my new home—have a smoke with my new female friend and hit the bed. Sleep comes for the first time in many months, a full nights sleep, not entirely induced by drink either.

I wake feeling bright and fresh. The bathroom is a bit disgusting, I'll sort that this evening, time to get ready for my first day!

FIRST DAYS—THE FIRST DAYS AT UNI

I arrive bright and fresh, the first time for a while not having a hangover, brilliant, I can sort this out at last, find myself, get a degree and a nice job, I'd been told the starting wage was in the 40K region, this sounded very nice to me, I'd sort myself out for this, get my life on track, about time I thought.

I get to the lecture hall, first day was always different, we needed to be told what we were going to be doing, what we need, what the years ahead would mean. We're told this is the smallest group for some years, the course is particularly challenging, wicked I think, I could do with getting the brain going again, it's stagnated for many years. We get told the software we're expected to use, given our logins, told to change our password on first login, all standard practise really.

Our student loan scheme is explained, awesome more funds! We have a light lunch and get to know each other, one of the girls there, I find particularly cute, there's only two in the class, there's only a dozen or so of us total. She's cute though, I wonder if something could happen, day dreaming . . . I snap back.

The group is then left alone, teachers gone, we all start talking. There's some mention by some of them they're looking to "score", I don't say anything, just give him a nod, I was living with people that could help there but I wasn't willing to be that open, not yet anyway . . .

He notices and we walk away to talk, he wants a tinth, no worries I tell him, £15, I deliver it later that day to him, what—I'm now a drug dealer? No, I'm just helping out a new friend I convince myself.

So it's happy days all round, the course is proving hard, very hard, no-one had told me the amount of math it would involve, very hardcore, it was Greek to me but I'd figure it out, I did, things were going well. I had new friends, I was an instant hit with them all, I had access to anything they wanted, could provide for all of them, I was helping, doing my best, being there for others, accepted by them, this was what I wanted!

I cut out the beer for a while and focused on working. The new computer I had I realised wasn't really good enough, I arranged to sell it to my flat mate, using my full student loan to buy parts for a new one, build a computer for the first time myself, I'd re-assembled the one I first had so I could do this!

My parts came, no expense spared, a "massive" 25GB IBM deskstar hard drive, being the prized component, that and a voodoo card, gaming at last would be good, well much better than before. £250 on a case to put it all into, a supermicro S750A—it was awesome.

I built my new computer, getting a student license of windows 98 and NT 4.0, all legal, this was cool. Ok I had no money now, just £140 a month to live off but that was do-able. I'd chip in to the house fund £10 and the other £25 would cover my beer and weed.

Nope, needed more, I go job hunting, I find one, the pizza shop round the corner, literally 2 minutes walk, what could be better!

He didn't pay me though, I made pizzas, from scratch, everything made by hand, he had someone else to help him, so we'd go and game on the play station, him providing me my weed. We even arranged that we could have a special code for uni mates and we could hide some weed under the pizza, this was awesome I thought!

So I've now setup a new life, the beer I'm cutting out, not totally but less, lots of new friends and things are going well, I'm finding the studies hard but I'll get there, just need to focus, only smoke the weed before sleep, to guide me to that peaceful place, that which I found so hard to find.

FIRST TERM COMPLETES—
END OF THE FIRST TERM AT UNI

So everything is going well, I've everything I need/want/desire, friends around me who like me, they're not taking advantage of me, if anything they're giving me more than I'm giving them, this was a first.

There's a few issues with the people I'm living with but we openly debate things, there's no hard feelings, one of the guys is "straight edge" meaning he doesn't drink, smoke, eat meat or animal products, doesn't do drugs, what I find to be most boring but he's interesting and we debate many things, in a good way. He also doesn't drive though, something I'm ok with. Yet he's late for his band meeting one night and asks me to drive him there, this I find a bit hypocritical and call him on it, he tells me no, it's my choice to drive and he can use me for that, ok I guess. It doesn't bother me.

I buy myself one of these new fangled "CD Writers", awesome, I can copy stuff for my friends now, backup my stuff, the CDs are expensive, £1 each but not to worry. Mum is also back in the UK, she's fallen out with her friend, her "friend" having taken her for a metric f*** tonne of cash. She'll recover though, she's strong, she's always been there for me, I worry little about this, a little angry about how she's been treated but not my decisions, the friend had been there for a long time, didn't think she'd be capable of doing the things she has but she did, her loss.

We have a Christmas ball, Roman themed, so I go with a Toga as my dress, jeans on of course! The term is at an end, it's been interesting, I'm known as "the man" my phone has been a hotline for the last 3 months, I'm constantly making new friends, we did a pub crawl and added a dozen or more people to my mobile, I had a mobile, no-one else did . . .

So the party continues, I seek out the little cutey that I liked, she tells me she has a boyfriend back home, I tell her it won't work, I'd seen it many times before, she didn't believe me, I pushed a little then left it, she laughed and gave me a friendly kiss on the cheek, telling me I was so kind to her, that's all I wanted anyway, to be friends, the other girl of the class takes a shine to me, she's not my type but I'm more than up for being friends.

I leave the party, head home, for a smoke, then some sleep, that which suddenly is coming to me on a regular basis, without getting myself shit faced, well tonight I was, I couldn't walk straight, fell over a few times and struggled to get home, it'd been a fun night, everyone was happy, I'd just got a bit carried away with my beers, oh well nothing some sleep won't cure!

Morning comes, my word, I can't move. My head is destroyed, I lay in bed wishing to make it better. The door knocks, I'm the only one in, I find the strength to get out of bed, only to open the door and have to excuse myself, to the toilet, vomit ensues. I return to the stunned visitor, explain no-one is in, I'm not very well, excuse me, I need to hit the bathroom again, then bed. I sleep. I wake feeling better. The term is now done, I've not done brilliantly but I'm passing at least, this is hard for me, my brain is still struggling to revive from stagnation, I'll force it—first though it's CHRISTMAS!

CHRISTMAS AWAY FROM UNI— THE CHRISTMAS SPENT AT MUMS

I go to my Mums for the Christmas holidays, we have some good times.

I get myself a part time job working at the hotel my sibling used to work at, I do well there, to a degree.

I offer to do the "splits", that's what my sibling did and if sibling could do it so could I. They agree and I start work. I'm there for 06:00 till 15:30 or so, then back again for 18:00 till 02:00, long day but I can cope, sibling did this so therefore I can, I've always one upped on the sibling.

One night I get sent home early, I'm too tired, not to worry. I return home, Mum there with step son, I have a few beers. I start to get a bit gobby, I get the "count".

Not sure if I've mentioned this but Mum always has this power over me, no matter my age, she starts to count, 1 . . . 2 . . . . I never found out what happens when she gets to 3, I'm in bed by then.

Christmas comes, I'm working the eve, the night is good, the place looks lovely, everyone has a nice night, I then get lumbered with the bar shift, knowing I'm working the next morning, staying at the hotel. I have to entertain some guests, they insist I match them drink for drink. I try to tell them I can't, I have to work so they say they'll go to bed then. I can't allow this, money away from the hotel, no chance, I agree.

I get woken the next day, hangover raging strong, I get ready and turn up for work, have an argument with my boss. We get over it quickly. The day goes smoothly, apart from some random guy returning two £500 bottles of champagne saying they were off! We tested them, nope he just didn't appreciate the finer things of life, obvious he's saved up for this event for his family but didn't have the taste, we dismiss it. I return home, open presents, have a few drinks and hit the bed, I'm knackered. Sleep comes again, this is pleasant, I enjoy my sleep but it comes so rarely to me . . .

2ND UNI TERM—THE UNIVERSITY CONTINUES

The term commences, I remember now the party before the end of the Christmas breakup, the reason I was so hammered, we started partying way before the party.

I went round some mates place, plenty of weed, a 24 pack of beer, we drank the lot before we went out, we also smoke a hell of a lot of weed, me making a make shift bong, me being the only one able to take the whole hit—several times. Everyone was in awe at my ability to keep going, several people elder than me dropped out cause they were too wasted, I kept my control, kept on going, pushing it further, surely I had a limit?

This was tested on the "Annual pub crawl" 14 pubs, the guys had to have a pint in each place, the ladies allowed a half, a pint? I counter that by having 2! I survive the evening, there's no stopping me!

I endured the evening, it was a good one, I finished it off by returning home after taking quite a long path of weaving around on the path, falling into the road a few times and rolling a nice large joint, that finished me off, sleep prevailed, oh the sleep I was enjoying so much.

All my fears I'd buried deep away, my losses I was forgetting about, my life was good, I was doing Ok, not brilliantly at Uni but this was hard, I could accept that, my fears though, my losses they were buried deep, deep down, they weren't coming back. I was going to graduate, be a success, be awesome!

(Awesome by the way is only a word I started to use later in my life, it feels appropriate to use it now though.)

I had friends, was always asked out for nights, was the life of the party, never shy of a penny, what more could I ask for—well something I didn't want came and bit me hard.

I'm chilling out one night, I don't have any weed so I game instead, maybe not even having a few beers, my mobile rings? No-one rings that, it's emergencies only, it's the Father.

Mo has passed, he hasn't been doing well for a while but I'd tried to put that in my past, bury it, deep.

I walk out my room dazed, my girl mate in the flat comes to see me asking what's up, she has a joint in hand, I tell her. She hands me the joint and tells me to finish it, she understands that I need it, I smoke it, the pain doesn't go away though. I'm gutted, the last of my family is now gone, just my Dad, Mum, Sister and one remaining grandparent remain, one that never showed me anything.

I retreat to my room, crying, the mate comes in again and gives me another joint, I accept willingly. Something has to make this pain go away, everything has risen from that deep place I put it, all of it—flooding back, Mo, the person who I got on so well with, now gone. I'm lost.

I lose interest in my study, how can this happen, I've never been religious but how, there is no logic to this world, it's ripped everything from me, all gone. I go and get some beers, the pain needs to be nulled, I consume 8 cans in less than 2 hours. My female friend trying to tell me it's going to be ok, how can it be ok, nothing much is left for me.

I now cry recalling the memory, that finished it for me, I didn't really want the course I was on, I only wanted to do it because I could prove I could. I decided then it was enough. I isolated myself once more. Carried on my learning on HTML, making stupid web pages that served no purpose, just because I could. I increased my drinking to almost lethal levels, my smoking too, money was now short though so it was rolling tobacco.

I didn't go back to Uni after this, for two months I continued, asking why, how, this shouldn't happen, yes being stupid, people die everyday but I was barely 19 and I'd lost almost everyone I cared about, all in such a short space of time, my head couldn't make sense of it, I'd seen so much, dealt with so much, I thought I was prepared but no, it destroyed me.

I eventually get an email from the uni . . .

THE EMAIL—THE EMAIL I GET FROM THE UNI

I say my goodbyes to Mo, although he probably didn't show me much right in this world, he loved me without condition, another one, **gone**.

I get an email from the Uni, asking why I've not showed up for the last few months, I have to go and explain myself.

I go there, see my tutor, tell him of my losses, breaking down in tears. I'm at this point deeply in debt to the government, thanks to the new rules for Uni funding. He tells me he understands, the course isn't for me, they'll keep me on the books but I can't work full time, not yet, I have to wait till the years end he'll mark me as failing, ESCAPE!

I'm sure he broke a few rules there, I can't even recall his name but he understood where I was at. I had to keep low for the next few months, so I did, I borrowed when I had to—my flat mates girlfriend being particularly kind to me, I tip my hat to her, she shared the same name as my second girlfriend, she lent me over £1000, that which I had to repay when requested, that came soon enough.

I had a building society account, £1,300 I had in there, I took it all out to repay her, they were off to Japan, they needed it, fair dos, they'd been good to me.

Eventually I can look for work, the term has ended, I've done nothing but drink myself to sleep, all the pain coming back, being a total wreck, stupid but I couldn't cope, my teenage years flooding back, the divorce, everything, it destroyed me.

I go for an interview, I think it's gone well, I get a call the following day or so, I've not got it. I leave it, look for more work. I need work, money is low, almost none existent.

I decide to ring them back, I speak with the guy that interviewed me, I ask him why I didn't get the job, what could I do to better myself for the next interview I faced? He tells me matter of factly that it wasn't anything I'd done wrong, just they found someone more suited. OK, I take this, I'm not that perfect afterall.

I seek more work.

Nothing is coming, I'm running out of money now, I have to ring the Mum, she comes up and buys me loads of food, no beer though, I shouldn't be drinking. Not a problem, I'm not—I need to focus. I find a way though, I always did, I needed to dull the pain that was ripping through me, all my loved ones gone, well most of them, I had a few left but not all of them, I couldn't change that, the drink would null that pain.

I get a phone call, I've got the job! Awesome, I get myself into my suit and a haircut, all looking good, go to see them to make sure it's ok. I ask what changed? Get told that the other guy turned out to be a liar and not what he said and because I'd called to ask what I could do to better myself, they thought me the right guy for the job! Awesome! I've got a job, £12,500 a year, not bad for a 19 year old in 1999! Help desk work, or hell desk depending on how you look at it—it was cushty though, I started, learning as much as I could!.

THE CAREER—THE CAREER STARTS

I walk to work most days, it saves on petrol for a start but my car is also showing its age, it was never good when I first got it, the brakes for a start were always shoddy at best, I had to pump them to make them work. I took it to be looked at many times but they could never find a problem, it was fine, just my luck!

I get welcomed into the company, there at the time being 5 other staff there, this is nice, they're friendly, we work over continents, there's a whole other office I have no idea about, two in fact, I get introduced to them also. I find an affinity instantly with one of the guys from the Canadian office, we just hit it off, think the same, have the same view on life. He shows me some site on the internet, such as http://slashdot.org/. It's not the same as it used to be, gone way down hill since then, being taken over by dice.com now, still it at the time was awesome.

I bought my own domain name—wanting to do more with this internet thing, it was truly awesome.

I mastered DNS lookups, the thing that converts http://www.foo.com/ to the IP address xxx.xxx.xxx.xx. that the host requires, it was awesome, all this new technology!

I was assigned to be technical document writer for the software we produced, I had no experience in this but I'd give it a go! I documented the changes, how to use the software, produced manuals, I was in my element, I'd found my home.

I continued my smokes, nipping out for lunch for a quick spliff, everyone knew I was doing this, it bothered them not though. I was preforming, doing more than they expected of me and more, I was unstoppable!

I'd also got myself a job at the local hotel, quite a posh one again, again I was doing split shifts there, working my balls off, I had debts now, I needed to clear them. One of the girls I worked with, you guessed it, I had a crush on, used to pick her up and take her to work. This was a hectic time in my life, things needed to be sorted. My debts cleared. I needed to stand on my own two feet. I would—I just needed a bit of time.

So I'm working two jobs again, back to what I knew, work work work, no playtime, things were good. I was drained constantly but the work kept me going, I thrived off it, doing good for so many people!

I met the guy who started cable and wireless, I think, at the hotel, we were talking one night at the bar, I didn't know who he was, he was just a customer, respect first and foremost, I'm the lowly worker afterall. I spill his drink and offer to refill it, coming out my wages, it was my mistake—I had to. He told me no don't be so stupid, what would I like to drink? I say a red bull please. I was living off these, that and Pro+—those tablets that kept me going till I crashed. So I pour him another red wine, my opening my can of red bull, duly noted on the tab.

He explains to me how he started his company by finding a scrap PBX system in the skip one night whilst drunk, took it home and toyed with it, getting his friends to use it too, it eventually evolved into NTL, now Virgin, how I've seen many people in my travels . . .

It's interesting to me now though how it was a "PBX" system, I didn't really know what that was but now I'm fully familiar with those . . . that will come later.

I got on well with the main managers at the hotel, one of them even using me to get his weed supply, we'd spend many nights I'd supposed to be working smoking in his office instead, he'd assure me he'd cover it—he always did.

I know this can't last though, I'm burning the candle at both ends and in the middle, something is going to snap. It does.

I go for my Saturday morning shift, breakfast, there for 06:30, I do my stuff, everything goes flawlessly, as it always did, me topping up on espressos, keeping the buzz going. Lunch comes, hell, I was supposed to have an hour break here, oh well on with it!

I can't take it—the boss here, a french lady, she did nothing to help, the other bosses always chipped in.

We had drink testing evenings, they were always there, a good laugh for the night, those were fun. So she's doing nothing, I'm busting my balls making sure the guests are served promptly, it's what I did, I've had maybe 6 hours sleep all week by now, it's now Friday. Lunch comes, I do my best, I feel totally drained so I sit on the stairs, only 5 to get to the restaurant floor, just a moment, I need to sit. Sleep comes.

My boss wakes me, tells me to go home, I can't I counter, I have to work this evening. Don't be a fool he tells me—you've done more hours this month than many departments combined, go home, sleep you need it.

Well I'd already taken 18 Pro+ tablets, had a dozen espressos and to finish that off, half a dozen red bulls, I do as he requests though, go home.

I'm greeted by a mate who the previous night I'd let use my car, to pick his brother up, he was petrified because the car wasn't working right, he hands me a spliff telling me that's the least I deserve, I'd drank the nigh before so couldn't drive, he did and nearly killed us! Oh well, spliff—lovely :)

We play Colin McRae on the play station, I'm that wired by now, I can't lose, I'm unstoppable again, no-one could beat me, they tried—they failed, I finally have enough, I can't keep my eyes open yet I'm still winning, time for bed, 06:30 again. I sleep till 18:00 the next day, how awesome is that, 12 hours of drink free sleep, yet lots of joints helped in that but I felt good, I ring work, my boss tells me tomorrow is fine, have the night off relax, I deserve it—so I took it.

RANDOM EVENTS—RANDOM EVENTS FOR THAT YEAR

So the year continues, I'm working my two jobs, getting no sleep, I don't need that anyway, I'm unstoppable!

I buy a new radio for my car, the previous one being stolen, didn't mention that before but I spent a lot of my car wage money on getting a huge amp and two 12" sub woofers, they were gone now, not to worry, I had two jobs again, £320 radio, no problem! My debts are cleared, well apart from the bank, it's only the bank what does that matter, they can blow me for all I care, they'll get it eventually.

Something has to stop though, I'm working stupid hours, I finish my career job and go straight to the hotel, I even have my clothes there ready for me, being washed if needed.

I meet a local business man, he runs a late night alcohol delivery service, Booze Brothers it got out the loop hole cause you had to order "bulk", awesome, I could now get beer anytime I wanted. He asks if I'd be willing to work for him, of course—I get discount then, my beer supply now cheaper!

I have three jobs now, the hotel has to go, I go see my boss at his home, an 1/8th in my pocket. We sit and smoke, I tell him I can't do it any longer, I need my "proper" job to work, he laughs and asks me what I think his job is if it's not proper. I feel shame, I tell him I didn't mean it like that, he was the manager but I was just a lowly worker and had a career going, he understood, we smoke lots and I walk home.

I now live in a new studio flat, the uni mates couldn't have me there any longer, since I was now working, that meant council tax, they asked me to go, I did so willingly. I didn't want to see them harmed.

The place is tiny, a kitchen that spanned half the length, a bathroom that was 4 shower trays squared, the living room just big enough for two single seat chairs and a desk, the "bedroom" the same, still I was happy, it was nice.

My old Uni mates used to come and see me, why would they not, I always had weed, that which I'd share so willingly with them, we played many games, Deus Ex, System Shock 2 come to mind, we could share those and take it in turn to play, the other doing the keyboard commands to initiate special "systems"—it worked well, we completed them in record time.

I met my neighbour, a shrink, he knocked one night to complain, my music as too loud, sorry, I'll keep that down, I did. We got on fine after that, I turned up one night quite drunk, he invited me in and his other mate was nasty to me, he defended me, telling his other mate it wasn't his case, back off, we laughed, let it slide. He was awesome. We spent many a night smoking the spliffs and relaxing, this was my life, stoned, gaming, we watched a film, the Big Lebowski, the main character being called "The Dude", that was me! I took to White Russians, "his" drink in the film.

I found happiness, I was content, always stoned, sometimes drunk but on White Russians, the off license told me they had to increase their buying of Kuala for me—awesome! 8 pints of milk I was getting through a week, just with the White Russians.

What more did I want, I visited the shop in the morning, prawn sandwich in the morning walk to work, to cure the hangover, ham and mustard for lunch, after that, anything was game!

I was the "dude", chilled out, nothing bothered me, I was happy, content, laid back nothing could bother me, this caught on quickly with my mates, no longer was I called my first name, just "dude". Everywhere I went, I was welcomed things were good.

THE DUDE—BECOMING THE "DUDE"

I AM THE "DUDE"—HOW IT'S GOOD

I continue my career, things weren't so good though, the big boss has put a hold on things, no pay rises, no climbing the ladder, we were all stuck.

I still continue my smoking of the spliffs, going for lunch with my boss and pulling out a pre-rolled joint, I'd smoke that on the way to pizza hut, he didn't mind—I busted my nuts off, the odd times we did go out, he'd ask me for a smoke too so he had no legs to stand on it he grassed me up, I was awesome, providing for my work mates, my uni mates, I was giving everyone everything I could. I was moon-lighting—working for the booze brothers, now defunct.

I did a delivery one night, one of my first, I made the mistake of leaving the keys in the ignition of the van! The people I was delivering to asked me why they shouldn't just take the van and leave me standing. I told them that they were good people and they really wouldn't want to see little old me left with a huge debt to repay and they weren't that bad, they got out the van and handed me the keys, paid me and let me go on my way. My Honesty was working.

So the booze brother comes round to discuss things, I'm quite well known now in the "underground" world, I'm the "dude", someone to trust, you can tell me anything and it goes no further. We need to address the festival in Nottingham, I tell him no problem, get me the flyers and I'll have it sorted, sorted I did, a record week! I went to the festival, seeing someone, I recognised him instantly even though he was camouflaged, the police were always on the lookout for him, he knew too many people, they needed him to talk. I dis-regarded it we spoke through other people, he used to

DJ at a night club, one I frequented often, we were allowed to smoke weed there, it was awesome, the owner being an ex copper, he had a free pass, we enjoyed this.

Many a night I spent there, getting stoned, drunk, hell enjoying life, I was always welcomed with warm hearts, everyone loved that I'd turn up, I'd found my home, people took me for me, the hopeless romantic that I was, just looking for love, everyone laughed at me because I was so desperate to find love, I didn't care though, I knew it would come, I'm the dude afterall, yeah it's going to take some time but it will come. I believe in myself, why would I not, I'm happy, content, everyone loves me, I'm welcomed with loving arms everywhere I go, happy I'm there, these are the good times, my sorrows I'm forgetting, my loses buried, hidden away, not to be released, they damaged me and I was no longer to be damaged, I had a life now!

CAREER ENDS—SO THIS COMES TO AN END . . .

I visit the parental units, Dads side for my birthday, I've been talking a lot to the local shop keeper, he sees me as useful, I'm learning PHP now, my first real programming language. He tells me he's thinking of setting up a training and recruitment business, would I be interested, Hell yes I would!

I'd already been in contact with this group of people through testing things for work, we needed new internet and could this wireless connection provide that, dd if=/dev/zero of=/home/user/outfile—s 512M was all I needed to test this with, it was good enough for the career, they'd offered to take me out to Vancouver—to meet the main guys, the big boss, the works.

I can't do this, my birthday I ring the vice president and tell him I'm looking elsewhere, I'm not happy. They've not provided me the training they said the would, broken all of their promises to me, I'm looking for a new job.

He thanks me for my honesty and tells me my job is safe for the time being, when I'm ready, they'll take the 4 weeks I need and let me have that as "holiday"—my honesty pays off again I think!

I start working for the local "internet cafe", the intentions being to turn it into a training and recruitment place. Here I meet some very interesting people.

The guy that was currently running it was well known to me already—he was quite ruthless, still I respected him, he knew code, I didn't—not yet anyway. There was also a character claiming to be the "henchman" from the Krays, I to this day know not if he was but he was very powerful, we befriended by mistake, him having his car stolen so I said he could use mine until his was recovered. That was it, I was in his protection now. I didn't need my car so I was more than happy to let him use it for work, my work was 2 minutes around the corner, why would I begrudge him using my car to earn a living?

So I'm now running a business, how many doors that opened! I open the internet cafe 10:00-22:00 everyday. All the other local business' recognise me, I have unlimited credit everywhere! All of a sudden I'm "someone", I'm known, I run a business. I make many friends all whom run businesses— I'm welcome there anytime. Night clubs, well hell I didn't have to queue any longer, I rang the owner and the door man would get me in, VIP, this was sweet, my past buried deeper and deeper, here I was, not even 20 and having the respect of everyone and everything around me, I'm a business man.

I keep in touch with my uni mates, spending what I earn on them, taking them out, showing them my life, hell I was drunk on the power I had, nothing could stop me now, past buried deep, what was that again, another life I told myself.

I had credit coming out my ears, I didn't pay for anything, I was "one of them", protected by the "ruler" of Nottingham. I quit smoking, I didn't need that anymore, the local beat bobby asks me about this, I tell him I've not smoked for months, I have a pack of Marlboro Lights in my top pocket, I always wore shirts then, to prove it. He asks what I was smoking then the night before, I've now moved into the business place, he could see me walking back from the pub . . . . oh that I say, nothing—him knowing full well it as a large joint, it's all I did, work hard, play harder, smoke insane amounts of weed, drink harder and party harder!

I have my old "dealers" party to attend, I go there, we go out, have a good night, come back and drinks are required, none in the house, not a problem, I pick up my mobile and make a call, 10 minutes later we have untold quantities of vodka, whiskey, beer, alcopops, you name it thanks to me. I see the birthday boy, tell him he's required to see his guests, he's busy with a girl, doesn't bother.

I tell the party that he's busy, drunk on the power I have, who else could have organised this, no-one, just me, all on credit £400 had just been spent. I'd pick that up later! My word being the only thing that allowed it to happen, my "word" something I never break, that's all that was needed. My tab now was close to £2,000 but it didn't matter, the booze brothers trusted me, they knew I was good for it, as did everywhere, in total I owed at this point nearly 20K all over the city almost all let it slide, I bought them more business than what I owed, I was the dude, the party man, without me they'd not have the debt but not the party I bought either, I was invincible!

WHAT CAN GO WRONG?—IT'S ALL GOOD!

So all is good, I have a good job, ok working 12 hours a day for peanuts but the life, it was awesome. No-one dared touch me, I was untouchable. Even the local bobby gave me a clean break, he wouldn't grass me up, I used to even smoke a joint in his presence, he turned a blind eye. He knew better than to mess around with the people I knew. I had drugs galore, I didn't care for those though, just my smokes, my weed, to chill me out, null the pain that was constantly nagging me, I could bury that though, I had an awesome life.

Not even 20 and I had all access to the city, clubs the life, whatever I wanted it was mine, I'm drunk on the power of this. Everyone wants to know me—they've heard about me, the guy in the internet cafe that gets you all access, why wouldn't they, I had the key to the city now, least the underground at least and believe me—all clubs have an underground connection—least they did in Nottingham.

So I'm living this life, most awesome, no-one dared touch me, I went out one night with one of the club owners, we finished the night and decided we'd head to mine for a joint or two, I always had copious amounts of weed lying around, and we run into a couple that had been at the bar earlier. He wants to start a fight with him, since he was a C U Next Tuesday to his staff. I wouldn't let him, instead I walk over, me being of frail form, not threatening, just me. I ask him what the problem was. He tells me to fuck off. I say I can't do that, it's obvious that there's a woman here in distress and well, if she's threatened, well let's not go there yet, what's the issue "mate".

He stands there looking at me—weighing me up, yes sure he can take me, can he though, would someone like me try something like this is if I didn't know something he didn't? He backs down, she tells me it's all ok, it's just got out of hand.

I retract, telling my mate on the sly to back down, I didn't need him anyway, I tell them to be careful, next time, it might not be someone so caring who comes over this shit, don't argue in the streets, keep it indoors! I walk away, 500m gone with my mate, I turn around and he's still stood their open jawed—how had I just done that, I believed in myself, I knew I was going to do something good, good I did, all I ever aim for.

I tell the Krays guy about this the next day, he tells me I was an idiot, I stopped something bad from happening though, I disregard him. I'm awesome, I stopped a woman getting hit that night, for that I'm proud, even though I was protected in that county, I knew he could stab me, I didn't care though, I had to protect the woman, that which I saw my Mum, me going back to being 13 and standing between my Dad and Mum, we have a smoke that night, sleep again comes, I've done good.

CONTRACT LANDED!—SO I LAND A NICE CONTRACT

I've been working now at the internet cafe a while, I land myself a contract, awesome over £1,500 a week, depending on hours, no worries, I can do the hours.

I'm up at 06:00 most mornings, I have to drive, now I nave the siblings Punto the same one I lent to the Kray guy . . .

I get there, it's computers, I've become good at these by now, they are after all simple input devices, I input they output, what could be hard about that?

I get to the destination most mornings at least an hour before they open, I'm awesome afterall! I wait, they come, I do my thing. An hour tops and I've finished.

I line the computers up, I have 4 discs to work from so I live my production line memories, feeding the discs one by one, working on the server as I do, these computer things I have an affinity with, I understand them, they're logical, I can work with this. I'm done within an hour or two at most. My employer challenges me, I employ a naughty tactic—the goose, the mother, she has a different surname to me.

I invite my employer to ring her, being my "financial advisor" he's unsure but takes up the challenge, challenge—something that shall be noted later. The goose does me proud, the employer relents, I get my pay cheque and continued work, I had caused a shit storm anyway, all the other guys working for the "client" backed me, I was right, they were wrong, they tried to relent on the minimum pay the promised, why should I get penalised because I was so good? It took me two hours to do what the other guys took 8 hours to do, I should have been paid double, I was that good at the computers now, that bent to my desire!

ON A ROLL—SO THINGS CAN'T GO WRONG . . .

So I'm loving life, I'm being paid well, have the key to the city, well least the clubs at least, nothing can go wrong for me.

I decide to step back a bit, get some focus, I focus on my code—this was afterall the reason I was here.

I sit back for a few weeks and read manuals on how to code, awesomeness—learning again! I meet a business man, he's looking for my skills, I entrust myself to him entirely.

Long story short, he ripped me off, several woman and left us all with nothing, brilliant! Didn't matter though, I had my business still, I was earning, still "the dude", no-one could touch me.

I enter chat rooms, I need to learn to type faster, I have to if I'm to fulfill my dreams, to be a proper coder, I'm talking to 20+ people at a time, typing faster than I thought possible, I'm now typing at 90+ words per minute, I can do real time typing of verbal communications, ok even now some words trip me up but I was there, it didn't take more than a few minutes to fix those mistakes. I'm doing what I saw my Dads secretary do when I was 9 or so, talking to others whilst still typing, looking around, not looking at the keyboard, what more could I do? I'd mastered my world, that being the online world, I could do without looking, even now I'm not looking at what I type, I can see my Mum accessing my server, reading this book, I can do this and know I'm not going to make a mistake—I'm that good at what I do, this at age 18/19—now 34 yet it still stands, my world is online, I live here, breath here, I know all that goes on, this will become an important part later in my life, not so much at this point though.

£1,500 a week gone, on making sure my mates were looked after, that's all I have to say, my "mates".

THE CHATS—WELL I HAD TO LEARN SOMEWHERE

I have nothing to do all day, just sitting waiting for clients, in the internet cafe. I enter more chat rooms, learning to type faster, I'm now up to 90wpm, this is cool, I can talk to 15-20 maybe more people at a time, I don't want to though, I'm pining now to find a love—I've not had a female companion now for over a year, 2, maybe 3, I'm missing it, I pine for it.

So I continue my talking, now we've moved, to a bigger place for the training to take side, I have many female friends, I "sleep" with many of them but only in a sibling fashion, I look back now and know there could have been more, I just didn't see it—blinded myself, trying to remain the nice guy, not pushy, always there, the "good guy".

It cost me dearly, one of the girls I used to know, from my "uni" mates, I had a huge crush on her. Why—I have no idea she herself would admit that she wasn't the most attractive of people, yet to me she was, there was nothing more I wanted in someone than her, not her looks, her. She was awesome, we used to spend many a night getting stoned, her quite often lying in my lap laughing, us both being stupid, she was awesome, I hope still is, it's been over 14 years since I last spoke with her. To me, she was snow white, nothing would I change about her, my heart pined for her, my hopeless romantic coming out, words can't describe her.

I meet someone through a chat room, we talk, lots. for nearly 5 months—I think there's something there.

I ring my Mum, I'm confused, I have this possible person online that I like and this other awesome person in my life, what should I do?

She tells me to go with my hearth, thanks, that helps no end. I visit my old neighbour, the shrink, he can't help me either, just advises me to invite the closest to me round and see how it goes.

I heed his advise, invite her round, show her round my new shop, she's not seen it yet, she's impressed. Why wouldn't she be? There's over 10K gone into it so far, all for me and my skills, she's impressed. We talk. We'd talked before but she tells me she's interested in another woman, ok fair dos, I can live with that, lesbians are cool, can I watch I joke? She smiles at me, gives me a hug and leaves after a quick peck on the cheek, telling me I've always been special to her!

THE ONLINE ROMANCE—HOW I MET MY FIRST "LOVE"

This is getting harder now for me to write, to start it was easier, easing the pain of my latest "family" loss now though, reliving it all I'm finding it hard, maybe the booze, yes I'm still on it, something I will address in the summary, I have it all planned. I've taken the week off work to complete "my book", hell I can type at over 120wpm now, I can do a book in a week, easily, it's only the Saturday and I'm half way though already, I need to tell my story though, I shall hold the tears back, maybe not, I don't know, I'm still 15 years from my current life so I can't tell, it will come though, all of it . . .

I speak with my Mum—telling her about my love, well not love but passion for these two woman I now have in my life, I've always been honest with my Mum, she tells me to follow my heart. My heart is telling me to continue with this woman who lives close to me, I disregard that and instead pursue this new woman, not far but far enough, we talk online for months, she sends me pictures of her, my mates telling me there's not a chance in hell—well that sounds like a challenge to me, I accept!

It takes me just two weeks after this to arrange our first meeting, it was hard, I did it though, she had problems with her internet, I sorted them for her, after telling her she shouldn't trust everyone on the intertubes! We laugh, I'm not that type of guy anyway, hell I just want the best, trying to revive what my parents had before it all went wrong. The hopeless romantic that I truly am, well apart from when my flaws tear that apart.

So we talk for nearly 7 months, have some webcam sessions, her lying to her parents to get said webcam, eventually I manage to speak with her parents, arrange a meeting, I go over, taking the train, her Dad picking me up, me bunch of flowers in hand, Mars bar milkshake in the other, she told me she liked them so I used my position in Nottingham to get that for her, didn't cost me a penny! I'd have paid the earth for them though, we'd fallen in love without even meeting, she told me this before she went offline, I had her number now though so called her to ask her why, she told me she was in love with me and didn't know how to deal with it, fair enough.

I turn up, Dad picking me up from the train station, him telling me if I hurt his little girl, he'll kill me, fair does I think, I do the same, I've not met her yet but can't do her harm, I can't harm anyone, I love this girl, lets ride this out.

We meet, the Dad giving us just enough space to have a kiss, it was awesome, the first real love of my life, I'd found happiness, nothing could stop that. We went to the pub next door, had a nice meal, we were all getting on great, the parents praising me, how nice I was, what could possibly go wrong here?

We went bowling, I took her home and stayed on the sofa, we had an awesome night just kissing, she was only 15—I had my honour, I'd not break that—I could wait.

THE PROGRESSION— HOW WE ENDED TOGETHER

So things are going well, I'm working hard, 12 hours a day, 7 days a week, I'm landing work as much as I can. I eat breakfast, small shop down the road from the cafe did a special, I had a laundry close by, all my washing done, ironed everything, all costing very little.

84 hours a week, all I was paid was £100, accommodation and electric paid for. This was less than I was earning washing cars, I'm starting to think this is taking the piss a little. I get a day off or weekend every other week or so, I visit my love, always taking her gifts, showing her my affections, we chat online constantly, usually over a webcam. She watches over my shop whilst I go for a joint, her ringing me if anyone comes in, this isn't so bad.

I read a lot, waiting for customers when things are slow, we've lost all the previous regulars since moving, we've turned into a training company more than anything now, there's no longer the laid back atmosphere. We used to have gaming sessions, everyone would come and have a drink and we'd play Unreal for hours, sometimes till 3 in the morning, this was all gone now. No drinking allowed in the shop.

I'm starting to feel my heart yearning to be with my love, I go over one weekend, talk with her Dad. He knows I've been feeling like I'm being used for sometime now. We spend the afternoon in the pub, talking at length. I tell him how much I love his daughter and want to be there for her. She's now turned 16, yet we're still not sleeping with each other, I'm waiting for the right moment.

He offers that he can have a word with his boss and see about me getting a job working with him, that I can move in with them! Well this was just music to my ears, I stay, literally with just what I was wearing and my wallet, not that there was any money in my bank, I'd spent all that on the mates in Nottingham, enjoying the life. We never queued to get in any of the clubs, I'd ring and we'd be told to meet "Bob" the head bouncer and he'd let us in the VIP lounge. I was bored of this now though, I couldn't keep on partying till 4, 5 sometimes 6 and getting up for work at 10. I wanted to settle, start a family maybe. I was in love now with this beautiful young lady, almost 6 years my junior but that didn't matter.

We'd cleared the lie that I was 21, not 20 like she'd told him, he wasn't too happy but since I didn't look my age, he said he could let it pass.

I ring my boss, well business partner to tell him I wouldn't be returning and would arrange to collect my things at a later date, he's not happy, tells me I've a mobile phone bill for over £300 that I have to pay, what I question him, it was all business calls that I'd made, well mostly. He tells me I should have used the phone in the shop, how could I do that when I was out on business, although I spent a lot of time in the shop there was considerable time spent travelling to clients, working out new deals, websites were the new thing and everyone wanted one, that which I could provide for them.

Well it was all over now, I was starting a new job, manual labour, this would be interesting. Air conditioning engineer was my title. I've little physical strength, I spent my days in front of a computer, then partying hard, I didn't have time to exercise, apart from walking I did little. I start eating properly, cooking for my new family, recalling my past experiences from the restaurant and re-creating dishes I'd only ever vaguely seen cooked, they worked, were a hit! Another skill I didn't realise I had until now, well I've always cooked, had to after the divorce but never tried to do anything exotic like these dishes.

The drink continues, the smokes continue, not cigarettes but the joints, I wasn't on cigarettes anymore, I was the dude still, just not having the endless parties, working hard all week, sometimes away from home, sometimes local, the Dad and I would always finish the day with a smoke and getting drunk, things were good, we were chilled out together, getting on great. Life with the lady was awesome, we'd spend our evenings watching TV together, or just talking in her room. My room was still the spare living room, this was nice enough, at least now I was getting a decent wage, working hard for it but getting it at least.

ENGINEER—I'M NOW AN ENGINEER

Working as an engineer was proving to be quite fun, there were puzzles to solve, how to route the ducting most efficiently. It's hard work, carrying all this tin around but I get to play with power tools! Grinding up ducting was fun, sparks everywhere, shoe laces were a problem though, the sparks would eat through them in no time.

My love tells me she's quitting smoking, her parents kinda knew she did but weren't happy, since I only had a joint before bed, well actually throughout most the day, she said she'd quit, two totally different types of smokes leave a very different taste/smell behind, so she's quit.

I'm proving to be quite good at this engineering business, my boss was shocked at my intelligence, he'd never met anyone who knew all his details from memory, NI number, bank details, everything was recalled the moment he asked me for them. I'm solving challenges with the ducting routing that the Dad was having issues with, he was impressed at the lateral thinking I was showing, turning out to be quite the asset to the company.

I've bulked out a bit now too, eating well and doing all this lifting, it was going to happen. I no longer moan about how heavy things are, just pick them up and get on with it, huge lengths of tin, straight up the ladder, no problem.

I've collected my possessions from Nottingham, seeing my old business partner, we'd had some arguments but we put it behind us, I wished him the best, my car now back with my Mum, I didn't need one anyway, I was happy with my love. I had no need to drive, we catch the bus instead, or get a taxi, money again was no problem, still spending as soon as I got it but managing to make a few savings each week. I'm doing lots of overtime, the Dad was renowned for working hard, possibly the hardest worker there so I had no choice, still it meant more beer tokens.

We now spend our evenings messing around on the computer, me still learning more programming, I've become quite good at producing websites so I keep on, the love showing an interest too so I teach her. I help her through her revision for GCSEs, this was easy compared to what I did, how they'd dumbed them down.

We're at it like rabbits now, her Dad having told me when we were ready, he'd pay for us to have a nice romantic weekend, how could I tell him that we were ready? It just happened one day when it felt right. We have to sneak around but we're good enough at that, she knows enough secluded areas so off we go, every chance we can, wind, rain or shine. There's the odd time or two we nearly get caught but we manage to find an excuse.

We're now 6 months into our relationship, I love this woman with everything I have, I'd given up everything to be with her, would do so again in a heartbeat back then. I'm working hard but I'm starting to get a little sick of this, I have my computer back, I'm not suited for this type of work, I need to be behind my keyboard again, I can earn more doing what I'm best at than this manual labour malarkey!

I go to Nottingham on a job with another of the work guys, he asks me what the hell I'm playing at, it's obvious I could be doing a better job without all the risks. It was always risky, we were fitting air conditioning ducting, that mean heights, ladders, scissor lifts to the roof tops. I tell him I'm thinking of trying to find something else but can't, the Dad is so proud of me for following in his foot steps. He tells me to fuck him off, take my love and move back to Nottingham, he'd heard the life I had here and thought I'd be better off heading to where I'd found my roots, found myself, become the dude.

I couldn't do this, the man, the dad had afterall taken me into his home when I was hitting a dark place, I put these thoughts out of my mind, carry on the work, save some money.

I speak with the Dad, ask him permission to marry his princess, will he accept me as his son-in-law? Of course! He's overjoyed. I spend the weekend seeking an engagement ring, I find the perfect one, I already know her ring size, it's pricey, only £400 but I only have £300 saved, I barter with them, I've always been good at this. It's settled, £330. Awesome, I have a little reserve I can draw on. The deal is done.

My love and I had joked before about marriage, even a fake proposal so I knew she'd say yes. I waited until her 17th. We went the pub for a meal to celebrate, the Dad knowing full well what was coming. He keeps winking at me whilst we're eating. We have a nice evening, the food was excellent, the drink plentiful.

Home we go, into the living room and I get down on one knee, ", will you give me the honour, the pleasure, the joy of becoming my wife" I say. Her eyes fill, ring extended towards her. "Yes, yes of course I will" she replies! The parents applaud, we kiss, the mother gives me a hug and a kiss on the cheek, the Dad grasping me and giving me a huge hug welcoming me to their family "proper" this time!

I still sleep in the spare room though, he knows things are happening but turns a blind eye, preferring to ignore it, thinking his princess the virgin still.

Work continues, I'm now very unhappy with it, I've heard many tales now about unpleasant working conditions, places I never wish to visit but know they'll come eventually. I speak with the secretary there.

She tells me I don't belong there and the Dad will understand eventually, he may be stubborn but he can tell it's not me, I'm a keyboard jockey, I should just talk to him. I wait the week out, until the weekend, there's no overtime this weekend so it should be the perfect time to have a chat.

MY SCREW UP, I—THE FIRST TIME I SCREWED THINGS UP

He can tell something's wrong though, he confronts me, I tell him I'd prefer to find another job, something that's more fitting for me. This is wrong, how can it be right for him, he has his GCSEs, he's intelligent and he loves the job, why can't I? He storms out the house telling me I best be gone by the time he comes home or he'll "smash your fucking face in".

I knew he was capable of this, the whole time I was there, I'd ignored all the arguments, him and his partner used to argue all the time. My love and I ignored them though, me blanking out the memories from my past, things trying so hard to take me back there, my parents, their arguments. I wouldn't go back there, I was moving on. My love and I just cuddled, made small talk and giggled.

Theirs was sometimes physical though, again I turned my eye to it, ignoring the searing pain that was trying to re-surface.

I'm now in panic mode though, where can I go? I have no friends here, I ring my Dad asking for advice. Next thing he's there with his partner, my Mum's here, they meet me at the pub, I explain the situation, they promise me they'll help sort things out.

The Dad returns from work, calmer now, he tells me I'm an idiot, why are my parents there? I explain I panicked, fearing for a beating, I'd never had a fight in my life and didn't want to start now. He tells me he's calmed down and things are good, he understands now I'm not suited to this work and everything is OK. We all go for an Indian. Drinks galore again, the pints keep on coming.

I can see his rage building, he's not fine with me at all, he can't accept why I don't want to follow his foot steps, things start to turn nasty, the more drink the nastier the conversation becomes. I'm trying to ignore this, just talking to my love, my Dads partner kicking me under the table mouthing for me to stop it. Stop what, talking to my love? I'm not doing any harm, I'm listening to what's going on and interacting when I have the chance, should I just sit here like a dummy? Not talk to my love?

"Fine, you want me gone, I'll go!" I stand up and shout, storming out, seeking out a taxi. I head towards the rank, I feel something on my shoulder, I'm spun around and punched in the face, it's the Dad! I fall over shrieking in shock, the step Mum jumps in, I'm shaking, angry, fist clenched, I know he's had a broken jaw before, one clean jab and it'll shatter, the Krays guy had taught me just enough to defend myself and put people out so I could escape. Could I hit him?

My thoughts are racing, I want to retaliate but if I do that there's a good chance I'll lose my love, no, I'll stick to the plan. Police see the commotion and come over. Things start to calm down. I'm asked if I want to press charges, NO I tell them, nothing has happened, I run to a taxi I see out the corner of my eye, just drive I tell him.

Where to? Nottingham. Nottingham?? Sorry mate that's too far. £60 I'll pay you, it'll cost you £15 in petrol and you'll have £45 for 90 minute of driving. OK the deal is done. I navigate him through the city, that which I knew like the back of my hand, these streets I'd driven down many times before, scaring my friends with the skill of driving down narrow roads, just 2 inches clearance—that didn't stop me though, I knew my car, knew myself I could navigate at speed.

I arrive at the Krays mans house, it takes me a few minutes to wake him up. He's furious, wants to go over and kick the living shit out of him, my face cut and bruised, he wasn't seeing this happen to me, no-one in Nottingham dared touch me, how dare this man. I tell him he can't, I don't want to see him harmed.

We go to sleep. I wake the next day and he tells me as much as he'd love to, I can't stay there, there's only one bedroom and his daughter comes over frequently, I can stay for a week or so but I have to find somewhere soon. I understand, he's very protective over his daughter. I head out to clear my head, returning some hours later.

My parents are there, we sit and talk. I'm in the wrong again, all I wanted was a chance to find a better job for myself. No I shouldn't have done that. I explain my boredom, how it was driving me crazy, doesn't matter, it was a job and I should have stuck with it. The Krays guy has my back though, he understands me. He'd seen me many times behind the keyboard, he knows that's where I belong.

I get given a mobile phone, so they can keep an eye on me, brilliant I think. At least I can keep in touch with my love now, off I go, get some credit and ring her, she can't talk and tells me to text. I tell her I'm OK, we'll sort something out soon. I love you, speak soon.

Nottingham II—
The return to Nottingham

Finding a home—Time to
find another home

I stay the night at the Krays man again, promising him that tomorrow I'll find somewhere else. We go the pub, I have my bank card and some money so why not? There's almost trouble in the pub but he just walks over, the trouble makers see him and shut up.

He tells me more tales from his past, he's over that though, having a daughter made him realise how precious life was. Back then though it was just business, you didn't pay you got hurt, or worse. Just business though.

I wake the next day, I have some of my possessions, get dressed and head out to see my old friends, those from Uni that I treated to so many nights of drink and drugs, anything they wanted, for months I was there to feed them that which they wanted.

I arrive, one of the house mates which I was never that close to is the only one in, she questions my bruises as I enter, her giving me a can of lager. I explain what's happened and why I suddenly vanished from Nottingham, they had wondered but had no way of contacting me. She's happy I've found my love but shocked at how things have suddenly ended. How could someone attack the dude, the pacifist that didn't hurt a fly? The others return from work and are pleased to see me but again confused why I'm bruised. I recount my story again, in a constant flow of tears, I've lost my love it seems. We get stoned, I get hammered. Sleep on the sofa, I'm welcome there. I feel safe, these are my friends, even the one who I was never that close to was warm towards me, feeling a connection that was never there before.

I wake the next day, I need to find work, would I be ok to crash here a while until I can afford the deposit? The main guy who I was friends with, my supplier, comes to talk to me, I have to go, I'm more than welcome to come round for their company but I have to find somewhere to sleep, out the door I go.

How could they not help me, I'm clearly in need of just a few days to get straight, they couldn't provide that for me, just a roof over my head was all I was needing, no they said it couldn't happen. How could they do this to me, everything I'd done for them? Drove them places at their request, treated them to nights out, welcomed them into my VIP world, free entry to all the top clubs, VIP no less. Free drinks in most of them, I scratched the owners back, they scratched mine.

Rejected from those who I truly thought would help me, I plod to the booze brothers head quarters, he'd grown from operating out of his house to having an office now, he's a bit shocked to see me but welcomes me in, drinks are offered, I accept.

Again I have to recount my story, he's appalled, again how could someone attack the dude? We talk all night, him taking calls when he has to, he no longer does many deliveries himself, he was 3 vans now and workers. He takes the last call of the night and puts the answer phone on, "Come on then" he tells me. Come on where?

"Well you obviously need somewhere to stay so you're coming home with me". Awesome! I knew he'd come through, after all of our "business" meetings we had, we'd become very close. I ask him about rent, bills etc, he tells me not to worry, get myself back on my feet then we can work that out. I can do some deliveries for him, that'll be a start—a job, awesome!

I know he can't really afford to take me on full time though, so the next morning head to sign on, at least that'll keep some money in my pocket. I sign on, two days and I get my first pay. I'm not being a dole dosser though, fuck that, I've never signed on in my life. Nottingham is a big town, I can cover it in those two days. I do.

I visit every shop possible asking for work, I have an address now and a mobile so I can be contacted. Pubs, clothes shops, restaurants, you name it, I entered asking for work, left my details and moved to the next. I must have visited 200+ places of business, it paid off. The following day I have two jobs, one in a pub, the other a restaurant—I have skills at this, it'll be easy, back to the good old days. I sign on for the first and last time of my life, thank them for the money and head to work. This is good, they pay for taxi's home if it's the late shift, can't be bad.

I get shown the ropes, at the pub. Simple enough, it's a pub, I've worked these before, I get food too, regular breaks, this is good, I've started smoking again, the stress, it was the first thing I did with the taxi driver, stop and get a pack of smokes.

I explain how I've two jobs, to both places, they're good with it, maybe even a little impressed—we agree to co-ordinate and make sure the shifts don't conflict.

REBUILDING—TIME TO REBUILD MYSELF

I settle quickly into my new role at the pub, not so much the restaurant, I'm getting on great with all my work mates but the restaurant doesn't feel like to me, the pub is where I'm suited most. I give it a few weeks, then have to quit, my hearts not in it there.

I'm spending stupid amounts on phone credit, I can't ring my love, her Dad won't let her speak to me yet, I can text though and text I do.

I walk to work, uphill half the way there, downhill the next, least it makes walking home easier. I'm feeling at home at the pub, get plenty of drinks bought for me, I save these up, having just one at the end of the night, I have unlimited beers at home anyway, the booze brother has given me an unlimited tab.

I work as many shifts as I can, I'm back in control, I quickly become trusted there, I'm given duties that aren't usually given for at least 6 months of service. My confidence quickly returns, that which I gained from running the internet cafe, I'm back, things are going to be ok. I save my money and instead extend my lines of credit where I can.

I visit many of my old haunts, things change quickly and in 9 months most the places have new owners, those that don't, well I no longer run a business so my privileges are revoked, this I expected, I can't scratch their backs any longer so why should I have them. Some keep good though and I'm more than welcome anytime, VIP style still.

My friends come and see me, have some drinks whilst I'm working then we chill out after my shift, drinking the pubs own special brew. We relax on the grass, my paranoia is now starting to get to me, my loves Dad has threatened to come and "see" me a few times, my smoking the weed isn't helping this but it's the only thing that aids with the sleep. We spend the afternoon drinking and smoking, my eyes now red it's obvious what I'm up to, everyone knows this though, I am the dude! It's summer and for once it's sunny out.

Everyone is getting a little annoyed at the amount of texting I'm doing, to my love, they let it slide though, they can see how much I'm hurting, missing my love. Things are getting better though, I've got some savings now, far outweighed by my credit lines but they don't matter, not yet anyway.

Things continue for a few months, I'm able to borrow one of the vans or his car, from the booze brothers, I sneak over to see my love as often as I can, I've been told to keep away until I can prove myself. I'm proving myself and you shall not keep me from my love. We sneak around, being passionate with each other, mostly in the back of the van if I had that. We get caught one day, man walking his dog, he laughs and walks off, we roll around laughing, good times are near, we can feel them, they're close.

I continue my drinking, my smoking—being the dude, party times are back! I start to relax, remembering who I really am, part of this was my fault, I handled things badly but I couldn't stand the work any longer, I needed my keyboard back. Oh well, time to fix things.

I text and ask if I can speak with the Dad—please. He rings me. I tell him all I'm doing to rebuild myself, prove that I'm worthy of his daughter, apologise for my behaviours. He accepts this and tells me when I can afford to move back, I can, I need to stay clear though until I've done this to prove myself.

FEAR—THE FEAR KICKS IN

Everything seems to be coming on, I've my friends back, the party life, I am again the dude. My supplier has a new girlfriend, we get along well too. I'm seeing my love as often as I can, extending my credit with petrol costs and borrowing the car/vans, it matters not though, I at least get to see my love.

The Dad gets wind that I might possibly be going over, he rings me to ask me, I can't lie, what do I tell him, when did they think I was over there? Ah awesome, no that couldn't possibly have been me, I was working that day, he can check with my boss if he likes, he relents, tells me to keep it up and soon I can be back.

I finish my shift and see my friends girlfriend, we go the pub, have a few there then decide it's such a nice day, we'll carry on in the park. We visit one of my usual off-licenses, I'm welcomed, we have a quick chat and off the two of us go, we relax in the park.

She asks me about my past with her boyfriend, I tell her he's an amazing guy, he's let stuff go that other guys would have made a big deal about. The one instance she pries from me being my other attraction back then. I recalled one of the parties we were having, I'd gone to the toilet, came out and she was there, she kissed me, I was overjoyed but thought something was wrong. I found out she was on and off with my mate, I confronted her the next day to tell her that she couldn't mess with my feelings like that, I felt deeply for her and didn't just do the casual thing, she apologised telling me she was drunk but did feel for me, was confused. He found out about this and told me he didn't believe that she'd contemplate even giving me a kiss, why would she, this is the dude, girls don't like me like that, I'm just a friend. I tell him I'm sorry and I'll not mention it again, we hug and make up. I tell her this to let her know how forgiving he is, what an awesome person he is and he'll get over things very quickly, we'd not spoken about it since.

She's a bit taken aback by this but seems ok, we finish our drinks, her on the cider, me my usual lagers, have a joint, I've always got that on me. We have more laughs, talking about how nice it is here, serene and relaxed, it was a nice afternoon.

I walk home, pop in for a quick pint in the local, no-one I know is there so leave after I finish my drink. Back home, I'm asked if I want to try an "e", well not really, I only do the smokes, still I figure what the hell, I'll have a half, I'm up for new experiences, I can't comment if I've not done it myself.

This does not go down well, I'm edgy, twitchy, can't relax, I don't like this, I'm off to bed.

Sleep doesn't come, the next day I'm asked how I could just sleep like that, I should have been wired, I explained how it didn't go down well, I'm told that's cause my head's in a bad place and usually it's a nice experience, I'll not go there again.

My phone goes, this must be my love, texting me, we've not texted for at least 8 hours, it's early morning.

"Get the fuck out of Nottingham or else" it reads, number unknown. I panic, what's this all about? I ring in work, explain I'm in a bit of a situation and will update them tomorrow, terribly sorrow but I can't make it today, they were aware of the whole mess anyway so it came as no surprise.

House mate goes to work, I'm panicking, a joint should help, help it does, in feeding the paranoia. I dress so I can't be recognised. I sneak my way through the streets, keeping to the back roads, those that no-one would use, no-one in their right mind, or protected at least. I run into someone from years back, bonus, I can score, get some more weed.

I get to the Krays house, this being the only part of my journey where I might be picked up on. He's furious, we ring through my contacts trying to find out what's happened. My "mate" who I'd just spent the day with his girlfriend owns up, he had to, he knew the Krays guy wouldn't take any lies. They'd been out the night before and he said he was fed up with me "messing" with his "girls". All I'd done was explain how kind and forgiving he was. He apologises but tells me to keep clear of them all, well that's not a problem, you've now shown me you really have no respect for me, just used me, I'll not give you anymore of my time, kindness, forget it.

I ring my Dad to tell him it's ok, we've figured it out, too late, we thought it was my loves Dad, he's rang to confront him, more damage to fix. I ring and explain what's happened, he laughs, knowing the paranoia that can come from the weed, tells me to sort myself out, then I can come back. Not so bad then, least I know who my true friends are.

I return to work the next day, explain it was a mis-understanding, my boss tosses it aside and tells me to get on with it, I was missed yesterday and had to make up, so I did.

RETURN TO MY LOVE—FINALLY, I'VE PROVEN MYSELF

Some 3 months have now passed since I was with my love, I've saved enough money now though to get rent a place. I ring the Dad, ask him if I'm ok to return now, I've learned from my mistakes and can prove myself, I need to find a place to live and a job.

He tells me that's fine, find a job first, then somewhere to live. So challenge is accepted, I borrow my friends car, head on over and start looking for work. Doesn't take me long, another pub job, I'm good at these—I can start as soon as I want, just let them know.

I begin searching for a house, my love now with me, we hold hands constantly whilst we drive around. I find a bedsit, it's tiny, just enough room for a bed, cupboard and chest of drawers, still it's close to my love, I'll make it there, it's not going to be for long anyway, I have plans!

I ring the pub, can I start Monday? Yes, looking forward to seeing you!

Back to my love—I return to the love of my life

Heading to my love— Leaving Nottingham again

I'm allowed to return! I have a job, a place to live, what more did I need, nothing, my love was there!

I move into my tiny room, meet a house mate, we get on good, there's a Chinese over the road, this is good, the kitchen is disgusting, I can't cook in there. I use none of the house apart from my room.

I start work on the Monday, first day introductions, the people seem nice, boss seems nice, owner seems nice, this is all good. I ask how many shifts I'm likely to get, calculating how much I need to survive. I'm told to start with just enough to cover my bills and have some spare change I calculate, if I prove to be good though, I can pretty much take the pick of the shifts.

Well you can't even call that a challenge, I've been doing this work for almost 4 years, at one point running a restaurant, working a conference place and doing a pub job, this is going to be awesome.

I tell my boss that won't be a problem, give me a week and he'll see I'm more than capable.

He laughs at my confidence, I smile in return, I'm the dude, I don't do nasty. He relaxes and tells me ok, he'll see what I've got.

The proposal, I've just realised came shortly after this, oh well, I've detailed it now, just it happens a few months from now, not when I first wrote it . . .

My love comes to see me, I'm almost finished with my first shift, I've done well, proven I'm capable of running the bar. I've acquired a few new friends too, she comes into the bar, I get her a drink. Shift finished I return to the other side of the bar and have a few beers, Dad wants to see me, he's back this evening. We leave, headed home, via the off-license, I should get him his usual drinks, a peace offering if you will.

We get to the home, I put the beers in the fridge, sit awaiting his return, I'm quite anxious. He comes in, the dogs telling us he's returned before he pulls into the drive. I stand awaiting to greet him, I tell him I've got his beers already, seeing he too has picked them up, he laughs, thanks me and gives me a hug. We sit, beers in hand. He tosses me some weed so I skin up a joint, we start talking. Things aren't so bad, he just wants the best for his princess, I can understand this, he feels I was running away from it but sees I just needed my keyboard back, we laugh about everything, the weed kicking in and giving us the giggles. Happy days return!

I ask if it would be ok for my love to spend the odd night with me at my new room? Not quite yet I get told but soon, respect for asking and not just assuming, we're back on track.

I get a taxi home, stopping via the local pool place, it's too late for the off license but I find a way, get some beers, head home. Drink some beer, watch some TV and have a few smokes, sleep comes, I'm happy again, I have my love, her Dad accepting me, things are good, it can't go wrong now—I won't let it.

THE PUB—CONTINUING AT THE PUB

Things are all going well, I'm saving money, have enough for my beers and smokes are never an issue, sleep is coming, I'm at peace.

I continue my work at the pub, it's going well, I'm liked by everyone, the kitchen staff, the bosses really like me, the owner telling me what a sweet young gentleman I am. My love can't really come there that often though, my boss has told me that I can't serve her, I know this anyway, so I have a laugh and joke with the customers, everything is going well, it couldn't be better.

I've as many shifts as I want, sometimes too many but I'm not turning the work down, I need to save, I have my plan! I feel some of the other staff are a bit put out by me, me the new boy and I'm getting everything I want, I have the experience though so I pass it off.

My love and I go out for meals with one of my work mates, he's a player, has a girlfriend whom we dine with, I know though that he's been sleeping with some of the other girls at the bar, I keep my mouth shut though, it's not my business. I know nothing.

Two of the local girls, I know they're underage but I've been told to turn a blind eye, their parents are good customers there, so I serve them under orders. My love comes in one night, she goes to the toilet and one of the girls comments how "I want your boyfriend". She's angry, I tell her there's nothing to worry about, I'm not that kind of guy. I wouldn't but the girl in question was stunning, was nice to know I was wanted by someone so stunning, she was a really nice person too, I didn't care though, I had my love!

I think by now we're engaged. Her wearing her ring proudly, she's started college too, doing a technology course, I help her with this. She doesn't seem to be getting it though.

I'm given a free pass at work, I can drink what I want, when I want, this is awesome, we go there for meals on weekends, or week days, whenever really, times were good now, nothing was making us unhappy.

We arrange our weeks according to my work schedule, if I'm working weekends, it matters not, we make a weekend mid week instead. This then causes a problem.

I'm asked to work a few more shifts that week, I'm already down for 4 splits and an evening, I refuse. My boss tells me I have to—I explain we've made plans, we're going the cinema, my love and I—he cares not. He warns me that I have to pick up the extras, I tell him I've asked someone else to cover, another girl that works there needed it more than I, he refuses, it has to be me.

I finish my shift, meeting my love outside when I'm done. I tell her what's happened, we decide to go job hunting, there's a new centre opened down the road, learning centre, I've experience with that, we go there first.

I ask to speak with the boss. We enter his office and I ask if there's any work going. He asks what I'm good at, I tell him my background, he's interested. I explain my situation, that I'm a loyal worker but I've been asked to break my plans that I made around work, work comes first and I'd broken my plans many times before but this was the first time we'd get to see each other for over a month, well for a few full days anyway.

He tells me there's nothing really there for me, I'm gutted. But he also has another company that's in the web design business, he'll take me on there but I'll most likely be doing more work for his other company, awesome, back to my keyboard!

We walk back to the pub, I ask to see the owner. She asks me what's wrong and I tell her I won't be returning, her son has asked too much of me and I have a new job now, sorry, thank you for you time but I'll no longer be of service. She's upset I'm leaving, angry at her son even, I apologise again and we leave, my love and I.

I run into one of the chefs on the way back to my loves house, I tell him what's happened, he tells me good for me, they're a bunch of c***s anyway, he's leaving the moment he can. Oh well another one down.

We return to my loves house, I tell the news to the Dad, he's happy, I should now be on better money, wages though were never discussed, I trusted the guy and he gave me the chance I was wanting, it can't go bad surely? Things were good, more beer, more weed, a taxi home, a new life coming again, a job that I've been seeking since I got my first computer and learned how to master it, my life is awesome, it's had it's ups and downs but it's getting there now, my past pains now buried deep, I can barely recall them, I have too much happiness piled on top of them, the happiness can't be shifted to allow those pains to re-surface, no, that's not happening.

LEARNING—BACK TO A LEARNING CENTRE

I go for my first day at work, find out a bit about it, it's a government scheme, money isn't an issue, wow this is cool I think!

I'm introduced to the other staff, the network admin there I at first couldn't stand, something didn't feel right, he was too much like me, too honest, I couldn't stand him at first, later though he became my best friend. The others were not the usual kind, the network admins brother was a bit messed up, later he ends up in a physc ward, the two girls being gypsies, this was cool, never mixed with those before.

Melded quite well with all but the network admin, I was nice to him though, could see he meant no harm.

I'm then told about the scheme, it's all online, I inspect the network, it's a mess. First job to fix that then.

I request a new server, I'm granted, I get to work, a windows 2000 server, I fix that up and get the DNS, DHCP working, group policies, everything that was needed. I then get to work on the workstations, copy of Ghost in hand, I make a master image, clone it to all the machines and things are looking up.

Next job, the physical side of things, I get permission to close the centre for a weekend to fix this, I cable everything up perfectly, swtiches installed under the desks, not a cable in sight.

Things have turned around in just the month I've been there, should be pay day now. I ask about the pay, what do I need I'm asked, well I'm a humble kinda guy, I explain my expenses, my "hobbies" and what I need to survive, no problem, I get a cheque for just enough so I won't struggle. Not so bad for a first month.

I still have my lines of credit to clear from Nottingham, don't worry, we'll get you sorted soon enough, we just need to wait 6 months to get the cash from the government, not a problem, they can wait another 6 months. They've waited this long, I'm not being hassled to clear them, it's not an issue.

I'm then tasked with looking at the database, something created by the bosses father, it was good but using access—we needed it web based, I go back to learning PHP, have my own space to work in, I soon push out something that's good enough for now, I'm working on it though, it's going to be better. At least people can manage their own accounts now though. My love comes to see me often, things are all good, they like her, she has a bit of a crush on the boss but I can understand that, he's a very good looking guy, oozes charisma by the bucket, we're happy though, in love, what does that matter, I've had crushes on other women, never acted even though I could have, quite certainly but no, my love was all I cared about.

The boss and I become good friends, he's also a smoker I find out, we spend the days getting stoned, he's worried though, he's seen where I live and it's not good, it's getting me down. He suggests I get a house, my plan all along, he'll provide the paperwork required.

HOUSE HUNTING—TIME TO FIND A FIRST HOUSE OF MY OWN!

So I have it, my plan is here at last, I can buy a home for my love and I!

We go looking, the first place we find, it's perfect, just the right price for what I've been told I can push to, we look around. It's a terrace, two up two down with an extension on the back for the bathroom, it's going to be cold in there in the winter but it's nice.

We finish looking around, I ask the owner what he's willing to accept, he tells me 3K less than what it's advertised for, I push, get another 1.5K off the price, we shake hands and agree. Deal done. I never take things for what they are, I always get a bargain!

My love and I head to the banks, I have no credit rating so all the mainstream banks won't touch me. This is causing a bit of a problem, I need to find this mortgage . . .

I've heard adverts for some place guaranteeing you'll get a mortgage, we head there. They're too busy today, can I come back tomorrow? No problem, we return the following day.

They take my details, my love can't be included on it just yet, she's still only 17 and that would harm the process I'm told. No problem, she trusts me. We trust each other implicitly. I complete the forms, it's done, a month before the funds are released, ok I can cope where I am for a month, or can I?

We return to her home, telling her Dad the good news, he's thrilled! Gutted also that his princess is leaving home so soon, he's agreed she can move in with me, that was the proving afterall. We have a drink and some smokes, it dawns on me, I could save a months rent if I could lodge here again, I propose the question, he tells me he was just about to ask me if I wanted to do that to save some pennies. Awesome, I stay the night on the sofa, things are happy again, happy times, my pains? They're buried now, still the happiness keeping them safe and deep, long forgotten memories, I had my love, a family that loved me, things were going well.

OUR FIRST HOUSE— MOVING TO OUR FIRST HOUSE

I arrange with work for the paper work needed for the mortgage, I'm given everything I need.

The mortgage isn't far away now, my boss is happy, he can see me changing already, things are good. I ring the owner to tell him it's just a few weeks now, he tells me he thought I'd backed out, no I tell him, two weeks tops now. ok that was close, thought I'd lost it for a moment there, nope, things are good.

I've told my Dad the good news, he's overjoyed, he's giving me £1000 house warming present, how awesome, thanks Dad, that'll help get us setup, there's nothing in there and it needs a lot of work.

The weeks pass quickly, Dad tells me he's also got us a dining suite, brilliant, how much more could go right now, apart from winning the lottery—not a lot.

I need a van, I ask my boss if he knows anyone who was one, has to be a closed one though, can't use the loves Dads ones, they're all open. He tells me he knows a guy, awesome. I go and sign, collect the keys, my love and I enter our first home, it's awesome. There's nothing in there but we don't care, it's ours!

I get the train to Liverpool, to collect the van, drive back to my love and we head to my Dads with her sibling, we need him to help load and unload.

We arrive, have dinner then we have to promptly leave, we go around and collect the furniture, I hug my Dad, give him a kiss and tell him I love him, we need to go though, it's late and I've a long drive ahead of us. Off we go, I drive, I'm tired but I can do this, my love falls asleep on the sofa we've also been given, the sibling keeping me company, radio blasting, the tunes are banging! I push hard, the van being battered by the wind, me struggling now to keep control. I keep control though, we make it back for 02:00, unload a few things, I have to get the van back in the morning.

My love and I put a couple of single mattresses together, cuddle up and sleep comes, I'm happy, I have a warm feeling in my heart, things are perfect now, we had our own house.

Sleep doesn't last though, I need to get the van back. Exhausted, I drive it back to Liverpool thank the guy and ask him how much he wants for his troubles, nothing he tells me, just so long as it did it's job, anytime just ask. Awesome, I get a taxi to the train station, I'm quite used to this now, my boss living there, I was always headed that way, I get back home and another taxi, I'm at home, my love there waiting for me. We decide to relax, new sofa thanks to Dad, we sleep there, for a few hours. We sort the house out the best we can.

Work is still going good, I'm coding away, I've been welcomed as a member into the other company, things were perfect.

LOAN—NEED A LOAN

The house is great but I want it to be perfect for us, I need money for that, I look into a loan.

I can't get a mainstream loan, my credit rating is still too poor for that, I find a way, 10K, it doesn't take long to clear. We buy everything we need, furniture, bed, new sofas. A washing machine, the only one left in the store was the display model, awesome! Can I speak with the manager please, I'd like to negotiate a deal since it's the display model, 20% discount, thank you!

I fit the laminate flooring, one night working far too late to finish it in the bedroom, the neighbours bang on the door, damn, ignore it, we head to the park to finish my cutting, I measure the floor, mark the flooring and we go, finish the cutting, that can be finished in the morning. The morning comes and it's all good, I finish the last little bit of the bedroom floor, the bed is in place, curtains, custom built dressing table for my love, drawers, it's all perfect.

I feel bad about keeping the neighbours up, I go the off license, literally on the corner of the road, get a bottle of white wine and some lagers, knock the neighbours door. She answers, I offer the bag of drinks to her, telling her sorry for the night before, I just got too carried away and needed to finish things. She tells me her husband is at work but thank you.

My love and I relax, enjoying our new house, everything now perfect, walls painted, laminate flooring in the bedroom and living room, all fitted by my own fair hands, I love creating things!

We get a knock, the neighbour is back from work. He tells me it wasn't needed—my apology, just he had to be up for work at 06:00, I apologise again, we laugh, sit outside and have a drink together. I have a smoke, he doesn't indulge in that, no worries, we get on great, life is coming together.

All in, we've got the house how my love and I want for 7.5K, not bad going, we'll save the rest, cover the payments for the first year, or for a rainy day.

CLEARING SOME CREDIT—TIME TO CLEAR SOME LINES OF CREDIT

Things are all going well for us, my love and I, she has everything she needs, wants, desires, I make sure of this, she's getting on with college, I'm doing my work for the learning centre.

I get a call from the booze brothers, he's in trouble, the business has failed, pubs can now open 24/7 and it's hurting his business model, he needs to have what I owe him.

No problem, I have my savings, he comes over.

We enjoy a good weekend, I write him a cheque, he's happy. We joke around all weekend, having lots to drink, smoking heavily and generally just having fun, he needs some speed, I get it for him. We're buzzing now, caning most of what he had, oh well—no sleep this weekend, nothing new for me. My love finds it hard to keep up, she tries though. We enjoy teasing him, her showing her affections for me quite implicitly, he's not bothered though, he's happy for us, we're amazing together, things are perfect.

My pains are long since forgotten.

For a laugh we decide to do a Ouija board, why not, it can't harm.

My Mum has since moved to Spain, asking if I'd mind, why would I—free holidays again! Awesome times.

So we start the board . . . nothing happens for a while, then the room goes strangely warm, the glass starts to move, we look at each other?? Nope not one of us is doing it, I'm barely touching the glass, we ask who it is. It's my Mums second husband, my mate now backs out, just my love and I continue.

We ask what it is he's wanting to share. The war in Iraq, he's worried I'll be called up for it, we ask if there's anything else, the glass then spells out my Mums real first name, she uses her second name mostly and no-one knows her real name, he did. My love didn't know this and I certainly didn't move the glass to spell this, "tell her I love her deeply" he tells us. "I love you too" and then it was gone.

I'm overwhelmed, how awesome was that! My mate's sceptical, yet how did the name, one that was never known get spelled out? I ring my Mum, it's very late, possibly 02:00 in the UK so 03:00 in Spain, she answers, quite not perplexed, I explain what's just happened. She thanks me then tells me she loves me, sleep tight, we hang up. The room has returned to being cold, time for bed, we've all consumed far too much, sleep doesn't come, my memories of my lost "Dad" haunting me, I find the sketch he did that I had from the Norfolk broads, I gaze into it, sleep comes finally, not long but more than I need to function.

JOB GONE—MY QUITTING ANOTHER JOB

Things were going well at the learning centre, I'd almost mastered PHP, things were good.

We'd cleaned up the filing cabinet, records were in order, everything was coming on great, yet the pay wasn't there. I was struggling to make my monthly payments. I pleaded with the boss to sort things out, he would, he kept promising me, it never happened.

One night we're at my place, I decide to go for a drink with the network admin, now a very close friend. We return, my boss is staying the night there, he did regularly, so we could work and get things sorted out with the website.

I come back to find the house destroyed, he's ordered Chinese, had the brother round and they've been drinking—lager cans all over the floor, lager causing the floor to warp. I'm furious.

I speak with my love outside, I'm raging, almost ready to punch him, how could he dis-respect our house like that, my hard work ruined, he hears us and walks out quite calmly, he's done nothing wrong. He tells me if that's how I feel, we're done, off he goes, I gain control of myself again, I'm not capable of hitting anyone, he's done me harm, my love and I go and relax, my mate already gone home, no loss, I can repair the damage, just need some cash first, that means a job, time to find one again.

SELF EMPLOYED?—COULD I DO THIS?

I decide to try and go it alone, work for myself, I contact a friend.

Whilst in Nottingham I made many new friends, chat rooms we'd meet, then arrange to meet in person. Made many good friends through this technique, many I'm still in contact with today.

I ask my friend if he was up for a new company, me doing the code, him the design, that which he's amazing at. We agree, we can do this.

So the rainy days come, we struggle to get clients, we get a few, just enough to cover the costs for a while, nothing good though.

I speak with a contact I'd made through the learning centre, he offers me some work. We'd never met, he was always awesome though, I really liked him. My old boss finds out and has a go at me for this, how could I contact one of his suppliers, well I did and we were now friends.

My love and I go and visit him, using most of the last savings I have, I book us a nice hotel room. We meet the friend, go out for something to eat, a Ruby, things were good again, he promised that he could give me work, happy days once more.

He tosses me a few websites, I get my designer to work them out, he gives me the PSDs, I make the site things are awesome. Problems though, the cash isn't coming, I need it now, I've just used my savings on an extravagant hotel for my love and I, I had to, make the most of it!

We have a fall out, work it out and get things back, my designer now decides he's coming over for a few weekends, he also DJs, awesome, weekends of music, drink and smokes, the life again, it was back, not much money now nor credit lines but we were there again. I'd find a way, I always did, I had to for my love, I wouldn't let her down, not like I was let down with everything, she wouldn't have to face the pain I'd felt, I'd protect her.

I bury my pain again, it's history, things aren't good right now but they'll come good, I'll make sure of it, I have to, the pain can't resurface, it's gone now, history.

I get a contract job through the learning friend, they need a network sorting, awesome, I can do this. I travel to Wales. We meet, go to our hotel and have some drinks, I sneak for a smoke.

The next day we work out what needs doing, we have just two days, no problem, we crack on, upgrading as we need. First day over and we're nearly done, just a few more bits left. We head back to the hotel, job well done, a few hours tomorrow and we're done, few hundred quid each, nice going for what was just one days work at this point. Nice meal, lots of drink, bed, sleep doesn't come though, I'm missing my love already.

Another hangover, oh well, deal with it, water please. We arrive on site, my website is working perfectly for them, does all they need, I've even hacked a solution that takes a security flaw to my advantage to make it work. One problem remains though, the emails aren't propagating properly, I could fix this. The other guy that was there was an "MS Expert", he dismissed me, I didn't have his certificates, what did I know?

For hours he tried to fix this problem, me insisting I knew the solution, finally they ask for my fix. I make not even 20 characters of changes, try that I say.

They go off, test it and what would you know, it works! My fix, the lowly knows nothing, not a certificate to my name, just a lowly GCSE keyboarding skills C grade, yet I'd fixed it. 4 hours later than needed we sign off the job, job done.

I have some money now, I can provide for my love again, keep her happy, working for myself might work afterall? The site was done, working, tested everything was good, we go home.

CLOSE TO LOSS—THINGS ARE GETTING BAD

I'm working, I've a few jobs lined up, I've met with my mates boss, the designer, he's offered me work, the pay isn't coming quick enough though, the spec comes in, I do it then it all changes, cash isn't released until they're happy.

I'm really struggling now, my love knows things are bad, she's worried too.

I speak with a financial advisor—I'm told I have possibly two weeks, otherwise I'll have it all taken!

I speak with my love, we hit the papers, her looking for anything that can be good for me, I'm feeling lost, how could I let this happen? We find something, I ring, interview arranged. I have two days to prepare, how can I make this work, I ask myself? I do what I know, I hit my computer, make my CV, recursive menus in javascript, it's awesome, looks like ass but functionality wise, it's awesome.

I upload this to my domain, that which I've had since 1998, decide to buy another, this one, upload it there too. If this doesn't get me the job nothing will.

I drive to the interview, 40 miles or so. This would be interesting, my cars not right either, something is making odd noises.

I meet my interviewer, he's nice enough, few years older than me, very good looking guy, confidence oozes from him, I like him. We talk, I show him my work, he tells me he's a bit of a coder himself but he's impressed, what he's seen is awesome! I go to leave, realise my car's oil is leaking, I ask him where a garage is, he gives me directions, I need a new oil filter. I have no money for this so I ring him, explain the humility me having to ask this, can I borrow £20 for a new oil filter, he laughs, no problem, he gives me the £20. I get my car fixed, head home, back to my love.

I'm filled with joy, I have the job I tell myself, there's no way he'd give me that money unless the job was mine, my love is happy, things are going to be ok, I promised her they would be, I've now done it, a year of hardship, we struggled but things would be good now. I've made that promise, it must come true.

It did.

More career—My next career

Job starts—Another new job, they come quick for me

I'm now just days away from having to make a payment, otherwise everything gets taken from me, my love, we'd be lost. I have a new job starting. I go for my first day.

There's just two other staff, this is ok, small company, I've done these before. I start two weeks before these though, I'm the network guy, IT specialist, I have to make things work before they can work.

I'm asked what I need, easy, a server, workstations, these will do, keep the costs low. We agree on the desks, lots of space for expansion, this is cool I'm the right hand man, he's trusting me, my opinions count!

I strike a deal, I get my first half pay cheque and I'll buy the stuff needed to network, done. I network the place up, saving costs by making most the cables myself, things are coming on nice, we have the three desks needed, 4 with the bosses, server setup, hell it's what I do, computers, I own them, they bow to my command. The work begins, I find out what we're really doing, advertising, not my bag but I'll roll with this, the guy is awesome I can do this.

Growth—How it grows

I "advertise", something I've been against my whole life—it's paying the bills though so has to be done, I'm responsible for making many sites, mostly crap. Still the bills are being paid, I have my love, things are good. The people I work with are nice, we all get along great.

The only issue is the distance, 40 miles, to get there for normal start time, I have to leave before 07:00—I strike a deal with the boss, I start work for 07:00 and can leave an hour and a half early, he gets an extra 30 minutes and I miss all the traffic, this is great! Gives me some time in the morning before the others arrive so I have some peace. I'm trusted with the office keys.

I deploy servers, backup solutions, everything we need. The business quickly grows, we take on more staff. I'm now making nicer websites too, things are all good.

There's a cafe on the premises, the people there are nice, they really like me, I eat there most days, not thinking to prepare food to take with me, besides it's not too expensive and I like supporting my new friends there.

Home life is good, money is tight though, the bills are more than expected, my love decides to get a job working with her Mum. This should help out, she contributes to 1/4 of the costs, more than enough.

HOMELIFE—LIFE IS GOOD AT HOME

Things are all good, work is going really well, I'm the right hand man, trusted explicitly with everything. My pain is buried deep, forgotten. The partying continues, we spend our evenings having a drink, just relaxing, passionate nights in.

We see the neighbours often, we're close friends now, he helps me with DIY, I help with his computer, we make a good team. Summer months come and we'll sit outside, having drinks, enjoying the sun when we have it.

My love usually comes home to make us dinner, I cook sometimes but it's mostly her realm now. She'll join us for drinks, happy times, nothing could go wrong. We visit my Mum for a holiday, my loves first time abroad, new and exciting for her, catching a plane, the airport, it's all good. We usually just relax whilst there, fiesta time if we can, there's usually one somewhere. First time experience for me though, driving on the wrong side of the road! We get friendly with the local restaurant owners, get taken out clubbing, the partying continues.

Back home things continue, we go out at the weekends, partying hard, always partying. Never a night passes without a drink. We rarely argue at this point, we're still deeply in love, infatuated with each other possibly, we didn't care though, we had each other, enough money to enjoy ourselves, whatever she wanted, I'd provide.

I get a bonus from work, well the TV is a little old, why don't I treat her for Christmas and get one of these new flat screen things. I go my usual haunt for things like this, there's always offers on and I'm in luck! I get her a nice 32" screen, more than big enough for our little house.

She loves it, I obviously couldn't hide that from her so she had it early, I put the other TV in the bedroom so we can watch films before sleep. The only room that's not complete is the spare bedroom, we don't mind though, we rarely have guests who stay over, those that do don't mind, it's got a few things in it, mainly my computer.

We spend the evenings apart, her watching her soaps, how I loathe those, I don't mind though, I can game, upgrades for the computer and I'm happy with it, all the latest games I play, we always spend a few hours together though before bed, watching a film or one of the series we both liked. There were loads of these so we had plenty to watch.

Work mates come up for her 18th birthday, we party it large, the night ending with her in the toilet ill, oh well, I aid her whilst she's ill, holding her hair back to tending to her. The night was good though at least. We avoided the usual fights that always happened—I don't fight and don't like seeing others, we kept ourselves to ourselves. Just enjoying our night out. One thing that did surprise me, her mate kissed me right in front of her, I was too shocked to do anything, we laugh it off as drunken stupidity. I have my love, that's all I need.

WORK CONTINUES—CARRYING ON WITH THE WORK

Things are really going well at work now, over Christmas our campaign was so successful, another 3 jumbo jets worth of product had to be ordered! We're quite pleased with ourselves, I'm not involved much on that side of things, I'm busy working on a new website to compete with a large advertising word network. I think it's a long shot but I have a plan, I always have a plan.

The plan is a bit large, my skills in programming are good but this is large, I make some mistakes but finally get the project completed, we pay a small fortune for the domain name. My car had broken down on the way home on the Monday, my loves Dad also had the same failure, what are the chances?

My boss comes to meet me at the nearest pub, to take me home, I tell him it's ok, the Dad is giving me his old one so I'll be back up in no time, well once he's fixed it anyway. We discuss what to do about the coming week, I suggest I could work from home maybe, I have remote access afterall. No, I'm needed in the office, not just for my skills but everyone enjoys my sense of humour, we're always crude with each other, in a nice way, my usual reply when asked to do something was "Ok for a blow job". Gaybar was one of the guys nicknames, he got this from the popular song at the time, we used to banter all day long, it was awesome.

We decide that I can stay with my boss, we're close friends now anyway so it's a pleasure. I get the train the following morning. That night we discuss the domain name—he's unsure to go with it or not, the name is fitting, almost too perfect, I know the state of the finances, I am afterall the network admin, I have full access, a privilege I'm trusted not to abuse. I know the state of the finances because he was always open, having a weekly meeting to explain things to the staff. We had to know, we were always needing at very large sum liquidity to maintain the campaigns. We have a few beers and watch TV, a film I think although what, I can't recall. His wife sits with us, she's stunning, not that I'm interested, I have my love back home. Another eye shot, I'm texting her constantly, missing not being at home with her, her being at her parents. I put my phone away.

We agree the domain name is the right one for the company, it's now time for bed. This continues for the week, me being invited along to his weekly film night, a 2 for 1 offer through a certain mobile phone company. Mid week I head home to see my love, getting the train back the following morning, taxi to work.

I'm usually the first one in but not this week, last in the office is unusual for me. Always first in first out, I had my deal, it meant I could be back in time for my love returning. Getting us drinks on the way home, friending the local girl at the off license, she was pleasant enough.

YEAR ANNIVERSARY— WE CELEBRATE THE FIRST YEAR

The first year has been a success, we're profitable, have no real debts, we're all pleased with ourselves. We arrange a day of go-carting to celebrate. I'm unstoppable! Being tall doesn't mean I'm heavy, I have a high metabolism so I can't easily gain weight, I'm easily the lightest there. I start in pole and stay there for the first race, lapping everyone else.

We go for a break and it's decided we're starting the next race in reverse finishing order—hell ok, I've lapped them all anyway, this'll make it more fun for me. Off we go, I'm soon up to the leaders, my boss being one of them, I see a line, he's not—I take it, forcing him off the track. I turn to see him spinning out on the grass, I grin and raise my finger to him, knew he'd love this!

I win again, lapping almost half of the others again, they all use the excuse that I'm so light, it doesn't make that much difference, I've always loved driving, play many driving games so I know the lines to take, doesn't take me long to figure out the limits of the vehicle I'm in and always push it to the limit. We head for a meal.

We hit the pub, I can't have a drink I'm driving, everyone knows I'll not drink whilst driving, my shyness has come back a bit but I'm in good company. We have a laugh and a joke, enjoying the company paid for event, we're told not to hold back, get whatever we want, it's been a good year, we deserve it!

I make my excuses and leave, thanking my boss, now close friend for everything, it's been an awesome day, I'll see him Monday, we shake hands, have a quick hug and off I go—returning to my love.

HEAD HUNTING—WHAT'S THIS, BEING HEAD HUNTED?

I'm at work one day, my mobile goes, no-one calls me whilst I'm at work unless it's an emergency, I don't recognise the number.

It's my old friend who I worked with before, in Wales, he's asking how I am, freakin' awesome dude, everything is working really well, my love and I are getting on great, I have a good job that I'm enjoying, good friends, how's things with you?

He tells me he's setup another new company and he's looking for someone with my skills, he trusts me, we've been close for a few years now, he can't afford to match my current wage though so we leave it at that, him saying he'll come see me soon, it's been years now. I miss him, he's always good company and we seemed to gel instantly on our first meeting.

Work though it starting to test my morals, those which I value so highly, my boss knows this so isn't asking me to do anything—yet—that would cross them. The business has become more competitive than ever, we're needing ever larger cash reserves. We're growing though so it can't be bad, have lots of new contacts, I'm taken to various meetings, introduced to various "partners", I'm trusted here, number 2. There's not many decisions that are made without extensive talks with me, why? I'm no business man, I'm just a geek, code monkey—I'm trusted though and have good intuition so my opinions are valued.

SIDE LINES—A MOVE TO SELF EMPLOYMENT AGAIN?

Work is now really testing my morals, I'm not asked to do anything illegal but all this online stuff is new, there's no precedent set yet, so things are a bit of a grey area. I don't do grey areas, things are black or white to me, nothing in between.

I somehow run into an old mate, from the training centre days, the second ones. He used to run a local shop I got some supplies from, he's been fired, setup by another and his brother didn't trust him. This is harsh, he's a nice guy. We go for a drink, my love coming with us, meeting his partner and friends at the pub. He tells me of his plans, this wonderful dream of doing everything I really loved, building websites and building computers, I'm tempted. We drink far too much, enjoying the summer sun. We agree that I'll think about it, I can't just quit though, it would have to be him running the shop until we had the cash reserves I required to keep my love happy.

How we got home I have no idea, we're both wasted, my love goes to work, I'm way to hungover to do this, I don't have hangovers though, I know how to deal with them, I'm not sure what's wrong, could someone have slipped something into my drink? My head is raging, I can't even ring work to tell them I'm too ill, I can hear my mobile ringing every hour, them trying to contact me. I bury my head under the pillow, my stomach churning, this can't be right, I've not felt anywhere near like this from drink apart from when I was in my early teens. Something else is wrong, I can feel it in my stomach.

Eventually I find it in me to answer my phone, I tell work I'm deeply sorry, I'll explain in the morning. I rack my brains trying to remember what happened the afternoon before, it was afternoon, we were back and in bed early, I'd had more than enough time to counter the effects of the booze. I recall there being a group of lads there, looking a bit too intently on my love and his partner, over the course of the afternoon they'd moved closer and closer, I'd hit the coke towards the end of the night, knowing I had to be up and driving, his partner was on coke since she was pregnant. I figured they must have spiked my drink thinking it was loves, it was the only thing that made sense. I ring my friend and he's fine, his partner hasn't been too good though, they'd put it down to morning sickness. We agree we're sticking to the plan, he's going to find a premises this week.

I head to work the next day, hangover—check but I'm ok, I took it easy the night before, just enough for the sleep to come. I enter the office and the boss is there, another work mate too, this is unusual. I'd missed a big day yesterday and he was on damage control—this was an important campaign.

My boss looks up as I sit down, simply asking "well?". I explain what happened, how indeed we'd been the pub but I was taking it easy, yes probably drank too much but laid off towards the end of the night and hit the coke instead. He's sceptical until I tell him about my mates partner, ok he laughs, you should drink bottles like I do, you can put your thumb over it when you're not drinking to stop this kind of thing!

No-one else questions me, they know better than to do that, I'm number 2 afterall. I get a few looks and those I trust most, I tell, over instant messenger, I was quite embarrassed, how did I not see this, I've been around this sort of thing for many of my years, the signs were there but I was too busy having fun with my friend and my love. I won't make that mistake again!

The week passes smoothly and the weekend arrives. My friend has found a premise for us, it's not in an ideal location but it'll do, we secure the property, he arranges for it to be kitted out. I head home and start working on the systems to power it all, first call, website, easy enough. I contact my designer friend, he does the design for me, I make it all work in a few hours.

So this could be an interesting one, let's see where it goes, I think, I've not invested anything so have nothing to lose.

PAIN SURFACES—THE PAIN STARTS TO BUBBLE UP

It's Sunday, I go round my neighbours for Sunday lunch, they used to cook for me since my love would visit her parents after work and not get back till late. We enjoy lunch, beers flowing freely, I help wash up, it's the least I can do, they've cooked for me!

We sit and game for a few hours, fishing today, how boring! It wasn't, we loved it! We'd compete to get the highest score, we'd do this for hours.

My love returns and comes around, I have her drinks ready for her, we sit and chat for a while, my house phone rings, cordless one that thankfully worked next door, why wouldn't it, the base station was only behind the wall. It's my Mum, her brother has passed. He had been suffering for a while now with cancer, asbestos related.

We leave, briefly saying what's happened. We're told to come round after we've talked if we need anything. I talk with my Mum, she's upset of course, I ask her if she wants me to come and see her, she tells me there's no need, she'll be ok. I was never close with my uncle but something was bubbling, I tried to prevent it. I hit the beers harder now, trying to dose the fire of pain that's starting to rage, all my memories flooding back, Mo, my "Dad", grandma, it's rising too fast, I can't control it!

My love goes to bed, I tell her I'll be in soon, I just need some time to think, I can't be here alone, my Mums alone, sibling half way round the world, I have to be there for her. I can't drive, I've had way too much drink for that, it's not dulling the pain though. I ring my now shadow partner, he agrees to take me to the airport. He's round promptly, I've already booked my flight, thankfully I had a few extra pennies this month. I email my boss to tell him I've had to go away—emergency, I'll ring him in a few days to explain, I'm very sorry but this has to be done.

It's pouring down, my mate tells me he has no petrol so we take my car, he has insurance to cover him 3rd party so it's fine. I have little on me, I've left a note for my love saying I've had to visit my Mum. I have my toothbrush and that's all. I thank my mate, tell him I'll update him as soon as I'm back and enter the terminal. There's confusion over my ticket, I'd only just booked it less than an hour ago, we eventually track it down. I go through security, I'm quite the expert at this by now and there's no hassle, I have everything prepared before I'm even at the metal detector, I pass swiftly through here and head to the bar.

The barman suggests I have a coffee, I'd been drinking heavily and it was showing, I suggest maybe not, he counters and insists I have a coffee. OK I understand this, I'm not allowed to fly if they suspect I'm drunk, yes I maybe a little but I'm upset, all my pain has surfaced, ripping through me, I won't show emotion though, not to strangers, that wasn't me, at least not at this point in time.

I have several coffees, it's late enough now, I should be boarding in a few minutes, I'd better ring my Mum to let her know. She answers and sounds relieved that I'm heading to see her, won't be long now, just 4 hours at most.

I arrive and we hug, I'm off the plane in minutes, I know this airport now, have no luggage so it takes me no time to get to her. I've not slept all night, I was too busy, things to do, places to get to, I was there now. We get back to her place and I ask if she minds if I take a quick nap. Of course not, she's happy I'm here and understands. Sleep comes for a few hours.

I wake and she's not there, I ring, she's had business to attend to, so I walk to meet her, stopping for a quick drink though, the pain is coming back again, I can't let it—I have to be strong for my Mum. We sit and talk and she tells me she's upset but it was expected, she's coping ok, it was better this way. He couldn't breath without tubes, he didn't want to live like that.

This is good, she's not suffering, we return home, speak with the sibling, she's impressed at my actions, for the first time I've showed my family strengths she tells me! That brings the searing pain of all I'd seen when she wasn't there, my standing in the way of my Dad when he was about to hit my Mum, she'd not seen this, she didn't know all that I went through with my Dad—when we were alone. Still I've done well, been there to support my Mum when I thought she needed it.

She transfers me money to cover the expense, I tell her not to, don't be silly she tells me, it was a really nice gesture and it's nothing for me, she knows I'm still struggling a bit with funds.

I spend a couple of nights with her then return home. I'm greeted to an empty house, my love knowing I'd be returning still not home, many hours after she'd finished work. No problem, I help myself to a drink, waiting her return. I roll a joint to help null the pain, everyone of my losses surfacing once more, bring back all the pain, fresh pain since I'd suppressed it for so long, the pain I'd buried.

She returns to find me sobbing, she consoles me. I question why she wasn't back sooner, her parents were fighting again, more memories return. She's angry that I just left, without evening saying good bye to her, I explain that she was sleeping and looking so beautiful that I didn't want to wake her, it was best for her not to get upset also. She couldn't have come with me, her work wasn't as understanding, I had to do it though I tried to reason.

I see cracks appearing in our strength, cracks that I'd ignored, she was my love afterall and I'd ignored everything that was wrong, her not being there after work, instead choosing to spend most her time with her parents. I'd ignored this, she was young afterall and possibly we moved into our house a bit too soon, we had known each other over two years though, in person well over one, surely that wasn't too soon.

I put it again to one side, she was my love, I could accept this, we'd be strong again, I was out of order for vanishing in the middle of the night, that was wrong of me? Hell no, she'd be there for her parents, quite often was when they needed her, I was acting correctly. Put it to rest, sleep, let it go.

There's no passion that night, sleep comes briefly, there hasn't been much of that these past 3 days, back to work, sanity is there, I need to explain myself anyway.

EXPLANATION—TIME TO EXPLAIN WHY I VANISHED

I return to work as promised, Thursday morning. My boss is there early, my friend.

Welcome back, where have you been, Spain I gather, what's up? He questions.

I ask if he wants a drink, it was always the first thing I did when arriving, put the kettle on, take my coat off, collect my mug and make a coffee. He comes over to my desk and I explain the events of the last few days. He's upset for me, it's not a problem, it can either come out of my holidays or sick day allowance I'm told. I ask why he's in so early, he was normally at least 30 minutes after me. A busy day ahead, I couldn't have vanished at a worse time, this was always the case.

I crack on with my tasks, determined to make up time, first though I make sure the backup completes, 3 days without a backup, that was not good. My custom script works as always and reports success, I unplug the drive and place it in the normal position ready to take home with me, that was my duty afterall, ensure data survived the worst possible failure. Anything critical I backed up on the fly, having my home server setup to be the device, a simple but effect way of making sure the vital data was secure.

Work mates arrive, I'm already deep into my code, barely noticing them arrive, until I'm asked if I'd like another drink. Awesome, coffee please, actually no a herbal tea instead, I've had too many coffees already. The day flies by, I get lunch early, I was allowed, I don't get hungry often and when I do, I need to act on it, I get others some toast.

The pain is bursting through now, I vanish to the toilets to have a little cry, they wouldn't see me upset, I was in control, they never saw me upset, I was always happy, having a laugh, joking around, fun to be with, they couldn't see this side of me.

My co-worker, side coding partner knows me well by now though and asks me what's wrong, I explain we've suffered a loss, I'll be ok though, we weren't that close, I'd not seen him in years anyway, hiding the real suffering that was eating away at me.

The week finishes, my love and I have had a few arguments now, we didn't argue, why now? I'm starting to see she's not really my partner, she moved in with me because she wanted her own space—to have her own house, that which I so willingly provided. She wasn't content with that though, she wanted "her life" to remain, doing what she wanted. Now it was frequent that she'd go out with her work mates, leaving me at home, this was fine I told myself, I could at least crack on with some code for my sideline business, this wasn't coming on as fast as we were hoping but no worries, we'll get there.

WORK & LIFE CONTINUING— THE WORK AND LIFE CONTINUES.

So things are going well, sort of. My love and I are arguing more now, the cracks have opened. Work is going brilliantly though, we've filled the office, time to find bigger premises.

I'm attending more meetings, sometimes rarely in the office for work—just arranging details, being techy, making sure my boss isn't taken for a ride. He knows some code but not like me, he trusts me to be there for him, ensuring he's not been fed a pack of lies. We've had many parties now, Christmas', birthdays you name it, we're all pretty close, things at work couldn't be better, well apart from the "grey" areas I'm being asked to work in. My boss sits me down and tells me he understands I have my morals and if there's anything I'm not 100% happy in completing, I'm not to do it. I need the job though, to provide for my love. I still stick to them though, nothing can falter me from those.

It's been almost 3 years now, since our first meeting, whilst in the office, we barely speak, he's a nice open view office he sits in with the new manager, we also get along well. I'm now into my 3rd car since starting, my love having passed her driving test and it was always a given that she'd have the car her Dad gave me, not a problem, I go and find one—a nice little sporty number. Nothing really but I was happy with it. At least this one was reliable, one of the previous ones I had, the lights failed on me one winters night heading home, I had no choice but to drive back in darkness, yearning for cars to come behind me, it mattered not though, I knew the road, every turn, every corner, I made it back and took the following morning to get the lights fixed. This one was in good shape, fast too when I needed it to overtake tractors or such, they were back roads afterall.

I now knew the road like the back of my hand, I could roll a smoke, I'm back on the rolling tobacco now, whilst driving and it wasn't a problem, I rarely touched my brakes, I knew everything about this route. My record was having to brake just 4 times, once at the top of my road, once arriving at work and the same on the return. 40 miles, 40 speed cameras, I knew exactly where they all are, I don't speed though, just be extra vigilant that I've not lost concentration for a moment coming down a hill and gained just that little extra to get me a ticket. I abide the law, well apart from smoking my joints, that's a plant, how can that be illegal, it's the same as cigarettes yet mellows me out, my morals tell me this is ok.

I get another call from my friend, asking me if I'll take his offer this time, it's too still low, I've a large bonus promised this year, we chat, things are good, he tells me one day I'll accept his offer. I tell him I hope so, I enjoyed working with him, we were very close mates and knew each other, "got" each other, it would also mean working from home, that would be nice, I could spend more time with my love.

Still this can't happen, it's not enough money, I'm still deep in debt and trying my hardest to clear it, I can't take a pay cut. My love and I are now arguing often, always drink involved. I can't say anything when I'm sober, I love her with my being, the drink though, I get the Dutch courage and speak out, always getting defence back, never her realising the problems I have are because of her not being there for me, like a partner should. I feel like I'm more a father to her. Providing everything I can yet her only wanting to be with me when it suites her. I always wake the next day and apologise, it was me being stupid—wasn't it?

We frequent the local, we're known in there, get on with the regulars, I'm known as "the student" thanks to my youthful looks, I'm nowhere near being student age but they still think so, it's nice. We all have nicknames, no-one knows the real name of anyone. We always have good times here, I know the owners, the staff, everyone, frequently I don't even have to buy my drinks, they're given to me for being such a good customer, my love takes this to full advantage and orders something special, a double or something, I stick to my usual, a pint, maybe, maybe once in a while a White Russian, in salute to my "dude" days.

We smoke outside, a joint rolled up covertly, everyone knows I always have some, giggle ensue, truly good times, until we get home. My love quite often now rejects me, telling me she's tired and has an early start. The only early start she has is because she's decided to go her parents again, leaving me alone, to dine with the neighbours. How hard would it be for her to come round with me, OUR good friends, they'd been there through some of the nastier arguments we had, sometimes even knocking because they could hear the shouting and trying to put a stop to us, we were a cute couple, everyone liked us. Still happy times, the sleep still comes at least, mostly, apart from when we argue. When we argue it takes me back, the pain rages through, ripping me into bits, I then hit the whiskey, to null the pain, often passing out on the floor next to my computer, not even bothered to make it the 10m to the bedroom. Probably not even 10m, more like 6 . . .

A WEDDING—THE SIBLING GETS MARRIED

So my sibling is getting married, awesome, my Mum pays for my love and I to go out, I'm a surprise Groom, this is going to be awesome.

We arrive after 24 hours of travelling, I'm exhausted, still it's the morning and the stag do is this evening, I can't let that get in the way. I try to get a quick hour or two, no good—the sleep doesn't come. Not to worry, I know the solution, a few beers, shower and I'm on form.

We have the races to go to first, it's going to be a long day, starting at 12:00, I can do this, mind over matter I tell myself. I pace myself, only having two beers over the course of the races, 3 hours, I keep in control. We leave the races, I'm starting to feel a little odd, not the drink, just exhaustion, the Dad is also with us.

We split into the males and females, off we go, night on the tiles here we come! We get some food, much needed by this point. I'm pushing into 36 hours now without sleep, I can cope though, these are happy days, my love I know is being looked after by my sibling, being so good at caring I knew my love was in safe hands.

We finish eating, head off to another bar, my head's now spinning, cloudy, simply exhausted. Still I'll continue, I'm unstoppable remember! There's some very lovely ladies at this bar, I'm suddenly alone, well why not talk to them, I'm feeling confident and let's see what the locals are like!

3 in total, all drinking very expensive cocktails. They're intrigued by my accent, I don't have a typical British accent, it's somewhat unplaceable. The conversation is good, they surf, enjoy various other sports, just finishing Uni and hope to become something or other, I forget my mind was half way asleep now—sleep, that which I missed so much. Still I can't go home yet, it's still early, well not home but to the hotel. The one that I find most attractive suddenly gives me a proposition, she wants me to go home with her and fuck her brains out, she's always fancied British guys and she's taken a very big shine to me, shall we leave—now! I'm shocked, somewhat flattered but I can't, I have my love afterall, I don't betray my love. I tell her thank you very much, I'm flattered but I can't, I'm engaged and I don't do that. She gives me a peck on the cheek and whispers into my ear how I'm missing out on the best night of my life, sure I won't reconsider? I give her a small hug, thank her and offer to buy them another round of drinks, nope, they're leaving now, if I'm not leaving with her then goodnight, was nice talking to you. Oh well, at least I have my love—she'll be at the hotel waiting for me, I didn't want anyone else.

We head off to the casino, my mind is totally blurred by now, I can't focus. I must, where's my Dad I wonder? Could do with a chat with him, he sorts me out, he'll tell me what to do. I ask one of the group if he's seen him, he hasn't but offers me his mobile to ring him, he was a friend from my childhood years it appears, I didn't remember him but he remembered I, he was more than happy for me to ring.

I try to focus, I know his number, I've dialled it a thousand times, I attempt to ring, number unknown.

The paranoia kicks in, I recalled hearing some Russians at the last bar, they'd said something that I somewhat understood, they were going to take someone, was that right? I didn't know, my head's clouded by lack of sleep, tiredness I'd not felt for some time taking a grip. I try again, frantic now to recall that number which I knew so well. 15 or so attempts later success! He's at the casino—fine and well, I'm relived. I thank the friend and give him his phone back, we're not far now.

I enter, give him a big hug, he takes me to the bar, tries to get me a drink, I'm refused, told I'm too drunk, I've hardly had anything, yes my eyes are red raw, I'm tired, I work at screens all day and don't blink I try to explain, no good. My Dad sneaks me a drink anyway, it's quickly picked up on by the bouncers, I relent and hand over the drink, I'm not ruining the night, I can go without tonight. I order a coke. That'll do.

My Mum has a man friend out there too, he's tired and wants to head back, awesome, hometime! I can barely walk now, my feet having swelled from the flights, agony but I'll get through this. I plead for him to get us a taxi, no, he's fit, we walk. I have no idea where we are, so follow his lead I do, almost sleep walking.

We talk on the way home, well to the hotel, he tells me how he feels for my Mum, I'm pleased, she needs a companion. More walking, my ankles are on fire, my feet I can't even feel. We get back to the hotel, I climb into the bed settee, next to my love, she wakes briefly and gives me a good night kiss. At last, sleep comes, the darkness falls, that which I'd lacked for so many hours, almost 40 by now.

WEDDING PREPARATIONS—THINGS NEEDED TO BE DONE FOR THE WEDDING

Everything needs sorting for the wedding, a visit to the tailors, this goes well, there's no hangover today, there should have been but the sleep was too deep. Well there shouldn't have been, I wasn't allowed to drink, the hangover should have been from the lack of sleep, I'm used to this though, it never gets me down.

The outfit is sorted, we arrange the rest of the plans, everything is coming on nicely. I sit with my love and we have some drinks in the hotel waiting the next moves.

The days pass quickly, the day is soon upon us. We arrive, things need doing, the "bar" needs setting up—my forte! I do this quickly, I've enough experience on this so it's no hardship, everything is prepared, we await the bride!

The location I recognise, something about it seems familiar, I later research and find out it's a set to a very famous film, awesome!

Awesome—a word I use a lot, it came from one of my work mates, he was always positive, I took this into me, to try and have that positive outlook on life, it remains with me to this day . . . sorry slight digression, back to the wedding.

My sibling comes down, sees me and winks, suspicions were there but it wasn't known for certain, the ceremony is beautiful, a military vessels passes and gives a salute, it was awesome!

The party afterwards was great, I get emotional, some friends that I knew should have been there but couldn't, friends of the sibling, I can't stop, it's not my place to cry but I had to, I'd not seen them in years, not even my friends but they meant much to me, to my sibling, never mind, I get over it, bury the pain, I've lots of space there, more room to bury pain, I miss my "Dad" I let it slide. Many tears later I rejoin the party, have a dance with my love, she's not comfortable dancing but does so—I dance with many friends, the day has been awesome, things couldn't be better. Ok I could have held back the tears but I couldn't, things got the better of me, for once I let some things bubble up, take over but it was awesome, my sibling now married, I was overjoyed.

My love is now also very drunk, we head back to the hotel, sleep, this comes, eventually, not for a few hours though, I'm replaying a lot of my life, missing my "Dad" why couldn't he be there to see this? Still at least my Mum had a new partner, content with that I allow the darkness to come.

ULURU—A HOLIDAY WITHIN A HOLIDAY!

I'd told my Mum that if I was visiting Australia I'd like very much to visit Uluru, Ayers Rock, I'd spent many hours searching for a reason, why I was here, something I may come back to later but not yet, I may not, it's very private to me.

Jackpot again! She'd booked a surprise, my sibling on honey-moon, my love and I are treated to a holiday here, awesome! I have no spare cash though so we can't do much, it matters not—she wants to do things, we can't, arguments ensue. Tearing more from me. She's been given all this, a trip half way around the world, thanks to my Mum, a holiday in a holiday and yet she's still not content, what more can I give her? She rejects me, my fears come flooding back, seeing my Dad threatening to hit my Mum, I shan't go there. I let it slide. The sleep doesn't come, I spend the night on the balcony, smoking much, what have I done wrong? We're half way across the world, enjoying life, my siblings wedding, a good night out for my love, I knew she was looked after, what more could I have done?

The sun is starting to come up, I try to get some darkness, sleep, I manage a few hours.

We wake, she's sorry, we have a passionate shower, something we'd done previously, only a few times when I was at the bedsit.

We go on the planned trip, to see the rock itself, there's something awesome about it—don't know what, we're told how it was formed yet there's this feeling of greatness here, I feel my strength building, I can forget the damage caused, it's my fault anyway, it's always my fault, we get back, have some passion and go for a meal with my Mum and her new guy . . . we then talk with some of the aborigines—we've been told to not get them a drink, how can I refuse, it's a good night, we go back, more passion and things are back on track, life is coming on.

I remember the good times, back when the pain was buried, that which I shall now do again, bury the pain, deep, deeper this time, it can't re-surface, it can't, my love I've almost lost, the pain has to go, it's destroying all I care for now, it's gotta go.

Vanquish I do, deep, deep down, buried, forgotten about again.

A TURN FOR THE WORSE—MY LOVE AND I START TO FALL APART

We've enjoyed ourselves, a nice break from everything, things can only get better I tell myself. We return to work, lives returning to normal from the holiday, well normal for us anyway.

My love starts coming home later each passing day, now opting to stay over her parents a few times a month, ok I can understand, she's close to her family, they've had a coloured life too. I'm starting to suspect she might be seeing someone else though, she's constantly talking about a work mate and how amazing he is. I talk with our neighbours one night, getting quite emotional, they reassure me that's not the case, she wouldn't do that to me. My love returns to find me upset, she assures me he's just a friend. OK maybe too much beer got the better of me that night, I put it to bed.

Works Christmas do is coming up, we have an evening planned, I book into a local bed and breakfast, I can't drive that evening, drinks are on the company afterall! I head from work, picking up some lagers en-route to the B&B. I grab a quick shower, have a few beers, I need the Dutch courage again and get ready. I arrive to find most the other work mates already there, things are going along nicely, the only food there is a buffet, I'm not too keen for those so I stick with a liquid diet.

We have our foreign workers over too, one of them is stunning, I find myself becoming quite attracted to her, what? My love is all I want, I remember my suspicions and convince myself she's cheating—I can have a bit of fun too. We flirt, much to my amazement, she's actually showing interest. We spend the evening laughing and giggling, having much fun. My work mates are stunned too, they know I only have eyes for my love, the evening soon passes, do I act on my male urges, she is stunning afterall. It would surely give me loads of kudos with my mates, I've never been one to have many women, have I missed out on all the fun?

Things start to get a bit blurry now, we've been playing drinking games— her telling me there's no way I can outpace her, well she doesn't know my relationship with drink, I know the tricks. We've mixed and matched though, this being one weakness, I usually avoid doing this.

We all say our goodbyes, everyone getting taxis home. There's just her, her friend and myself left now, do I jump in her taxi with her? She's given me all the signs, signs that I'm now capable of seeing, we wait. I give her my coat since it's cold, I've enough beer in me to keep me strong, I don't like the cold but I have to be a gentleman. Her taxi arrives, she gives me a kiss on the cheek, we may even have had a proper kiss, my memory is very vague. She puts her hand out the taxi for me, I instead take my coat, this is not who I am, I'm loyal to her. I wish them a good night and close the door, almost—I had faith in myself though, I remained strong.

I get a taxi back to the B&B, have another beer and collapse, easily the last one to make it to bed. Morning arrives, as was tradition, I always turned up late for work after these events, today would be no different. The hangover is raging, I'd broken my rule and mixed my drinks, I knew this was coming. I stop at the shop to get some supplies, lucozade and lots of it. I realise I've cut my jeans with the key, it was just a long bit of metal, quite sharp so half my bottom is exposed, good job I've got a long coat that covers it, it's breezy though, cold on my bare skin.

I'm greeted with applause, my boss giving me his usual grin, the party animal has surfaced! I explain my situation and go get change into my trousers from the night before. Making a coffee as I do so.

I sit down, the lady from the night before a desk over from me, I was always backed in the corner, to have command over the room. She's looking rather worse for wear, still stunning but eyes a bit baggy, it's obvious she's not had much time to get ready. She glances up at me, I smile at her, nodding in thanks for a lovely evening. One of the lads catches this and he suddenly remembers, the outrageous flirtations that took place the night before.

He slides over to me, a single word written on a post it note, her name. I look at him, stoned faced. "Well?" he says and rolls back to his desk, to continue over IM, she's sat directly opposite him. Well what, he's not convinced. I ask him would I really have turned up at a different time if anything had happened. He's still not convinced saying I'd plan for something like, to make it look like nothing happened. I eventually convince him nothing happened, although it never really sunk in with everyone, there was always the odd whisper about it.

Not much work takes place, there's hangovers all round, the boss was expecting this though, we usually had a laid back environment anyway so it mattered not.

Things with my love and I are getting quite bad, we argue more than ever, always after a drink. One Saturday we're going at it again, she's pushing my buttons, knowing exactly what to say to wind me up. She's getting ready to go out, me staying in again. She's on the bed now, acting all superior, sarcasm oozing from her, it was never fitting for her. She says something that cuts deep into old wounds, the pain surfaces, I raise my fist!

I look at myself, how had she driven me to this. I start crying, I can't hit anyone and I was about to hit my love, I knew I'd never manage it but this was the closest I'd ever come. I sob, she realises we've gone too far with this one, we hug and make up, this won't happen again. We go out the following day for something to eat, make up and all is good again.

WORK NOT SO GOOD—THE WORK IS NO LONGER ENJOYABLE

I'm starting to resent work now, it's getting harder and harder and riskier moves are having to be made, nothing illegal still, just not what I'm comfortable doing. I look for other work, there's nothing suitable at the moment, economic times are hard. I'll stick with it, the work mates are all good, the office is full now.

There's a new girl too, she's rather nice, we hit it off instantly, having playful flirts with each other all day, much to the amusement of others. She's a smoker too, the only other one in the office, we take our breaks together, chatting about everything and anything. She's having problems with her ex, I listen, things aren't so good for her. Several times she gets upset so I give her a hug. She smiles, I'm there for her.

The new manager there is getting married, we're all invited to the party, awesome, I arrange for a hotel room, there's only a few spaces and it's too far for a taxi.

Still the work is bugging me, where's my friend—shortly into this time he rings me, he has an offer for me, it's slightly less than I'm on now but I'll be working from home, I quickly do some calculations. In the savings in petrol and being able to eat at home, it works out I'll be better off. I tell him I accept, now to hand in my notice, this is going to be difficult.

We all head to the chip shop for lunch, this was the custom on Fridays, I ask the new manager to hold back, I need to talk with him. I explain my situation, the work isn't as fun as it used to be and the driving is starting to take its toll on me, it's not a huge distance but the early starts aren't my style. He asks about the money, if they offer me more will I stay. I explain it's not about the money, that's never been it for me, that's just a means to an end. He wishes me well and the best of luck, will I serve out my notice period or is it instant. Of course I'll serve my notice, I'm contracted to and I wish no bad feelings, am I still welcome to the wedding? Don't be silly, of course you are, I've invited just my friends.

We return and eat lunch, he's telling my boss, my friend the bad news. I'm summoned into the office. I explain the same to my friend. He understands, the driving isn't something he'd want to be doing either, he does though ask I tell everyone else I've got a better offer. Well technically I haven't but with the cost savings, it does work out better so I agree.

I keep quiet for a while, telling just a few of my closer friends there, the new girl asks me for a favour, "Yeah ok if you suck my dick" I reply, my usual retort. She smiles and tells me if she could find it she would. The office is laughing. I knew she wouldn't take offence to it, we were always joking and flirting, it was how we got on. Next thing, I'm summoned to the office again. My boss, friend is struggling to contain his grin, he knows what I said was in a harmless fashion and she'd take it as the joke it was meant. Someone had reported me, I know how it was but the manager has to give me an official warning. OK, that was worthwhile, I've just handed in my notice anyway, thinking sexual equality—what a joke, it was ok to say that to the lads but to a friend, oh well, only a few weeks to go, I'll just keep my head down.

The weeks pass quickly, I prepare our spare bedroom, converting it to mostly an office with bed, build another custom desk with the help of my neighbour. The carpet's a bit shoddy but it doesn't matter, I have the perfect workstation now, dual screens, powerful computer (I always kept that upgraded), coffee machine for the mornings everything I needed to work from home.

I start my last day, it's a cold winters day, the office is cold until everyone else arrives. I'm a bit low, I'm going to miss these guys, we've shared several years together, had some good times, still a new job awaited me, something I'd be happy doing. Lunch passes and the weather takes a turn for the worst. It's starting to snow, little anxious now, we've been forecast heavy snow for a while now, it appears to finally have arrived. It starts to come down thick and fast, settling quickly. This could make the journey home interesting.

I decide it prudent to ask if I can leave, my friend, my boss tells me of course, he was expecting this question an hour or more ago. I wish my farewell to my mates, we'll keep in touch though we promise.

The snow is coming down heavy now, settling quickly on my coat. Everyone else it seems has the same idea, I get as far as the town and hit deadlock. The journey is tedious, it takes me almost 4 hours to cover just 10 miles. I contemplate a different route, tune in the radio to get a status update—no good, everywhere is same. I guess I just have to sit this one out. I'm now only half way home, the off license is shutting in the next hours, I ring my neighbours and ask them to get me my supplies, celebrations are needed—I'm starting a new job!

Suddenly all the traffic just vanishes, the roads are clear, snowy but clear, I can make it back in time now! I drive faster now, being careful of the conditions, slowing well in advance of the turns, the bends, this has been my road now for years, I'd driven it in darkness before now when my headlights failed me, I knew my car, new my abilities, drive I would.

As it turns out I made it back in time for the off license, doesn't matter though, I go to see my neighbours.

The drinks are already chilled for me, we sit back and relax, talking bout my new job, what will it be like working from home? I'm excited, I know the guy, he's a good friend, he'll sort me right I'm sure.

I spend the weekend preparing my computer, the programs I needed. I had most already, I had worked from home on evenings anyway so it wasn't much of a change, just the new office, everything was set, my love and I talk, happy that I'll be at home more, so we can spend more time together, her not having to worry about my driving so far each day. I'd had a lucky escape one day, I stopped to get some smokes, I was planning on quitting but this day I really fancied one. On the way back, a lorry had crossed the road and steam rolled two other cars, I find out later that very nearly could have been me, it happened just 10 minutes before my arrival, the 10 minutes it took me to get my smokes.

There was no fear of this now!

Working from home—The Job Starts, Working from Home

1st Days at Home—The Life at Home, Working

I start my first day bright and fresh, only having to be up 15 minutes before work, enough time to put the coffee machine on, ready for a fresh cup. This was certainly a refreshing change, I'd normally be into my 3rd hour of waking by now.

I've my work equipment set, we talk about what my role will be, duties, responsibilities and what would be expected of me, we'd been over this before, it was just a formality. I'm introduced to the other staff and given access to what I need. Lots of learning to be done, this is stuff I don't really know, I'd started preparing weeks before though so was a little prepared.

I'm really enjoying this, learning new things, I'm working till late at night, trying to give a good impression. My love is fine with this, she comes back later in the evening, watching soaps. I try to make a few hours for her but find I end up getting caught up with my work, thriving on the new things I was learning.

I feel us drifting apart—she's rarely at home apart from later in the evening and then I'm always working, it's a new job though, she'll understand, it's just till things are settled, a few months at most. I tell myself, then we'll get back on track. She seems quite content though, going out with her mates, having fun, we still have the party life, not quite as much now. My work is consuming me so I don't have time for that any longer, well apart from the weekends, then we party hard, work hard, play harder is my moto!

I have to go away to sort out some personal business, just a couple of days but it has to be done. I'm away, having tended to business I take some down time, first time I've done for a few months. I'm enjoying a glass of wine on a balcony, a nice cigar and reading a good book, basking in the sun. It suddenly dawns on me, I work from home, there's internet here, maybe, just maybe I could live the dream and move out to the sun!

I return home, business all sorted for now and speak with my boss, my friend. The only concern he has is if I can get internet, not a problem I tell him, great when do you want to go? It's going to take a few months to organise but I think this is what I want to do.

I need to speak with my love, see how she feels about it, we'd mentioned it years before but now it was a reality. A friend rings and we go to the pub. I get an angry phone call a few hours later, where was I? Where were you my love, you finished work hours ago, I wasn't waiting around for you, you never do for me. She comes and joins us, we continue drinking, playing pool.

I've discussed this with my mate, he thinks it's a great idea, I just have to see how she feels now. We get home and I mention it, she's not instantly thrilled like I thought she would be, ok let's work this out, there's a way we can do this. We agree that I'll go and she'll come and join me a few months later, she has to finish off a few things first. I tell her that things will be different there, we'll go out, the place is really nice I've selected, lovely area, the people are all great, we can settle there and make it our home, actually spend time with each other, be how we used to be at the beginning.

Plans are made, I've a week holiday in which to do this. I have to wait until things are sorted the other side first though, making sure the internet connection is working before I can do anything. A few months pass and the move is finally upon us, my love staying at our house until she decides. The weekend comes, time to pack, this is upsetting for both of us, everything's boxed up ready, we both drive to the freight section at the airport, I have a bit of difficulty arranging this, I'd been told previously that I just needed to turn up, that turns out not to be the case.

Eventually everything is sorted, we drive home, my flight not for another two days. We have a night of passion, we're finding our connection again. She looks at me and tells me she can't be without me, she'll hand her notice in as soon as she can and be out with me, Awesome things are going to get back on track, just my love and I, happy in the sun.

I take my car to the friend from the shop, I've told her she can have it and pay me monthly, it's doing me no good anymore, she's overjoyed, she even has the insurance paid for the rest of the year, transferred into her name.

My other friend comes to pick me up, I've an early flight so have to stay at friends near the airport, it's too early for me to expect anyone to take me and too costly for a taxi. He stays for a quick drink but then has to head home, he was work in the morning. I thank him greatly for all his help, we have a quick hug and away he goes. I chat with the friends, enjoying a few more drinks, they've been really good over the years.

I wake to the sound of rain pouring onto the windows, no more of this I think, soon I'll have the life, the life in the sun! I'm feeling no regrets, my love and I will have the dream that so many want, all thanks to my landing a nice job! I promised myself to make things the best I could for her, ready for when she arrives in hopefully just two weeks.

My friend checks on me to make sure I'm awake, taxi has been ordered. I shower and prepare my belongings, excited at the new start ahead. I thank them for their hospitality, offer to pay for my time there, don't be stupid they tell me.

My taxi arrives and off I go, excited at my new start.

LIFE IN THE SUN—STARTING A NEW LIFE

I arrive at the airport, check my bags in and head through security, having mastered getting through in minutes now. It's too early for a drink, I have a coffee instead, drinks can be had when I arrive! I drink my coffee— watching the board intently for my gate opening.

It does, it's early, great, I know these flights, that means I'll be there early, my travel arranged there. I'm in no hurry to board the plane though, I wait for the queues to die down before I make my way. I take my coat off, place it in the lockers and take a seat, just a few hours more now and I'll be there!

The flight passes, I'm off, waiting for my bags, they take a while but it matters not. I meet my lift, off to collect the rest of my things. We load the car, everything just fits, a bit of unboxing needed to make it work but it's done. To my new apartment!

Supplies need to be bought so I just unload things and leave them in boxes, off for furniture, it doesn't take long before I've everything set, a nice new office to work in, TV is installed, new bed sofa, everything is set, I test the computers to make sure they're not damaged, all is good, I'm ready to work and 2 days spare, I might as well check out the area.

I already know someone there, I'm told of a new bar that's opened, so decide to see what it's like, I'd missed the opening night, was too busy unpacking. Lovely young couple are trying their hand at being publicans, they're really nice, she's a lovely, young, bright bubbly person, she's always happy it seems. We become friends, their place now officially my local. I spend the evenings there, returning to speak to my love.

The drinks are cheap here, stupidly cheap I think, ok the party life is going to go but I can a few weeks to enjoy myself first, I quickly figure out the area, finding the shops I need. Food is also cheap so I eat out most nights.

Work continues, I'm doing well, the odd occasion doing a full 24 hour day, my love coming soon, life is going to be great again, we'll be awesome once more. I'm enjoying my evenings, going and seeing my new friends, enjoying a drink outside in the sun, this is the life I tell myself. Everyone here is really laid back, a totally different life style to back home, there's no rush for anything, relaxed and calm. I'm certain I've made the right decision here, my love will fall in love with it like I have.

The weeks pass quickly and soon she's arriving, I have to work though so I arrange her travel. She arrives, we're thrilled to see each other, give each other a big kiss and hug, we're connecting again, I can feel the bond again, this will work. The pain is gone again, buried deep.

THE GOODLIFE—HOW THINGS ARE SO GOOD

We've rented our house out to the friend from the shop, she's trusted, I know she'll pay on time, this is helping, life out here is much cheaper, my love doesn't have to work, instead just enjoy life, relax and be cared for. Money isn't copious but we have enough to enjoy the life.

My love's enjoying how cheap things are, smokes and drinks are always in stock. We dine out frequently, finding out all the places we like, sampling the local foods, tasting the wines. My love doesn't have to work, she's finding she's a bit bored, lazing around watching TV or sometimes sunbathing—we're getting along like we used to, passionate with each other.

We go out and celebrate Halloween, the first time ever, I dress up in fancy dress, the grim reaper, the night is fun and long, talking with more new people.

Christmas comes and my love returns to spend it with her family, I have a friend come out to see me, a close friend. We have a good time, enjoying the holidays we have, we drink far too much most nights and stagger home. He's shocked at how nice people are, one night suggesting we cross the road rather than walk through a group hanging outside one of the clubs, I tell him there's no need, watch. So we simply walk towards the group, they all see us and move out the way, wishing us a good day. He's in awe, he's never seen this before, he realises how much happier I am here, the life is much better than where I was, he too thinks I've made the right decision.

My love returns for my birthday and we celebrate, trying out a new steak house I've heard is good. It turns out to be excellent, we'll add this to the list of regulars. New year comes and we celebrate that with friends, we're making many of those now, it's a small community so all the Brits tend to know each other. We play pool, drink cocktails, spirits are large, my mate asks for a double, I tell him this is a bad idea, he doesn't listen to me, continues anyway. We enjoy the night head home, carrying my mate. We head to bed, having one last drink first, whilst we're drinking that we hear a crash from where my mate's staying, oh well we can sort that tomorrow.

We get up and spend the day lazing around, happy again, with each other, the friend finally arrives early evening, very worse for wear. We have a good laugh at his expense, he returns to sleep more, so we relax and watch TV, no going out tonight, we've partied too much and need a break, doesn't stop us having a few drinks though, enjoying the life.

My love is starting to want to work again though, it's going to be tough, she doesn't know the language here and isn't really happy about learning it, not a problem, we look to finding her some work, I ask my boss, we're in luck, there's an opening and she's just the person needed to fill it. We have more equipment sent over and she begins work, me training her partly, I'd done that role before and knew what I was doing.

Summer is fast approaching and it's getting warmer by the day, gone the few months of the year where there's any chance of rain, we're excited, BBQs again, the party life on the weekends can commence again, not that they really stopped, it was just harder when things were cold.

ALONE FOR SUMMER—I SPEND MY FIRST SUMMER ALONE

My love decides that she's missing her parents, I can understand that, so heads back home to be with them, just for a few months, we can talk as much as we like anyway, we've both got webcams, it's not going to be hard, it's only a few months.

I spend my days working, evenings gaming, always with beers in. I have many friends now, they're a bit surprised she'd want to spend the summer at home rather than here but I don't let it bother me, we talk most nights— well apart from when we're out. She's out with her mates again and I'm out with my new found friends.

I've been having problems with my tenant, she wasn't paying for our house, well some but not all, the car I find out has been crushed so there's no chance of ever getting that now. I ring to try and arrange something with her. She explains she's lost her job and is having difficulty paying. I understand this, I've been there before and almost lost everything, I could give her a break. She promises she'll pay me as soon as possible for everything, the debt is now quite sizeable. I knew legally she had me, we only used an off the shelf contract and I'm sure there were loopholes there, she was a friend, I trusted her anyway, it mattered not, she'd find work soon enough.

I spend the summer with my new found friends, partying hard at the fiestas, there's one in town, awesome. Fair ground rides and partying till the early hours of the morning, I'm in my element again, happy to have so many new friends around. Everywhere I would go, I'd meet someone, I couldn't even walk to a restaurant at the end of the road, maybe 200m without running into a friend, asking how I was, me happy to ask them about their lives, it did mean quick visits to the shops were out but it mattered not, life was laid back and easy here.

I worked, earning a pay rise, happy times! That should help out with the bills. Not that we struggled, I always found a way to provide. I have a car now too, a friend helping me to get a good deal, what more could I want.

I host BBQs for all my friends, a full days event. Get up and take the stuff to the roof, get it setup and prepare the food. Light the BBQ then relax with a lager whilst it settled down, greet my guests and start cooking. The BBQ was barely bigger than a disposable one, it sufficed though, I liked it, it was cute. I'd spend the day cooking, drinking, feast galore! I always made sure my guests were satisfied first though, so by the time I'd come to eat, I'd gone past it, besides, it was time to get ready and hit a club by this point. We'd go out and party hard, doing the one thing I had forgotten about, mixing my drinks again.

Every round we'd get a small shooter, as is the custom, foolishly I drank it, not to worry though, I'm not at work for a couple of days, I can manage the hangover. Recover for work on the Monday.

I'm pining for my love though, when's she coming how, I've still no date.

The summer comes and goes and the intense sun relents, the partying dies down a little, there's always something going on but not as much now, no longer full weekends worth of partying. Things are quieter now—I get phone calls once in a while, I'm not out as much now, yearning for my love to return, I use the excuse that I'm too busy, sorry can't come out. Eventually she returns.

I pick her up from the airport, delighted she's back, we embrace, happy times again, it's been a few months but now we're back, surely she'll settle now.

CHRISTMAS IN THE SUN— ANOTHER CHRISTMAS WITHOUT THE SUN

Another Christmas is approaching, my love decides to spent it away again, this causes a lot of pain, I'd suffered the first without her, not another one surely, it starts an argument, both of us having far too much to drink. We were very much alike in that way, we wouldn't like to upset each other when sober but come the drink, we let rip. We'd started to have fiery arguments again and this was just another to add to that list.

We awake the following day, her having slept on the sofa, my eyes take in the picture before me and I remember the promises I'd made to her, to make her happy, not get upset if she wanted to return home, she wakes, we talk, I apologise and tell her it's ok, she can go home and we'll repeat the last year ritual.

We continue to have a few more fights, always after a night out, we'd usually sort these by the end of the night though, our passions continued, they were some awesome passions too, sometimes quite adventurous too, things were good, not perfect, not brilliant either but good enough, we knew this was going to be hard but tried to put it behind us.

She heads off again, promising to be back for my birthday, my mate coming out again, I'd not seen him in a year, barely spoken with him, we were too busy living the life, partying, enjoying it all. That's when it was a "we" and not at home for the Summer, oh well least I was enjoying myself.

He comes over, staying in his usual place, we continue our routine, holidays from work so out we go, we party hard, he remembers to avoid ordering a double of anything though, he's learned that lesson already!

We visit all the locals, places where I'm known, always welcomed, how you been, it's been a while. I apologise for that and explain work has been busy, well it was either that or we'd been other places—trying to keep things varied. We again enjoy Christmas day, recover boxing day by chilling with a few beers and watching some TV, or films, didn't really matter, we were just relaxing, taking some down time, much needed by now.

Work had seen a good year, tiring but good, I'd learnt many new skills and was progressing nicely. I speak with my love, the flight is all arranged, she'll be back in time for my birthday.

We drive to the city closest to the airport the next day, might as well make a day of it before she arrives we say, I show him around, I've been here just a few times myself.

We stop for a quick drink, I allow myself a small beer, I have to drive in a few hours but a small beer won't hurt, we're going to eat shortly so I'll drink lots of water too, it'll be out my system by the time we have to drive. Food time, so of all places, we visit the golden arches, how not typical cuisine I comment! Still it's his holiday so he gets to do what he wants, I'm happy to be host.

I get a text, it's my love, she's missed the flight, sorry but Dads paid for the day after tomorrow. I'm gutted, the pain of my having birthdays with one or the other parents tearing through my heart. Not to worry, at least she's still coming home, we'll celebrate tomorrow. We walk around a bit more and after a few hours return home, first point of call, get changed, then hit the bars. Hit the bars we did, we were good at this, it's what we did, we'd worked hard all year, now it's time to play harder! Reward ourselves for another hard year of work.

Eventually my love returns, she's so sorry, explains road works were the cause, I kinda buy it but really, if she wanted to make sure, you check the road reports. She tells me it was an accident that happened after they left, ok, it matters not, my love is with me again, we party for the rest of the holiday times, enjoying it most we can.

I feel something isn't right though, the arguments are more frequent now, over silly things, things that were never a problem. I keep burying the pain, I can get over this. My monster won't be fed, it won't come out.

ANOTHER YEAR—MORE WORK, ANOTHER YEAR, LIFE CONTINUES

We both continue working, I'm still spending too much time either working or gaming, I've started that back up now, after upgrading my PC I decided to get some games to test it out, how I've missed those. She also games, sometimes we game together, often not, me leaving her alone to watch TV.

We start arguing more and more, almost daily it seems. We still keep on going out though, putting on the happy face that we're still good with each other. The cracks are really starting to show now, this isn't right but I ignore them, I can't split with her, I'd made a promise to this woman, this, my love—I would keep that no matter what. I start backing down in arguments, letting her win, sometimes she was right, others not, all I was bothered about was keeping to my promise of keeping her happy, it seems I was failing at that.

I get a cleaner, that was one of her arguments that I didn't help out, I did sometimes but ok, not enough, my reasoning being I was too busy with work, often times that was gaming, I lied to myself thinking it was work.

Our friends from the bar are also leaving, they can't take the heat any longer so are moving back home. We're sorry for them but understand, we spend many a night with them, me helping them at the bar, as I'd always done, I knew bar work and it wasn't any hardship to chip in once in a while, they'd been good to us.

We reach breaking point, it's no good, we're not working, my love wishes to return to the UK for another summer, I suggest we have a trial separation—see how things work out, we won't talk about details to each other but we're free to see other people, if after a few months we're still lusting for each other, loving each other, then we'll give it another shot.

This being my suggestion, she readily agrees but tells me she'll not see anyone else, she knows the answer just needs some time. I concur, I only have eyes for her afterall. I take her on her way, we promise we'll keep in touch, just not every day like we used to, a catchup maybe once a week, they do say, absence makes the heart grow stronger. Most of our friends have been suggesting we do something like this, we're not working as it stands so maybe we need drastic measures to get back on track. We agree and off she goes, back to her home, our home.

We leave on good terms, we both know this is only going to a short term thing, to re-kindle our love, her to find her space and return to me.

ALONE FOR SUMMER AGAIN—ANOTHER YEAR LONE, DURING THE BEST TIME OF THE YEAR

It doesn't take long for the news to spread, everyone is concerned and ask if things are going to be OK, sure I tell them, it's just something we need to do, we just need a bit of space, we've being in each others pockets for too long, it'll work out.

I soon find out there's a few other ladies who've expressed interest in me. Now I'm feeling a little tempted, I have a free pass afterall, we're allowed to if we want, just not to tell each other. I decide no it's not worth it, I can wait, I have faith in my love.

A month or so passes, we're hardly talking now, as per our deal, I'm finding it hard, missing my love, a companion, someone to share the time with. I go see our friends in the bar, there's one of the said ladies there, we have some drinks, she's obviously very into me but I show no interest, instead remaining my thoughts on my love. Sure we have a bit of a flirt, that was something I did anyway having found my confidence years ago, it was harmless though, nothing would come of it.

A few more weeks pass and I'm yearning for some companionship, my love once more but we're still not talking much, she's living in our house and the odd times we do chat, I remember the good times we had there, the place still very much the same. It upsets me but I remind myself that it won't be long now, it's coming, soon we'll be back, my love and I.

I found out again, the lady who I flirted with was still expressing much interest in me, I consider it for a moment but soon dismiss it, I'm out this evening anyway, that'll take my mind of it, I can have a few drinks and a laugh with my friends, go home and wait.

I'm out, the night is going well, drinks flowing, laughs all round, good company, happy times. I get a phone call, it's my friend from the bar, said lady is there asking if I'd care to join her for a drink . . .

Well I've had a few too many and I'm not thinking straight, I'm also very horny by now, been several months since companionship, I decide why not, arrange a taxi and I'm headed off, one night won't hurt, I'll use protection, it's just to release my needs, I do have them at the end of the day so I'll tend to those and await my loves return.

I arrive at the bar, she's talking to my friends, I offer her a drink, we sit and talk. Things are going well, I'm a bit of a mess, though, I've been out all day and since we were with friends I'd not bothered getting ready, just out for a quick bite and a few drinks and I was coming home, it wasn't intended as a proper night out. I joke about this with her, she laughs and says it doesn't matter. We're the only ones in the bar and I know my friends are tired, they work long hours and I try to ease when I can.

I suggest to them that if they want to go home, it's fine, we'll continue this at my place and they can get some much needed sleep, they see this as the hint that it is and agree, besides they want some time and sleep themselves.

We head back to my apartment, she's obviously a little nervous, she was talking lots, she'd already told me she talks lots when she's nervous, I listen, chuckling to myself at some of the things she's saying, she really was very nervous! Changing topics without even finishing what she was talking about.

We get back, drinks are poured and I turn to face her whilst she continues her ramblings, I ask her to stop for a moment, she puts her drink down and asks me why, I reply with "Well this might shut you up and relax you for a moment" move in, put my hand behind her head tenderly and give her a kiss, she reciprocates, very much so.

We spend the next few days with each other, passionate like something I'd forgotten, it was years since I'd felt this passion, yet I had no feelings for this woman, sure I liked her but nothing like I had for my love, it had to stop. She's left several of her things round mine, they have to go, I talk to my friend and he says he can have a word, she's not likely to take it well, she's really taken to me. I feel like a coward for backing out but he's known her longer and I'm terrible at these things, my foot always ends up firmly placed in my mouth.

She comes round to collect her things, I apologise but I did make it clear that things weren't ever going to go anywhere, it was always just a fling. She smiles, it's ok she tells me, I understand, we can still be friends though. Gives me a friendly peck on the cheek and away she goes.

Relieved I sit back and enjoy a beer, that could have been a lot worse, still we can remain friends, my love will never know and she'll be back soon. I feel guilty for what I've done, the drink nulls that feeling, it was ok, we had an arrangement didn't we? I didn't do anything she didn't say I couldn't? No it was all good, she'd never know.

DARK YEARS APPROACH— THE DARK YEARS ARE LOOMING

Little to my knowledge though, a friend had reported back my activities to my love, the reasoning I was behaving badly, wrong. He didn't know the agreement we had though, why did he meddle? Still I couldn't blame him—he thought he was doing the right thing.

I get a phone call from my love, she's furious with me, how could I do such a thing!

I calmly explain it wasn't something she didn't know could happen, it meant nothing and I'd not seen her in days, had no intention of doing so. She's coming back, it's made her realise how much she does indeed love and it what was she needed, quickly calming and turning to upset, we sob together me saying I'm sorry but it was a moment of weakness. She comes home quickly.

Not quite how I was expecting things to happen but it had worked! I still wasn't happy with how it had come to this, I should have waited but it had done the trick. She was back. I picked her up and bought her home, a day of passion, how we'd missed each other.

The damage was done though, the fling somehow managed to appear everywhere we went, me having to explain I'd taken her to "our" place to dine one night. I only took her there since it felt like the right thing to do after our drunken first night. Things quickly start to fall apart again.

We hobble on for a few months, we argue, always the fling being the topic of her attack on me. I can't rationalise with her that she'd agreed to this, we knew it would happen, I regret it deeply but it happened, never again but it did, we need to move on.

This was the only year my love had spent with me during summer months, she enjoyed it, sunbathing when she could, even doing so on her lunch breaks, I thought this was going to be ok, she'd finally seen the life we had, everything we wanted.

We'd go out lots now, me trying to make up for the mistake I'd made, it was an agreement but one neither thought we'd act on, me more surprised than her, still it was done. We get back one night after an evening of wining and dining. We argued. I lost my temper and threw a wine glass, not at her but over the sink, I can't take it any longer, she won't let this drop.

It shocked her, so we talk more calmly now, she accepts it's happened, we'll move forward.

Our friends are now close to selling the bar, we're asked to go down, as place holders, to make it look like the place is busier than it is, sometimes we oblige but it feels wrong so excuse ourselves most times.

The arguments return, she can't handle it. This is something I never wanted to happen, I'm devastated but can't fix it, my pains starting to bubble to the surface again. I can't bury them, this has happened before, not just with my parents but hers also, we're both recalling so much hurt, it's tearing us apart.

We try to resolve it, talk it through calmly, without drinking, we reach an agreement, we'll put it behind us, if one of us starts about it, we'll just walk away from it, reminding each other of the agreement. It's done.

The bar is sold, our friends go, we're sad to see them leave but soon get on with the new owners, we'd spoken with them many times already so it wasn't hard. We spend some time there, getting to know them well, things aren't so bad afterall, we've made it through this, we can make it through anything. Work continues, it's all good, we party, we live our lives, there's arguments still but we stick to our arrangement, not biting with each others problems.

Christmas is looming again, how I hate this time of year, it brings back all my memories and pain of my parents splitting, it fears me for it to come along, I know the pain will surface, I can't bury it around this time, my first Christmas alone with my Dad, my Mum absent, it haunts me so very much. Those times that were always so good, suddenly so empty and filled with sorrow.

My love tells me she's going back home, just this one last Christmas, she left in such a rush it has to be done. I agree it's the right think to do, she packs just a small amount, she won't miss my birthday again she promises.

I drive her to the airport, we've had a night of passion and we're sure things are going to be ok, we talk all the way there. Arriving I even park for a change, something I never used to do—walk her over to the terminal. She tells me it's not necessary for me to go in and wait with her, she's done this many times now and is confident—I should get back, I've an evening out remember and lots to do.

I embrace her into my arms, giving her a deep passionate kiss, one my gut is now screaming at me this will be the last. I give her one last hug, tell her I love her, she tells me the same. I turn and walk away—I don't turn back.

Dark years—The Dark Years come

Leaving the airport—My journey home, the dark years fast approaching

I leave the airport, get into my car and do myself a roll up, I've not looked back, my gut is screaming at me this is the end, I'll never see my love again. I question where this feeling is coming from, put it down to past experiences, her missing her return flights, I bury the felling, light my smoke and turn on the radio. It's playing one of our tunes, one from an outing to a town over an hour away. I treated her to a weekend away, 5 star spa hotel, we had an awesome time there.

I focus on this, our weekend away, the fun we had, everything was awesome. She sampled many new things that weekend, money was no question, whatever she wanted we had.

I focus on this as I exit the airport, we've sorted things for good now, how could they not get better? We've suffered through the pain of "an affair" even though we'd since agreed it wasn't. Nothing could stop us now, I'd see her for my birthday, my love would return and things would return to the good times.

There's not long till Christmas, well it's far enough but I understand my love needs to finalise things with her family—to finally be whole with me, it's been nearly 10 years but we've finally gotten there.

My friend messages me, he's coming out for Xmas again, this is becoming a ritual. I continue my work, we've a new project starting, a huge one, it's going to take up my time now so this should keep me busy, it's about time—it's been a long time coming. It'll help keep my mind busy until my love returns.

The few months till Christmas pass quickly, I know my love will be back soon, I ignore my gut, it's having an off day I lie to myself. Yet another off day, well things have been long and hard, it's bound to get a bit confused once in a while, again lying to myself.

I ring my love, to see if she's arranged the flights as planned. She has something to tell me, she's not returning. I'm stunned, I thought we'd worked it all out, everything was going to be good again, what's changed? I ask if it's someone else, she sobs to me that yes, someone else is now her love, I am no longer.

My world again falls apart, I'm hysterical, how could this happen again, all my buried pain now seeing a way through, all coming out, ripping at me as it does, it's getting its payback. She's crying too, telling me she's sorry, it didn't mean to happen but just did, she still loves me but not like she used to, not like her new guy, I feel like I'm going to explode, wishing my head to do so, free me from this pain.

I ring my boss and ask for the day off work, I'm ruined once more, I'm told no can do, I need to work on things, compassion is there but this is business afterall. I ask for the next available days off, I'm granted but it's not till the end of the week.

I struggle to do work, I've been sliced into a million pieces, my world has now gone, again, everything for the last nearly 10 years vanished, never to be seen again.

THEY KICK IN—THE DARK YEARS TAKE HOLD

My world is ending, I can't focus, work is becoming a hardship, I ask my boss if he wants me to quit, I'm a mess, he understands tells me it's all going to be ok, I'll get over this.

How can I possibly, this is all I've know for the last 1/3rd of my life, my love now gone for good. I do the only thing I've ever known, ever been taught, I hit the booze and hit it hard I do. Forget my promises of keeping off the hard stuff, I'll save that for just before bed, I up my beer count to at least 24 cans, buying from all over the place to avoid the questioning looks that you get when seeing the same people, always just buying beers. Couple of bottles of wine can't hurt either. I limit myself to a bottle of whiskey a week, sometimes two.

I go out constantly, sobbing almost everywhere I go, people are no longer pleased to see me, I'm a wreck. I can't help myself though. I'm lost without her, my love for almost 10 years, gone into the abyss.

My friend comes out earlier than planned, he can tell how upset I am, I take more time off work. They've known us for a long time now and understand what I'm going through, well they don't—they've not been here themselves but at least can associate.

I restrict myself though, I don't start drinking till later on in the day, at least 17:30 but then they come thick and fast, using the only method I know to bury my pain, it's all come back, I can't bury it, the drink is the only way I know how though. Christmas comes and goes, a blur, me being no company at all. I try to put a happy face on, it's no good. It's not working, I excuse myself and find places to be alone. My birthday arrives, supposed to be a big one—a happy one, a landmark. I can't do this, I just want to be alone, well not alone but with my love, that which I know I can't have any longer.

I maintain enough to get through it, then return to sob myself to sleep. I know the drink isn't helping me, I'm an intelligent guy but I know nothing else, it's all I've seen my entire life. I torture myself to music that reminds me of her, again sobbing deeply, self pity taking hold and a hold it takes.

My friend has to return home, he tells me to keep my chin up, he's there for me if I need him, just give him a shout, this is nice, he's been there for me for a long time, as have I—we understand the pains, different pains but the pains none the less.

I go out lots now, challenging myself to drink as much as possible and remain in control, I generally fail, my mind is too weak now, it's nothing left—all the pain is there, nothing else. I pass out one day in the local, to wake finding someone drinking my beer, I don't like this, I've never drank anyone elses beer and that's mine—sacred, I pull the pint from him pouring the remaining contents over him, he's a big guy, I'm not a fighter but I tell him never steal my beer. Thankfully I'm backed up—he offers to buy me another beer. No, it's time to head home, hope the darkness will come.

The darkness hasn't come for some time, the sleep just isn't happening. I'm exhausted, I'm not eating just drinking surely I should sleep soon?

Friends tell me to go see someone, talking will help, I need help. I refuse, I'm stronger than this, I shall beat it, my mind just needs some time to work it out, time it would seem it did—almost 4 years.

DECLINE—HOW I DECLINE, ALMOST TO DEATH

It continues, day after day, week after week, the pain just keeps on coming back, my work is suffering, I'm not performing, I'm doing kinda ok but nothing like I should be, I keep on offering to quit, give me a reason to end myself. Thoughts of suicide rampant in my mind, I contemplate it one night, have it all prepared, the knife, the bathroom clean and ready for me, I'll do no harm, I'll do it cleanly, in the bath.

I drink myself stupid, ready to do it, climb into the bath, knife at the ready. I hear an email, an old friend knows of my problems, he talks me out of it ringing me—soothing me to bed. The darkness comes, I have a good sleep and wake feeling a little better, still ruined but I can do a days work at least, I have to do some, work won't take this for much longer.

I can't eat, it's been nearly 3 months since I ate something properly, all my friends besides themselves with me, snap out of it they tell me. I try, I fail.

I awake one day, something isn't right, I can feel my body in pain, something I've not felt for years. It's been some 16 years since I last had to see a doctor, I call a friend. He arrives with another friend in tow, they look at me, I'm weak, a frail form of my former self. They leave some food for me and tell me if I'm still not feeling better tomorrow ring.

I sleep again for just a few short hours, if not minutes. I can't do this, I'm in need of help so I send a text message. The friend comes and picks me up not 30 minutes later, off to the medical centre she takes me.

I'm told I'm moments away from being taken into intensive care, mass dehydration—how can that be, I'm drinking like a fish—ah the wrong type of drink. I get a jab, the first needle breaking since it was to the bottom, me clenching at the thought of a man touching my bottom. My female friend turning around, embarrassed to see me like this. I get told to go and get various supplies, drugs from the chemist, fluids from the supermarket. One of the pills is to stop me vomiting, I've not even been able to hold down a glass of water now for a week, everytime it comes straight back up.

I take the meds, give it 30 minutes as told and drink the fluids I've been told to get. They stay, things are looking up. I try some solids later on that night, it seems to be working, I can bounce back from this, I've been through worse. I've not even been able to drink the beer to null the pain—something I should have kept up but I couldn't, the pain is ripping my every limb by now.

HELP—A FRIEND COMES TO MY AID

I'm off work for a week to recover, my emotions uncontrollable. I think about taking my life several times, never carrying it through, that's the easy way out I've been told. I'm unable to eat, my stomach not wanting it, instead I'm wasting away.

A close friend comes around, early in the morning, he tells me he's cooking me breakfast, I'm not interested in eating but he makes me anyway. He tells me things will get better and heads out for work, only to return to cook me lunch. I'm again not willing to eat but since he's put the effort in, it would be rude to refuse. Again he heads of to work, only to return in the early evening, food in hand for dinner. He's bought us steak. This is very kind of him, I thank him for the 3rd time that day.

We spend the evening watching TV, talking about old times, some good some bad, always interesting though. It's been some months since my love had told me she wasn't returning, still I couldn't hold back the tears. He's telling me I'll get over it, it hurts but the pain will fade eventually. I'm not convinced but we're enjoying ourselves, just passing the time, enjoying a few beers. I'm still drinking heavily but I'm no longer on the warpath to total destruction, just enough to help the darkness come.

He continues to do this for me for a month, maybe more. I return to work, keen to get back on with it, get myself straight. My door bell goes, this annoys me, everyone knows not to bother me whilst I'm working, I've made that clear. I open the door to find my friend there, tins of paint with him. Since the apartment has memories, he's decided that he's going to paint it for me, give me a fresh start, remove the memories. This though will clear his debt to me, I'd always been good to him lending him money when he was stuck.

Awesome, I'd just made enquiries myself and it would have cost about the same, it not more to have someone else come and do it, he was good too. He spends the week decorating, cooking, making sure I eat. I'm starting to feel a little better now, the pain is easing but still very much there. I miss my love, how could she have lost what we had, to find someone else.

I spend my evenings thinking about what I did wrong, I neglected her, spent no time with her. Instead I chose to spend my time gaming, working anything really, the only time we spent together was when we were out. We used to go out frequently I recall, why wasn't that enough? I think deeper into this, really thinking about it I used to spend the time with other people, mixing with my new friends, our friends. She was shy though and stuck to just the close few she knew, knew well. I vow not to make this mistake, the next love I find, I'll dedicate myself to them, give them everything I had, like I used to in the beginning with my lost love.

FIESTAS!—SUMMER COMES, IT'S FIESTA TIME

The summer arrives, fiesta time! I take a couple of weeks off work, I know this is going to be fun times but the hangovers are likely to be intense, I can't make any more mistakes with work.

There were many of these, always somewhere there'd be one taking place. I'm missing companionship but my shyness has returned. I'd had it ripped from me when my lost love left. I felt like I'd failed. I could get this back.

I offer to help a new friend, do a few shifts for him, to give him a night off. I expect no pay for this, I'm doing this for myself, I'd ridden the shyness from me before doing this, I could do it again. He's thrilled, tells me I can have a few beers as payment, deal done! He entrust me with the keys, knowing I'm trusted.

We head out one evening, it was quiet in the bar so we closed early to go to a fiesta. It's huge, later I find out it was on local TV, I'd seen the camera man but I wasn't getting caught on that, I don't do cameras. We have a few drinks then decide to hit the dance floor, the music is banging, just what I need. We're crazy with our dancing, not holding back, a small square of space is formed around us, everyone cheering us on, or most likely laughing at us, we had no rhythm but it mattered not.

We return to get some more drinks and take a break for a bit, taking a place just close enough to watch the action. I notice a very nice hottie, I nudge my friend to show him. He tells me to go for it—what harm could be done, the worst she can do is say no. I'm not feeling confident though, I have enough Dutch courage in me by now but I'm holding back. he pushes me, just hard enough that I brush into her. I immediately apologise to her, she smiles, says its ok, no problem. I ask if I can buy her a drink, she accepts! I give my friend a smile in thanks as I take her to the bar. We start talking, getting a few drinks and going somewhere where there's less noise, it's hard talking when there's several thousand watts of music being pumped out.

We talk for a while, the Dutch courage now kicking in, she's really nice, I'm taking quite a shine to her, I contemplate asking her if she'd like to go for a meal with me this coming weekend. Not quite yet, let's get to know her a bit better. The chat continues, she's obviously flirting with me, she's incredibly stunning, beautiful blue eyes, long blonde hair, a figure to die for, this has to be worth I shot I tell myself, what is the worse that can happen afterall. I ask if she's seeing someone, just to test the waters a bit.

The response I got took me back, I was shocked. She tells me she's been seeing her partner for a few years but she's really taken a liking to me, she'd be willing to come back with me for a night of passion but that would be it, just the once. She explains she lives just far enough away that no-one would find out and we could enjoy one very long night of fun! I'm flattered, this stunning young woman was willing to cheat with me on her long term partner. I consider taking her hand and finding a taxi, intending to text my mate I'd left and see him tomorrow, or maybe the next day, depends how long this lasts.

My morals kick in, I recall the hurt on finding out my lost love was seeing someone else, I couldn't do this, I couldn't hurt someone else. I explain this to her, that I very much want to take her, for a night of passion but I can't, it's wrong for her to cheat. She looks a little disappointed, I hand her my card, tell her to keep it safe and if she ever does break up with her partner, please give me a call, chances are I'll still be single anyway.

We part company, me kicking myself for what I'd just done, it was the right thing though I tell myself. I find my friend and we get more drinks. Having found a new confidence in myself, I mingle through the crowd, trying my luck with anyone that catches my eye. I've had too much to drink now though, we head home, my friend coming back to mine, more drinks before bed.

The morning comes, the hangover as expected is there, I now have a better cure than before though, the drink I was told to have when I was ill, the only time I'd been ill for years. I knew this would rehydrate me quickly so I always kept many of them in the fridge, stocked up in my store cupboard.

We recount the evening, my friend laughing at me for turning down such a chance, still he'd do the same, it wasn't right.

I'm meeting more new people, welcomed into their group, the party times are here again! We party hard all summer, enjoying the life, travelling to the nearest fiesta. Things are starting to look up, I'm still hurting deeply though, my lost love never to return.

PARTY LIFE IS BACK—THE LIFE OF PARTYING RETURNS

Having found more new friends, the party life starts up again, I'm careful to not go too overboard on work days, I falter a few times and work suffers. They understand though, I'm still hurting.

This life continues for 3 years, I'm running out of money though, I have my other house to pay for, no tenant and I wasn't making that mistake again, instead I was trying to sell it, I priced it as low as I could, just enough to cover my debts, debts that were increasing each month, paying for two places to live was expensive and my party life, although cheap, was adding up.

I have access to anything I want, I decline though, I'd been there before and the come downs weren't worth it, I was depressed enough as it was. I only really enjoyed my joints, they mellowed me out, helped with the darkness. The darkness now would be for 5 hours at most. I could cope on this though, I was the party man was I not.

The money dries up, I can't afford to go out as much as I wanted to, my friends ring me inviting me out, constantly. They enjoy my company, want me there, I'm always the loving drunk, stupid and funny, I make them smile and laugh. I tell them I can't, I don't have enough money. Why didn't you tell us that, it's not a problem, we'll buy you drinks, come on out.

So out I go, I pay when I can, a little bit extra here and I treat my friends that are looking after me, they've treated me to so many nights, it's the least I can do.

I've not a woman for over a year now, they tell me to just go for it, there's no-one around that I like though, I'd tried to get back in touch with my fling, she was having none of that though, I'd rejected her and she wanted more, she wasn't making that mistake again. I'm taken to a brothel, I'm given the pick of the bunch, I elect for not the one I desire, I'd leave her for my friend who was paying for me, we head off—she's not my type and I don't enjoy it, not even reaching climax.

Home time comes—one of my friends stops with me, few more drinks and the darkness comes.

TAKEN ADVANTAGE OF—MY "FRIEND" GOES A BIT OVER THE TOP

The friend who helped me get through the rough times is starting to become a bit of a hassle now, he's coming round at all hours, just wanting to see me, have a laugh and a few beers, I'm working though, I can't do this. I've had several warnings from work and I'm trying to sort things out there, I owe it to them, they've been good to me. I should have been fired but my friendship kept it going, I couldn't strain that relationship any longer.

One morning he arrives at 06:30, ringing my doorbell. He knows I work and don't go to bed till 02:00 and need just 6 hours, still he's wanting to come and have a drink. I ignore it, for 2 hours, he's ringing constantly, it's woken all the neighbours and they're banging now too, I have to sort it out. I open asking who's died, this is out of order, he threatens me telling me to shut up and let's have a drink, he has a lady with him. I can't have a drink now, I've work shortly. He takes some drinks and leaves, I try to get a bit more sleep, it doesn't come. We've had a few fall outs in the past now, always something stupid that he takes way over the top, he's threatened me a few times now.

I decide enough is enough, I've got to stop the party life, focus on my work, sort myself out. I'm still deeply depressed but the pain I've once again buried, it's staying there and if I can make a clean break, it can stay there.

I start looking for an apartment, these things always seem to come easy for me, the first one I find is perfect. I negotiate on the price and get a good discount, I'm quite good at this by now. It's a week or so before I can move in, we sign the contracts, it's all done. It's more than my current place but it's a lot bigger. I was suffocating in there, it was like a shoe box. My other house has sold so I can afford this, keep my cleaner, I can make a new start here, get my life back on track.

It's far enough that I can leave the life behind but close enough that I can still keep in touch. I speak with a trusted friend, one who's now become very close to me. He thinks I'm making a mistake, moving away from him, the group of friends we have. There was no messing with us, no trouble, just good friends always enjoying a night out. I explain the problems with my other friend, he understands and tells me I'm more than welcome to go over and stay any time and go out.

Reborn—A new place, a new life

New beginnings—Time to sort myself out

I move, my friends helping me, they don't accept any money, they're happy to help me. The place is awesome, large open space for my office, a large living area, the kitchen is a bit small but it doesn't matter, I rarely cook for myself, it's cheaper to eat out. There's several bars close by, they serve food, local cuisine, this is perfect for me.

The place needs a bit of work, to make it my home. Again, I fit it out to how I want it, a display piece for the living room, costly but quality. It quickly comes together, getting a new desk for my office space, my computer is getting bigger now so I need more space, using my other desk as another workstation to fix friends computers on. I order a new TV, fancy plasma 3D model, a friend shipping it over for me, it takes him a bit of time but it comes, with a fancy new office chair I've ordered. I spend much time now gaming, working so figured it was worth the investment.

I unpack the TV, it fits the unit perfectly, I'd not thought to measure first but luck was on my side, it couldn't have been better if I'd tried. I look for the glasses, odd, they don't appear to be in here. I'm a bit puzzled, eventually figuring out they'd send me the wrong one, the 2D model instead. I email the supplier, they tell me they've made a mistake and if I ship the unit back, they'll give me a full refund.

This is a bit of a problem, it's going to take more time to ship it back and well, let's be honest, 3D is a bit of a gimmick. I reply to them stating it's going to cost more than the TV is worth to ship it back, it's now in a different country, a small white lie but it would have, if I didn't have a friend who was more than willing to do it for me. Instead I suggest, they refund me the difference, between the one I had and the 3D model. I hear nothing back from them for a few weeks. I joke I'm going to get it for free, I'm good at being a complaint customer, if things go wrong, I make sure it's put right. My job afterall, I make one typo and things break, others can do the same surely. I'm never rude with the support staff, I've done that work and know to be polite and you'll get better service. I am to the point though and take no excuses, just what's needed to fix things.

Since it was from a large online store, I wake one morning to find an email, they've refunded me the entire cost, the other company wasn't responding to my offer so they'd just given it to me! I'm cuffed, brand new awesomely big TV, all the latest gadgets with it, for free!

My new life is here, my apartment is now exactly how I want, I've left the party life, for good this time I tell myself, time to concentrate on myself, my work, keeping that pain buried deep.

I'm back to my old self, work is back on track, I'm enjoying my work again, things are awesome. My apartment is awesome, everything I want, I spend time watching films, just relaxing, finding peace with myself again.

My friend who helped to save me rings, he's needing a place to stay for a week, no problem I tell him, you're more than welcome here, things were a little off with us but we'd put that under the bridge. He comes with some stuff and I show him the bed sofa he can sleep on, he knew it well, he'd spent many a night on it before.

Work has just won an award too, I'm sent it and place it proudly in my display unit, I'm working for an award winning company. My friend and I go out for a celebratory drink, we meet a couple of girls, I knew them already so we offer to buy them a drink, they accept. We chat, one of them I'm taking a shining too, would they come back for a drink with us? They do, we go back and continue talking, it's obvious she's not interested in me though, still we have a good time, they're impressed at the award I have, not many people have things like this, it's quite unique! They leave and my friend and I watch TV, chilling out having a few drinks, the sleep comes well this night.

I decide to host a house warming party, arrange with a friend who does catering, food all sorted, drinks in, apartment arranged, I await the guests, expecting my friend who's staying with me to turn up. He doesn't, I'm gutted by this. Still I have all my other good friends here, ok most of them are older than me but I enjoy their company, they have many tales to tell and they're intriguing. The night is a tranquil affair, no crazy partying like I was used to, this was nice.

The following morning he returns, I tell him I was upset he didn't turn up. He throws a torrent of abuse at me and heads for a shower. He comes out and tells me he's leaving anyway, he'll be back for his stuff later and he's going to smash my fucking face in then my computers. He storms out.

I'm in panic mode again, I'd moved away from him yet welcomed him back, he'd been a good friend to me in the past, we could patch things up, besides he needed somewhere and I couldn't turn my back on him.

I arrange for his things to be collected, he's phoned and told to not come near me. It's the last I see of him. I decide enough's enough, I'm not going back to that life anyway, I'm focusing on my work, sorting myself out, fixing the issues I have, again kidding myself, I'm just burying them deeper still.

BONUS!—UNEXPECTED BONUS

I've cleaned up my act, I've cut the drinking down, it's not out my life but it's now to levels that aren't so lethal to me. I work hard, why shouldn't I have a drink in the evening, to help with the darkness, that which comes with much difficulty.

Work is happy with me, I'm performing like I should be again, getting my jobs done in a timely fashion, back to who I should be. We have our annual review and I'm in luck, I've got a bonus and pay rise! I tell my boss I don't deserve it, I've not been good for a few years but I'm back now.

I'm told that's why I've been given it. Awesome I think, I'm really back to being me, the person who I am, good at my job, caring for my friends and family, I'm happy again, all the pains have gone, well buried at least. They definitely are staying there this time.

I upgrade my computer with the bonus, it now looks like mission control, screens everywhere. I've purchases that many games I don't have enough time to play them all but they can wait for a rainy day. I spend my days working, then gaming, keen to complete the latest ones. I've even bought games I didn't know, in a special bundle from a popular online gaming store. These are fun, never thought I'd like this type of game but it's fun, I get into it quickly and get the rest of the series.

I'm having no free time, well I am but it's been filled, I no longer sit around missing my lost love. I'm finally over her, almost 4 years later.

I can begin my life again.

A HOBBY—AN UNEXPECTED HOBBY

I get a phone call from a good friend, I've known him for years now, we don't see each other often but he's always got my back. He's met someone who could use my help, would I be willing to do that which I do best for him? Sure I say, let's arrange a meeting, see what he needs and I can make what he needs.

I'm told about the guy we'll be meeting, to take him with a pinch of salt, he may be a bit crude but he has a good heart. That doesn't bother me, I can banter with the best of them, I've done enough bar work to have dealt with just about anything, I'm quite thick skinned by now.

We meet at his house, he seems nice enough, had a rough time but who hasn't, I can help though, do what I do best. I tell him I'll not charge him for this, he's been ripped off and I can't see that in my line of work, I'll do it to show him we're not all that bad.

He tells me in return he'll let me enjoy what they do, something I've always wanted to do, car racing! Stock cars but none the less, racing, I'm finally going to get a chance to do what I wanted as very young child.

I produce what's needed within a week, plans made to improve it. I start going the racing, quickly getting very involved with it all. The people there are all awesome, I was nervous because I'm not a racing type at all and thought they'd all take the piss out of me, they didn't. All just happy to see a new face, someone else helping out.

My first day there, people are out testing their cars, we're stood in the middle of the track when I see a car lose control, he comes heading straight towards us, there's a van in the way but still panic. I run, I do exactly what I've always said is stupid, I run away from the car but in the direction it's heading, straight into another van. The first van has stopped the car though, my heart is racing, this is dangerous but fun! I'm allowed to take a car for a little drive, I'm shaking with excitement, the guy notices this, he takes the piss, I don't care though, I'm in a racing car, the noise is awesome, the vibrations, it's amazing. I take it for a little spin before putting it where it needed to be. I get out shaking still, I've always done this when I'm excited about doing things I enjoy, he jokes more at me, something that would be an on-running joke for a while, did I care, no I'm a racing driver—well a potential one, I've yet to see if I can actually race, I have the chance though.

Life now couldn't be better, I have a new group of friends, a hobby, something that's keeping me away from the beer, work is going well, what more could I possibly want? The only thing missing was someone to share my love with, that would come though, I'll stop looking and just see what fate brings, I'm back to being me, happy, caring, content and doing all I can to help my friends, this is all I've ever wanted.

HOBBY CONTINUES—THE HOBBY CONTINUES

The racing takes place every fortnight, having meetings a few days after to discuss this. I'm in charge of handling many aspects of it, keeping people safe, making sure things are looked after, even doing some Marshaling.

This is dangerous, being so close to the cars but the smell of the petrol, the rubber burning, it's awesome, I'm thoroughly enjoying this.

Race days are a bit stressful, it's a bit of organised chaos but I see ways to help improve that, I start work on those.

No longer do I spend my days in my apartment, I'm getting out, meeting new people, making new friends. At least 6 days a month I'm out, that's without the other friends I go out with, birthdays etc.

The only problem I'm having is the darkness, it's eluding me greatly now, days without sleep are turning into weeks. I try and sleep on my lunch break but that's no good, I'm above the garage and there's always someone coming or going, usually just as I'm about to finally drift off.

This is fine though, I've coped without sleep for my entire life, well since being 7, I can survive, I'll do what I've always done, keep on going then when I can take no more, I'll drink myself to sleep and crash out for a weekend, I have to plan this around the racing though. I don't need to do it often though, just once every 2 or 3 months, I'm used to this.

Christmas comes and I spend it with some friends, one my now long time buddy, the other a new one from the racing. My long time buddy creates a feast for us, I drink freely, knowing I have no work, I don't have to drive, I'm welcome to stay the night. We watch TV, me drinking hoping for the darkness to come that night. The others go to bed and I'm left to the sofa. I finish my beer and settle for the night, trying to relax my mind. Everything is good, the year has been good, my job is safe again, I've a new hobby, an amazing group of new friends and something to keep me away from the beer.

I can't sleep though, the darkness refusing to come. I drift for a while, still fully aware of what's around me though, the dogs moving around, hearing them breathing.

The morning arrives, I thank my friend very much for his hospitality, it was a very nice day, quiet and tranquil, just what was needed. He tells me I'm more than welcome, it's his pleasure and see me soon, racing starts again soon. I head home, driving slower than usual, I know I'm not as aware as I usually am, I'll not make a mistake, I'll just take it easy.

A BIRTHDAY—ANOTHER BIRTHDAY EVENT

I'm invited to one of the racing guys birthdays, I'm chuffed, I've only known them a few months but I really like them all, it seems they want me involved too.

I have to drive but that's no biggie, I don't have to have a drink—I can enjoy myself without it, I'm just so very tired though, it's been at least 3 months since I remember having a full nights sleep, fuelled by the beer of course.

I'm a little uncomfortable upon arriving, there's going to be people there that I know but haven't really talked to, not to worry, I put on my confidence, feeling good about the last few months, everything has been awesome.

The barmaid there is really quite nice, honest and it seems caring, I can get an understanding of people very quickly. The main guy tells me she's interested in me, I'm keen but my shyness takes over. Another lady starts talking to me, convinced she knows me. One of the other drivers asks how I'm doing it, I don't know—I'm not talking, I've entered my shell again.

We eat and the main guy tells the bar maid I fancy her. My cheeks burn, I'm the same colour as the bright red table clothe, something another friend picks up on. Everyone is laughing at me now, still I don't care. He goes off—telling me he's going to get her number for me, after a while he returns and hands me a number, wow I think, he wasn't just taking the piss. We leave and I smile at her and tell her I'll ring her. She says ok, tomorrow is good.

I head home, yearning for sleep, the darkness that hasn't come. I drink a bottle of wine whilst watching a film, happy that this might be someone who likes me, I'll ring her tomorrow and talk to her. Sleep doesn't come so the next morning I make it my mission to acquire some sleeping tablets, I do, prescriptions that aren't my own. I know this is stupid but I'm desperate for sleep now, it's been almost 4 months, I have to do something.

I try to ring the number, no answer. ok I've done my day at work, let's go relax and watch some TV, I have a few beers and decide to take a tablet. Surely this has to work.

I head to bed for before midnight, quite unusual for me, only to wake again by 03:00, I'm annoyed but at least I've had a few hours, I do some work and head back to bed again, hoping for a few hours before I have to start again. It doesn't come. The week is nearing an end so I figure I can do my usual, drink myself into a slumber, it may not be quality sleep but at least it's better than lying there all evening, wishing for that which won't come.

OVERDOSE—OH HOW THINGS CAN GO WRONG

I've finally rang and found out the number was a joke. I'm upset and threaten to pull out from the racing. I'm told it was just a joke and to let it slide, it's not worth giving up my hobby over. I head the advise of my friend and arrange to see the racing guy, the one who thought this was funny.

My head's now hardly able to focus, it's just yearning for the darkness, I decide I'll take 2 tablets tonight, that with a few beers should certainly do the trick, not too many though, I'll just have 4 small cans. That won't mix too badly. I head to bed.

I wake late the next day, shit I'm in trouble with work, I'm feeling drowsy still so think I've had a good nights sleep. I ring my boss to apologise, he tells me to take the day off, awesome I think, he's known I've been suffering and he's given me a free pass to try and get some sleep in. I look at the packet of tablets, odd I think, I'm sure there were more than that after I took two last night, it's empty. I'm sure it was a full pack of 12, I head back to bed, determined to take advantage of the drowsiness I was feeling.

Sleep comes, I wake for the first time feeling quite refreshed, the drowsiness gone, it's 18:00, I've managed almost 8 full hours! This is incredible. I get up, remembering the empty pack of tablets. Strange my computer was on, I'm sure I turned that off too when I went to bed. I check through my call records, there were calls made whilst I thought I was sleeping, I listen to the recordings. I'm making sense in them but not, I sound like a zombie. I check my computer, I've had several chats with people, sent a load of text messages, WTF was I doing? Some of it makes sense, I'm explaining I'm annoyed at the joke that was played on me, don't mess with my feelings.

I've only just gotten over my last heartbreak and didn't want to relapse, it was done with. This type of messing with my heart though I know could set me off again, I couldn't, I'd buried those thoughts, they couldn't come back.

The other messages are gibberish, I can put together typos that I make, even whole sentences based on the layout of the keyboard, I'm a touch typist afterall but these were making no sense, the odd one would but mostly it looked like I'd just bashed the keyboard. What the hell had I done last night?

The only thing that made sense was I was sleep walking, I'd done it a few years ago, well many years ago, my friends thought I was fully awake but the next day I had no memory of it. I check the tablets, sure enough it's empty, I'd taken another 10 after going to bed, after getting up and sleep walking. How did I manage to login to my computer? Well I could explain that easily enough, I'd been doing it for 15 years, I don't need to look at my keyboard, it's instinct.

I ring around those I've rang during my sleep, apologising to them and explaining what I thought had happened, well the only thing that could have happened, I couldn't have done it drunk and forgotten, I had nothing in my memory of it, there was always something if I was drunk, I'd not drank enough for that either, knowing not to mix meds with beer.

I put the tablets somewhere I know I'll never think to look when I'm sleep walking, get rid of the beer and head to bed, I wasn't going to make that mistake again.

The sleep doesn't come though, I'm trying to remember what happened the previous hours, eventually I manage a few hours, then work comes.

I ring my boss to explain what's happened. He's cross with me, my behaviour could have caused much damage to the company, I'm almost fired. I'm given the chance to see a doctor to sort it out, my insomnia needs to be put to an end. I've not seen a doctor in years, well just that once a few years ago but I agree, it's the only thing that will save my job.

I head to see the doctor—getting an emergency appointment. I explain what's happened to him. He's not surprised, he's seen this in many professionals who use screens a lot, I'm surround 180° by them, it's no wonder. The screens deplete melatonin levels, that which regulates sleep and I've fully depleted mine. I have to spend two hours a day without any kind of screen on in my presence, no TV, no computers, not even a mobile phone I'm supposed to look at. Instead I need to switch off at 20:00 and read for at least two hours, go out if I like but not if screens will be around. I also need to have at least 20 minutes of daylight, not through windows but direct sunlight, this will help. I have to get a report to give to my boss, this can't happen, it's illegal to do so, I beg, 4 times for one, saying it's the only thing that will save my job. He can't comply, I'll have to explain this.

I return home, after getting some tablets prescribed to me, I can only take these for 5 days for each 3 month period. They're highly addictive hallucinogens. I'm not happy with this, I've never taken meds in my life, not even for a hangover cure, apart from the tablets for my acne but they were relatively limited in their affects.

I call my boss to explain the doctors diagnosis. He accepts this but I'm cut off from all work access when I'm not working, when I can be kept an eye on, I'm grateful I've not just lost my job.

I stick to the doctors advise, promptly turning off my screens at 20:00, 20:30 at the very latest and go and read. I've a huge book case full of books, finally I have a reason to read them. I'm not happy though, I'd rather be gaming but this has to be done. The beers go too, I'm not risking anything now, I lost control—not just lost control but went on a rampage, I could have killed myself, I was making sure that wouldn't happen again.

MAKING AMMENDS—
SPEAKING WITH THOSE I'D UPSET

I meet with the race guy, he's upset that he's upset me, he didn't know my situation and thought it was just a prank. I tell him I'm all up for pranks but don't pull shit like that on me, I've only just fixed my broken heart, I'm in tears telling him this. He's deeply sorry and promises not to do it again. We go back to his for something to eat. He asks if I've stopped messaging the barmaid, I tell him I didn't have any clue I was, another race mate shows me the messages he received from me. It was obvious this wasn't me in control. If I could have had any memory of this, I'd have gone red in the face at my shame, I didn't though, I just had no idea of what was going on—a few hours of my life that I'd totally no control over, I'd not let this happen again.

We put it behind us, me knowing the action I must take, I cut the drink out, continue my pills and within a week of following the advise, I'm suddenly sleeping, without aid, nothing but natural sleep. Only 6 hours but that was enough, I could push the computers and TV till midnight and still have enough time to read for two hours before having to head to work. Awesome, things are back on track, I'm off the drink, I'm sleeping naturally for the first time in over 20 years, I have a hobby, good friends, I'm just lacking someone to share my love with, I decide to do what my mate did, sign up to a dating site, he'd met his wife on one of those so it must work, I sign up, fill out my profile and leave it at that, I'll check back in a few weeks maybe, I'd been a "member" for years but never paid, never put a picture up or anything really, just testing the waters.

It wouldn't take long, the profile was about my new life, my hobbies, what I enjoyed doing.

My love—I find a new love

Introduction—A small explanation

A small note is needed here, it doesn't really sound like I've been much of a hopeless romantic so far, I can't detail the memories I have from back in the early years, my first real love, I've moved on from those, let those feelings free. I'm now close to the end of my journey though, here I shall reveal what a truly hopeless romantic I am, the measures I'm prepared to go to, the sacrifices I'll make for the one I love.

The "Date"—Our first date

I've taken a week off work, I've not taken any holidays all year and I've lost my allowance, luckily I manage to sneak a week in, at least some down time to relax with.

It's only a week or two after the incident with the tablets so I'm still having the effects in my system, they'll take at least a month to get out my system. This is fine though—I'm enjoying reading, it's nice to get back to that, something I used to spend much time doing but forgot about when I found my computer.

I've decided I'm going to take things into my own hands, I'll find a love myself, as I said, I've signed up for a dating site, so I join another or more. I look through the profiles and send a few messages, not expecting much but my gut is telling me I'll have someone to take with me for the first race meeting of the year, I'm sure of it.

The few hours I do spend on my computer, I'm working on making things good for the racing, I've bought a bar code scanner to help with the whole process, automate it, I hate doing repetitive tasks. It's coming on well, a few more weeks and it'll be complete.

I'm reading a series of books about a popular young wizard, I've seen the films and the books are always better, I'm making good progress with them. My drinking is now at the lowest levels of all time, for 22 years, I'm drinking just 3 pints a night, it's aiding with the sleep but more so because I enjoy the taste of a beer and it's a long time thing I've done, it's a routine to have a drink before sleep but it's now at minimal levels, still too much but for me it's a massive step. I'm happy with this, the hangovers have gone, I'm feeling good, I'm cutting down my smoking, just one pack of tobacco a week now, sometimes it lasts me almost two weeks, I'm getting my life together, for the first time ever.

My pain is forgotten, I've buried it deep down and put a cap on it, it's not going to come back and haunt me any longer, I've moved on. My lost love is now just a friend, someone who I spent some good times with but I'm happy for her, she has a child now and is happy, this pleases me. I'm again content with my life, happy with myself, I'm awesome afterall, good job, awesome apartment, everything I want, I relish in this whist reading, my life is how it should be.

I hear my computer receive an email, I can't check now, it's past my self imposed curfew, I'll look in the morning. I finish reading and head to bed, the darkness now coming rapidly. My mind is finally at rest, at peace, tranquil times are upon me.

I wake the next day, early but I'm refreshed, no hangover—clear head feeling good. I check my emails, remembering there was at least one come in the night before. It's a contact from a dating site, intrigued I view the profile. It's a lady a few years my elder, she looks stunning though, I read the message.

She tells me she knows she's too old for me but feels we're kindred spirits— enjoys motor sport and would I be interested in being friends and showing her the hobby I'm now thoroughly enjoying. I debate this for several hours, not if she can come and be friends, the more the merrier but if I could be with an elder lady. I consult with a friend, he comes over for a beer, pizza and gaming evening. He tells me go for it, what's the worst that could happen? (hah how that will come back to bite me in the ass.)

I think some more, decide why not so message her back, suggesting first we meet though, since I know the driving lot and they can be a bit crude, I feel I need to warn her about this. We contact each other on instant messaging and start talking. I tell her the first race meeting is this weekend, it's now Tuesday, so we should really meet first.

She'd like me to go over and meet somewhere mutual, I tell her it's not needed, she can come over here and I'll take her out for the evening, she can have my bed and I'll sleep on my bed settee—I'm a gentleman afterall. The conversation gets a bit flirty but I'm telling myself we'll just be friends, she's far too stunning to have an interest in me anyway, I'll do what I do best, just be a friend for her and welcome her into my new life, my hobby and show her a good time. She's not sure, I give her my address, contact numbers of my friends to reassure her, I'm not a stalker or an axe murderer!

We discuss a taxi, she's told me where she lives and I know the cost is too great, would be far too expensive for just meeting as friends, I'm not a threat, I've never even killed a spider! She laughs, she'll get back to me.

I spend the day gaming, awaiting her response. It comes. ok she says, she'll come over Thursday, we can go for drinks and discuss the racing crew, the intention just to be friends and her come along and enjoy the day. She tells me she's not just wanting to use me to get her in for free, I don't pay neither do my guests, I'm number 3 there in some areas so have my privileges.

The Thursday comes and I'm anxious, I've not been on a date for years, I decide to return to my old friend, the lager for some Dutch courage, not many though, just 2 or 3 halves to give me that little boost, I don't really need it but feel I do. My phone rings, an unknown number, I'd given her my number but not taken hers. She's here, where's my apartment. I look out my window and see this stunning woman—phone to ear, I tell her to walk the way she's headed and it's the first block on her left—no her other left as she goes right. The buzzer goes and I let her in.

I wait with the door open, heart pounding, I've not done this for quite some years, sure I used to meet strangers in Nottingham all the time but always on mutual ground, never my home first. My home was awesome though, I was proud of it, I knew she'd like it. I can hear her foot steps coming up the stairs, any moment now, 6, 5, 4, 3, 2—I can see her arm, 1 and she's there.

My thoughts of just being friends fly out the window, faster than the speed of light, she was utterly stunning, she walks towards me, me taking in everything about her, my word I think. Where has this woman been all my life. My heart pounding, she's still 5m away from me but my heart knows it's found a new love, I could make this one work, I've learned from my past mistakes, I hide my thoughts, playing it cool, even though I know already this is the woman I want to spend the rest of my days with.

I greet her with the typical two cheek kiss, welcoming her to my home. I ask if she'd like a drink first or would she like to go out to the pub?

I'd already asked her what her choice of drink was, a certain bourbon and coke, well it took me all day to locate the bourbon but locate it I did, nearly 100 miles I drove to find it, I now knew where to find it though.

She says we'll have a quick first drink, then go out to the pub. I pour her drink, not making it too strong and get myself another small can of lager, putting it in the holder I have to keep it cool. I give her the drink, it's not strong enough so I make it so. I tell her the mission I had to find her drink, she laughs, that's sweet she says.

As I write this, American Authors—Best Day Of My Life is playing, this was how I was feeling, this was going to be the best day of my life! The start of a new love, I knew now she was the one for me, there was something between us already, we'd not even kissed, well just the cheeks but she was amazing.

I put some music on the TV, streaming from my computer. She'd already commented how my computer looked like mission control, commander of the world! I laughed and tossed it aside as it's just for my work, I'm a geek but love it, she'd already told me she was a bit of a data geek. My setup was impressive though, several friends had taken photos of it—just because they were in awe at the awesomeness of it.

We sit and talk for a bit, the first drink quickly going, I suggest I take her to the local, I've ensured I've enough money for whatever she wants for the night. She agrees and we leave, I want to hold her hand but refrain, it's only round the corner. I ask if she wants her drink of preference, "of course". I ask if she minds sitting outside, it's cold being February but there's a heater on, we can't smoke inside and I'm smoking my roll ups. She says that's fine, we enter though to order the drinks. The owner is working tonight, he greets me with the usual welcome he does, he's pleased I'm there, sneaks a look at this wondrous woman I'm with and gives me a wink whilst she's not looking.

He tells me to take a seat, I explain we're going outside so I can smoke, he tells me it's ok, directs me to a table hidden from view and puts an ashtray down for me, it's ok, just keep it subtle, well that I can do. I keep the ash tray on the floor, away from the lady, she's not a smoker so I try to keep my smoking down. We talk, I ask her if she's done this whole online dating thing before. She recounts a couple of dates she's been on, the guys she met lied in their profiles one saying he was 6'0" but turned out to be a midget, she tells me since she's so tall—it's important for her to have someone taller than her, thankfully I am by 3".

I tell her that she has no worries with me about that, I'm an honest person, I can't lie (well apart to myself) and that what she's read about me is all the truth, I challenge her to question me about anything I've written. She laughs. We briefly then move onto the racing, I tell her about the guys there, she laughs, not a problem, she's been around guys like that all her life, she can handle it. Awesome I think, this woman is so strong, so stunning, absolutely beautiful, everything I've been looking for, I've found love again.

I forget the rest of the conversations, I was just gazing into her eyes, her having glitter on her cheeks, highlighting her beauty, could I really be so lucky? She tells me she has a child, I knew this already so enquire about her, the child sounds lovely, loving caring, they're more like sisters she says, I can believe this, she's amazing!

We've had several drinks now, I ask if she'd like one more, she tells me no, it's ok, I think she's trying to be polite, I've already told her this night is on me, I don't believe in going Dutch, it's the mans duty to pay. I get myself one more and order one for her, the owner telling me to go and sit, as he has done with all the drinks I've ordered. We've known each other for almost a year now, I'm a regular there and he's happy to see me with a lovely lady, rather than being alone like I mostly am. He brings our drinks over and she's telling me she didn't want it, drink it she does though, we make that our last one.

We head back to mine, it's not far just a minutes walk, I take her hand, she accepts, well I tried to first "link" with her but she says that's for grandparents and takes my hand instead.

We get back in, her sitting in the "command seat". This is amazing she says, what's it all do. I explain the various screens, how it all works and the work I do. She wastes no time in logging into my dating profile. Well you're a nice guy she says, we better find you some more dates. I'm a little taken back but figure what the hell, I've told her we're just going to be friends, she sends a few messages to a few other profiles. I'm not taking this any longer, I need to let her know that I'm wanting more than just being friends.

I use my tactic from my fling, I look at her and say "I'm going to have to do something to stop you doing this", she looks back, "what's that then", I learn in an kiss her, with a compassion I didn't know I was capable of, me kneeling on the floor since she was in the "command seat". She later tells me she was totally overwhelmed by the passion in my kiss that time, our first kiss.

She'd told me in our online chats that it wasn't me she didn't trust, it was her, she takes what she wants. We move to the living room, me stopping for a moment to put some chilled out music on again. It doesn't take me long to unclothe her, me remaining fully clothed. I pleasure her for some time, she knocks her drink over, that which I'd poured when we returned. I dismiss it, she asks if I have something? I tell her no, that's what I meant when I said she bring the only things she wanted to have with her. ok no problem I continue for a while. I can feel my heart bonding with this woman, she's absolutely amazing. We stop, she looks at me and says "Please this is no reflection on what you've just done, that was amazing but I've had to much to drink", she then proceeds to "find" the bathroom, I tell her turn right, she turns left, she never was good with directions, ends up in the kitchen. I go to aid her, holding her beautiful long hair back whilst she's in the sink. She finishes, I mop up some of the drink, it doesn't matter, my cleaner will sort that for me.

She says she needs to go to bed now, I've already shown her where it is, she put her bag in there when she arrived, I prepare to get the sofa out, for my bed. She shouts through to me "You're more than welcome to join me", well I didn't need to hear that twice, I turn all the lights off and we get into bed, I cuddle her, getting as close as I can to her, she should surely feel my passion for her, the love that I already know I have for her. She falls asleep quickly, as do I, the first time I've had a lot to drink in weeks. My last thoughts before the darkness slides over me, "I'm in love, this woman is amazing, she is everything I want, has a child, wants no more, this is just too perfect, I can't be so lucky", the darkness slides down—peace, happiness, I'd found love again, I would do everything it took to make this work, anything, she was now all I wanted.

THE MORNING AFTER—A HANGOVER FOR THE FIRST TIME IN A WHILE

I awake to finding myself hungover, this beautiful amazing woman next to me, I quickly recall the evening, what was her name, oh yes I remember, I'm in love with her you fool, you can't forget that!

I call her name, softly to see if she's also awake—nothing. Ok she's still sleeping. She later tells me she wasn't, she just couldn't remember where she was, what had happened, something she was used to happening and just needed time to recall.

45 minute pass, at least, I can't tell, I have no clock I can see, she eventually says "morning" to me, I ask her how she's feeling? "Like shit" she tells me, I cuddle into her, trying to reassure her I'm not just there for the one night. "I've known a woman who has a good cure for hangovers" I whisper to her, "what's that?" she asks, I show her, going down saying a good climax

always helps clear the head. I spend 30 minutes or so, her making noises I take as she's enjoying.

She has to get back though for work, we'd woken early, we get dressed, well me in my dressing gown, she shows no shyness of being naked around me, I take this as a good sign. I show her out, asking if she has everything she needs, give her a kiss a big hug and tell her I'll ring her soon, for the racing. She reciprocates and thanks for me for a good night. Awesome! I'm still feeling like shit though, I have no work today, it's the last day of my week off so I figure why not, head back to bed. I sleep through again till nearly 18:30, drink induced sleep but still the sleep was coming now, the darkness, no longer was it becoming a problem.

My heart is overjoyed, I'd not had any satisfaction myself last night but I'd had an awesome evening, this beautiful, amazing, caring woman had entered my life, I could make this work. I wanted it to work and when I want something, I get it—well if it's something I can control, this I could, I could be the person she deserved, she'd had a loss recently, I knew those all too well, I could be there for her, to support her, be her shoulder to cry on, this I knew was the start of something beautiful, at least I was hoping so.

THE TEXT—I GET AN SMS MESSAGE

I'm sat playing some games, it's not my curfew time yet and it's the weekend, well weekend is coming it's the last day of my holiday. I hear my phone go, a message has come in.

I take my phone off charge to see what it is, a message from my date, saying "I don't think it will work with us, I can't be with a smoker, sorry. I also think it's best I don't come to the racing". I'm curious now. I've quit smoking before, I know I can do it again, can I do it for this woman, this woman that had somehow captured my heart in such few hours. I think on it for a while, well I've been wanting to quit again for a while. I think some more. I can't sleep, I really want this to work, this woman, I can do this. I send her an email saying if that's the only deal breaker, I'll quit, I'd love you to come to the races anyway, even just as friends.

She replies, thanks for the email, if you'd still like me to come I'd love to, as for the smoking, we'll talk OK?

Awesome, this can work, I want to quit smoking anyway, this is the perfect reason to, she is perfect. I text asking her how she prefers her men, at this point I've grown my hair, it's almost shoulder length but swept back, grown a beard, that I keep trimmed and neat. She tells me "short hair and cleaned shaved, a groomed man is sexy", awesome I think, hairdressers tomorrow.

I go the hair dressers, my usual at this point, tell him it's all got to go. I cringe lower in my seat as he gets the clippers out and starts taking it off, he asks if I'm sure. Yep, it has to go I reply. It does, there's masses of hair on the floor, wow it really was long. I get home to shave, there we go, all neat and "groomed". I text her I've a surprise her for her, she's intrigued. Tomorrow I'll pick her up for the racing, hope she likes my new look, I've had the old for 2 years but back to being groomed!

FIRST RACE—THE FIRST RACE DAY WITH MY NEW LOVE

I skip my usual routine of having a smoke when I get up, I don't want to smell of it afterall. We've arranged I'll pick her up, near her house, I get there early, she's already said she's always late so I'm expecting a wait, I've told her we can't be late though, I'm needed to help sort out the racing, get things setup.

I see her walking up to the meeting place, I get out the car to open the door for her, she's smiling, I ask if she likes my new look, "Much better" she tells me. We talk, heading to pick my mate up. She tells me she had a really nice night, apart from the little incident she had, let's see how it goes, don't quit smoking, just don't smoke around me please.

Awesome, how understanding is this woman, I want to quit but I can still have the odd one so long as I'm not seeing her, best of both worlds! I'm overjoyed, this woman is the one for me, she's so understanding and caring, indeed I do love this woman! I can't be too obvious though, it's far too soon I tell myself, I have to keep this inside for a while.

We pick my mate up, he has a fright, she reminds him of one of his ex girlfriends he tells me. We drive to the race track, about 40 minutes away. We have a good laugh and joke whilst driving down, my mate doing most of the talking, I'm too busy concentrating on driving, motorways require concentration.

We approach the track and I go to say something, forgetting my new loves name for a moment, I have to refer to her as "the woman", she doesn't notice and just laughs. We arrive and I take her to introduce her to the boss, expecting the normal banter back from him. She responds well, joking how knickers are really ankle warmers, she puts him in his place. She's awesome, she gives as good as she takes and she'd just taken a load from the boss. I speak with him, making arrangements of what needs to be done. He asks if she's my new girlfriend, a bit stunned I've found someone so soon after the birthday incident. I tell him I'm working on it, hope so but we'll see.

I do my usual duties and see if I'm needed to marshal, yep, so I change into my gear. I've bought her some drinks already, holding her hand where ever we walk. I ask if she's ok for another drink, get the water for the marhsals, give her a quick peck on the lips and tell her I'll see her in a bit, over there's the best place to watch from.

The racing starts, I'm inches from the cars again, adrenaline pumping. We only manage a few races before I get a phone call, my mates Mrs has hurt herself, she needs him to come home. I find my mate and tell him, we arrange to leave. I go find my love and apologise but something's happened and we have to go, she's ok with this, only got to view a few races but it was fun none the less. We drive back to my mates, working out the plans for if he needs me to take her to the hospital, this is a bit of a problem, I have to get my love home too. It's ok, he's sorted something so we head back.

As we're nearing my place, I ask if she'd like to come back for a drink, she accepts, awesome! I pour her a bourbon and coke and get myself a beer, we relax to some TV, me thinking she's staying the night, I'd gone out the day after our first date to get some protection but not tonight, I'm being a gentleman. She lays her head back on my lap, me stroking her hair tenderly. She tells me this is strange, she feels really comfortable around me, I concur. I ask if she'd like another drink, no she tells me—can I take her home please, the child is expecting her. I feel foolish for assuming she was stopping the night, it passes though, I'd forgotten for a moment about the child.

I stop drinking, I don't drink and drive, I've had half a small can of lager, I'm safe to drive, I'll take it steady though. We head back to hers, talking constantly, we're so alike, have the same outlook on life, share the same passions, this is too good to be true. She jokes about how she can never remember her phone number, I tell her I've memorised it already, recall it for her, I'm good with numbers, they stick in my brain. We near where I picked her up, she tells me to carry on, her house number, I pull up outside. Thank her for a lovely day and give her a kiss, another deep passionate kiss. I tell her it could be done, that I can be a gentlemen and I stood by my word, she laughs telling me yes, I'd succeeded but I was boring for doing so, she wanted some fun! I smile, I'd proven I wasn't just after her for a "quickie". I ask if she'd like to come for diner, not this week, she's away, maybe next Saturday, ok "that works". I tell her I'll text her and head home.

I'm overjoyed, I have this beautiful, intelligent, strong caring woman in my life, everything had happened as I'd hoped, I'd sorted myself out, cut the drinking down to reasonable levels, now had a reason to quit smoking, my apartment was awesome, I was sleeping reasonable well, what more could I want. Nothing, I had it all now, well I'd like her to officially be my girlfriend but we've only had two dates, can't happen just yet, that'll come when it's ready.

MY OTHER DATE—THE OTHER DATE I WENT ON

I'd already arranged before meeting my new love that I'd see someone else, well I can't be rude, I've promised her dinner. Besides, we're not official yet, people see other people until they become official don't they?

I drive to meet her, it's quite late at night, lovely evening, not too cold, it never is really here. She comes up to me from behind, querying my name as she approaches, yes I reply, turning to meet her. I give her the customary two cheek kisses and ask where she'd like to go. She knows a lovely place she tells me, first though I need to go to the bank, I'd not had time to earlier.

We'd been talking over IMs for a while so knew a fair bit about each other, we enter the bar and get seated. We order, me having a beer to start then moving on to the coke. We talk, it's easy, no feeling uncomfortable, we're getting on well, she's nice. We talk about our pasts, how we are where we are today, the conversation coming easily.

We finish eating and I ask for the bill and I pay, I'm a gentleman afterall. She thanks me for a lovely evening, asks if I'd like to come back to her place for more drinks. I decline, using the excuse of work in the morning, I can't do this, I've found love, this was just a night out to meet a new friend. I walk at a half run back to my car, glad I'd not made the mistake of going with another woman, I'll make this work I tell myself, this woman is amazing, my new love.

Second date—An evening of joy

I email asking if she'd like to go for dinner the following Saturday, she agrees, I've already booked the table, I knew she would. The week can't go fast enough, I bury myself in work, sending her texts on the evening, having a few beers, some getting a bit too soppy, well I'm a sop at heart, she knew this. She's not romantic though, having turned down a valentines night, saying she was busy. She does get a little romantic with a few replies though, she tells me she's trying to meet me half way.

The night comes and I pick her up, I've been waiting all week for this, it's going to be awesome. We head back to mine for a quick drink first, I allow myself one small beer and pour her the usual bourbon and coke, she jokes she might not be able to drink it after the last time! We decide it's time to go eat, it's way later than she's used to eating. I take her to the restaurant, a place I frequent and know everyone there. We're greeted and seated, ordering a bottle of wine, we can get a taxi home, my car will be safe here. The owner walks by and gives me a wink, I can tell she thinks my new love is nice.

We talk over the meal, the food is exquisite here, the portions look small but they're very rich and filling. The conversation is easy, she tells about her previous marriage and her ex relationship, how she was almost married again. Marriage is important to her, she's fiercely loyal to her partner and this symbolises that bond. I tell her I've been engaged before but we never really saw the need to get married, still it's something I'm willing to do, so long as it's not religious. She agrees but tells me her first marriage was in a church, even though that wasn't her she'd done so to give her father the chance to walk her down the isle.

It's sweet time, I tell her I don't usually do sweets, I have to she says, she's not having one otherwise. Ok, I agree, order something light, her getting her favourite, crème brûlée. We continue talking, everything about us right, we share the same thoughts, we're so comfortable around each, natural, this is definitely the one for me I think. I ask for a taxi to be ordered, no problem. I pay the bill, she's offering to pay half, I tell her not to be so silly, chivalry isn't dead in me! I see the chef and thank him for a wonderful meal, see him soon. Give the owner the usual kiss, thanking her too and we get into the taxi. We talk as I direct the taxi back home, I'll get the car in the morning.

We get back, I pay the taxi driver and open the door, holding it for her. We enter the apartment and start kissing immediately, passion driving us, this is amazing, I've fallen for this woman totally. We have an evening of passion, pausing the film we're watching to do so. The evening was nothing short of amazing, I'd not been with a woman for years now but this woman was worth it, the wait, it could have been longer if I'd known it would be with her.

We wake the following morning, more passion ensues. She has to get home though, the child is expecting her, no problem, she showers and I get dressed, take her home, giving her a kiss as she leaves. That was more like it she tells me, much better than being a "gentlemen" she jokes at me!

I drive home, I'm cooking for her next week, I check what I have in my kitchen, hmm it would appear I'm missing cooking wares, shopping I go. I get everything I need to cook a roast, haven't cooked really for years now, I'll be ok though, I have my experience, I can make an awesome meal.

There's party coming up, in another country, will my new love be my girlfriend by then I wonder, of course, I'll make this work, I book a room in the hotel for the two of us, the top suite there, I'll make sure our first "holiday" is perfect for us, I'm a little concerned since the ex will be there but it won't matter, I'll have my new lady with me, the one I'm now already thinking of marrying.

COOKING AGAIN—I COOK FOR THE FIRST TIME IN A WHILE

I'm preparing the meal for us, I haven't done this for years but I still remember. She comes round and I offer her the usual drink, no wine to start with she says. I'm running a little late with the food, it doesn't matter, she's content watching a series I've enjoyed. I keep on popping in to make sure she's ok, just get the food done, I'm hungry she laughs. I top her drink up.

Finally the food is ready, I've no idea what it's going to be like, is the meat too tough, lamb her favourite, I couldn't get the joint I'd wanted so made do with another cut. She's impressed, "you've missed your calling" she jokes, I'd thought about being a chef before but I'd worked those hours, there was no life doing that work. We continue watching the series, pausing it a few times for some passion. Several times we have to pause, our lust too great for each other.

Sleep is now coming easy, I'm sync'ing with her routine, getting up way before I need to since that's the time she gets up, going to bed much earlier than usual, the same time as my love does. Our lives are already forming into one.

I enquire into the child, what they do, hobbies etc, they sound really interesting, I'm keen to meet them and the parents, I can't be too quick though, we've only had 3 dates. Their birthday is coming up, I've heard how a new music player is wanted, that's settled then. I buy it, ready for the birthday.

We continue dating, her coming round and bringing DVDs which she leaves, a series she's enjoyed, I always cook for her, make sure there's her bourbon and wine in for her. She's impressed even more at my cooking skills, well I have spent many hours in kitchens watching the chefs, it's easy for me. The passion is intense, we can't get enough of each other. She comes round two or three times a week, staying over and working the mornings with me, having some passion when lunch time arrives before she has to head off home.

I start cooking for myself again, rather than going out, I'm enjoying it again, my heart is filled with joy at this new love, I can't stop talking about how amazing she is, how we're getting on and feel at home with each other.

I talk with a friend, my rent contract is up for renewal, do I suggest we move in together, not just yet, there's 3 months before I need to decide. He tells me to slow down a bit, I'll scare her away, I know this but I'm just thinking out loud. We've only been seeing each other a month, it's far to soon to think such things.

I'm gaming one night, texting her as I do, I'm quite soppy in all my texts. I'm having a few drinks, not many now, I'm cutting back, realising I can have a happy life without it, just a few to help with the darkness but that's coming easy now, I'm happy, in love have everything I want. I have the urge to tell her I love her, I text her. I get a reply the following morning, "alco-shame much?" she asks. I tell her not at all, I meant what I said, fearing I've moved to fast I ask if she's heading for her running shoes. Not yet she tells me, I'm a bit full on, am I always like this? I tell her I'm just a hopeless romantic and want to lavish her with my affections. She laughs.

I push to meet her family, the child, her parents, she says it's a little soon but she's spoken with her Mum, getting told that yes I probably do love her, the way I've been treating her to everything, she tells me soon.

BECOMING THE GIRLFRIEND—I FIND MYSELF A GIRLFRIEND.

I'm cooking for her again, I'm enjoying this. Cottage pie this evening, never made one before but how hard can it be. I've told her there's a treat for the starter. She arrives and has a shower, she's just been to the gym. She comes out and says "So, I guess you're the starter then?" I smile, go over to her and we head to the bedroom for some passion, she tells me she's feeling a really strong connection with me, how special that just was. I agree, she's not even accepting the label of girlfriend yet but we're feeling a special bond already.

She continues to watch the series whilst I finish the dinner, another master piece, she's thoroughly enjoyed it and asks for more. We relax and continue watching one of her DVDs, deciding to spend the night in the living room on the bed sofa. I prepare the bed and we continue watching the DVD, pausing for some passion, we can't get enough. We're relaxing, talking about how we're so fitting with each other, she whispers something, did I just hear that right? I ask her, did you just say what I thought? yes, I'm want to accept that label now, be your girlfriend!

Overjoyed I kiss her, passionately. I then tell her I'll let her know the secret I've been hiding from her, I've already booked us a holiday for a birthday do. Wow, you really do put your money where your mouth is don't you? She tells me. I tell her I was confident this was going to happen, I knew we were right for each other, I was going anyway so it didn't make much difference, just another flight. It wasn't a gamble anyway, I have faith in us. She cuddles into me and we sleep.

We wake the next day, I prepare her breakfast. I'm looking out the window, getting some fresh air, where's her car? I ask where she's parked it, this isn't good, it's been towed. How could this shadow the joys of the night before. Not to worry, we'll go recover it. I message work to say I might be a bit late, I have to sort this out. We go pay the fine and wait for them to open the compound. She's cuddling into me, talking about how typical this was for her. She has to take her parents to the airport this morning too and needs to be there soon. I offer for her to take my car, she can't drive an automatic. She can't wait any longer and rings her parents to explain what's happened, she didn't want to since this is so typical for her but can't let her parents down. Just as she's explaining the man comes to open the compound.

Typical, she could have got away with it, her parents had told her two hours early, since she's usually late they didn't trust her so bought themselves some extra time. She recovers her car, we kiss and off she goes, we'll see each other again soon.

MEET THE PARENTS— INTRODUCTION TO THE FAMILY

I'm nervous, I can't have a drink I have to drive so Dutch courage is out the window. I text her to say I'm shaking with nerves, she replies telling me to chillax, there's nothing to worry about. I get ready after I finish work, struggling to shave, I manage though and look smart enough, casual smart.

I head over, shaking with the thought of what's about to happen. I buzz to be let in, meeting the child for the first time. They're lovely, obviously has a big heart and is very kind, we shake hands. To the parents we head, bottle of wine in hand. I'm told it wasn't needed but it was the least I could do, they're cooking afterall.

I'm welcomed into the home, they're very nice people, very down to earth, just the sort I like. We dine and I have a beer, them having wine all round. I'm not sure if I'll be allowed to stay over, the child has to decide that so I can't have more than the one, I might have to drive.

We head back home, I'm told I can stay, the child really likes me. Awesome! We watch some TV, the dog going mad at me, I've told my love the dog won't take long to get used to me, I have an affinity with animals, it takes no time before she's laying next to me, no longer barking. My love is amazed, this has never happened with anyone before, it usually takes weeks.

We head to bed, another night of passion in store. We talk, her resting her head on my chest, me stroking her hair lovingly. She asks me if I really did mean what I said, about loving her. I tell her of course, she asks me to explain how I know this.

I tell her my reasons, how I knew from the moment I laid my eyes upon her that she was the one for me, I have good intuition and knew this was going to happen. I come clean about my other date, how I could have had a night of passion but my heart wasn't there, it was with my love. She sits on top of me know, asking me to tell her again. Tell you what? I love you, well I do—I love you with all my heart. She tells me she loves me too, she doesn't give her love easily but I'm amazing and she's fallen for me! I'm so happy words can't explain it, we make love, sweet tender love. Sleep comes easy after this, me being close to my love, her loving me too. How things are good, nothing could make things any better.

We wake the next day, I cook her and child breakfast, time to leave though, I have plans for the day. We kiss and tell each other our love. I head home, my heart pounding with pleasure, I've found a love, one that loves me to. I get in and email a close friend, explaining how good things are, he replies the following day expressing his happiness for me, I like to keep him updated on my life, we're close friends but live many miles apart, we've never even met in person but he has a good understanding on life and gives me advise to help me on my path.

FIRST BIRTHDAY—THE CHILDS FIRST BIRTHDAY I SHARE

We've been seeing each other lots now, three or four times a week, always passionate nights, we struggle to actually watch any of the programs we have lined up. We engage in role play, me having bought her some kinky outfits, how things are amazing, the connection we have is unbreakable, I'm sure this is the woman I'm going to marry now, nothing is going to stop that.

We go out for a meal the night before the birthday, me staying there, we're alternating between the two places now. We enjoy the night and head home, preparing for the morning. The main present has been had already, a trip away for school. I give my gift, I've done well, it's loved, I get a big hug and kiss and many thanks. I'm pleased, I've provided joy for the child, the gift being something that's wanted.

We go out for the day, treating them to lunch. Bit of a mistake though, they don't take cards, quick visit to the bank solves that—leaving the child there to make sure we return, not that I'd skip paying my bill, I always pay, even if it is the next day as used to happen back in my party years, the dark years.

I'm hardly drinking now, hoping that I'll get invited over, can't do that if I've had a drink. This happens a few times, I'm racing one day to get a message asking "impulsive idea, want to come back here when you're finished?" Silly question, of course I reply. I skip out my usual duties to head there, going through the tolls, it'll save a few minutes, to get to my love quicker.

The dog now is excited to see me, quite unusual for her, she even recognises my car and starts barking for me. I've been smoking though, something I wasn't doing if I was seeing my love that day, she asks me. I tell her I didn't think I'd be seeing her. She explains she was moping and the child suggested it, that I go round to please the Mum. I'm happy, obviously I'm liked. I'm whispering sweet nothings into my loves ear, kissing it softly. We're like love struck teenagers. The child thinks we're talking about them though and heads to the bedroom. Mum goes to fix it, comes out and tells me it's all my fault! Of course it is, it's always my fault I smile, she's smiling too so I know it's all ok. I'm told to behave, stop whispering sweet nothings and kissing her on her neck, I try to oblige but slip up every now and then. I move in my seat and trap the dogs paw. She yelps and snaps, doesn't touch me but it was close. My love asks if I'm ok, sure I say, I've had dogs go for me before, I can handle that, I explain it was my fault anyway. The dog settles again next to me, content with me stroking her.

We're spending almost every night with each other now, all but the one they had reserved for their time together. My love spends the mornings with me, working on my spare desk, I rig her laptop up to a spare monitor I have, this is much easier to work from she explains.

SMALL BREAK—A LITTLE BREAK AWAY, FOR THE BIRTHDAY

We head away for the weekend, I've arranged a hire car, we're going to visit her sister first though, I'd offered since they'd not seen each other for some time. My love didn't want to ask since it was our holiday, not for her to see family. Well why not, it's close to where we're headed anyway so what's the harm, I'd like to meet her anyway.

The flight is full so we can't sit next to each other. Not to worry, it's a short flight. We arrive and quickly get through to the terminal. First things first, food, we're both starving by now. We get some supplies, the liquids and stuff that can't be taken on flights anymore. She rings her sister whilst I go and sort out the hire car, it takes a while but we're done eventually.

We start the drive to her sisters, talking constantly, I'm nervous but she tells me it's fine, just take it as it comes. It's rush hour so it takes us some time. We arrive and we're welcomed, her sister being silly with my love, as siblings do. It's cute I think. I'm introduced to the boyfriend. They both seem really nice. They crack open a bottle of wine and we order pizza, I just have a water, I'm the driver! We have a nice evening, my love pleased to see her sister. It's getting late though so we have to get going, we ring the hotel to ask what time's the latest we can arrive, well ideally already but as soon as we can, the night porter will let us in.

We arrive and we're let in. The hotel is lovely, very old and full of character. We're shown to our room, my love tells me it's beautiful, we put our stuff away and climb into bed, we have an early start, have presents to buy and more supplies. We wake during the early hours, more passion is had, we have to make the most of it, soon she's off limits. There's only us in the hotel but the staff have put on a full breakfast for us, food galore, we chat over breakfast, she tells me she can be stubborn, I challenge her to that and she can't stop talking for more than 5 minutes, laughing as I say so. She accepts the challenge and doesn't talk to me, refuses for a while. I tell her I'm sorry give her a kiss and she laughs, told you she says. We take a walk around the gardens, holding hands, they're nice, it's a lovely day, we're happy.

We go shopping, find a lovely present and get other bits, I drive on the wrong side of the road, forgetting where I am for a moment. She laughs at me. We get back to the hotel and relax with a drink or two. It's not long now, we'd better get ready. I order some food to be sent up, my love relaxes in the bath eating her sandwich, I have a quick shower in the other bathroom. I came back and she's not feeling well, migraine setting in. She doesn't think she can make it. I tell her not to worry, try and sleep it off and see how you feel in a bit. She promises she'll be down in a bit.

I head off, knowing I'll see have to face my ex, alone, where's my new love they'll be thinking. I hit the bar awaiting the others. It's a surprise party so we talk for a while, then get shuffled into rooms to await the birthday girl. She's truly surprised, shocked to see me there having travelled so far. I've not seen them for years now, it's nice to see them. We catch up and carry on at the bar. I'm chatting to new people, making new friends continuing to drink. I'm nervous still about my ex, I see her but don't go and talk with her. My love comes down just over 2 hours into the event. She finds me at the bar but won't risk a drink herself. I continue on the lagers. We go to eat, another buffet so I'm not fussed. We're both talking to friends, some I've not seen since they were little, they can barely remember the times I saw them.

The night continues, dancing commences and my love and I dance, very dirty dancing. I'm quite drunk now so head to bed, my love to follow soon. I'm in bed awaiting my love, she doesn't come so I go looking for her, half naked. She's not impressed with the state I'm in. I apologise in tears, I've ruined what should have been our perfect first little holiday together. She tells me she doesn't know if we can continue. I'm heartbroken. I sleep, awake in the morning remembering the shame, I was nervous though, my love wasn't with me to start and I did what I know, drink to get the courage to face things.

We don't talk much on the way to the airport, nor on the flight. I'm kicking myself, why did I get so drunk, it was foolish of me. I take her home, not even getting a kiss back. I head home, devastated, thinking I've blown everything. I email my close friend, explaining my stupidity but it's also kind of expected of me, I'm the party boy, the life of the party.

He replies quickly telling me I'm stupid, it's time to grow up, stop being the party boy, it just makes me look like the joker. I realise my mistakes, yes it's time to stop it, be responsible for a change. I email my love apologising again. She's calmed down now so tells me it's ok, she was more concerned about me not being fit to drive and missing the flight. Awesome, we're still on, I'll cut the drink out and that'll be that. I've already left most of my party life behind, I don't see my friends any longer, I'm leaving that life, time to grow up.

DISASTER STRIKES—TIME TO MOVE THINGS UP A GEAR

Things are going well, my love comes round, we have a few drinks, watching TV series and enjoying ourselves. I spend some evenings over there, still turning up with a bottle of wine for my love and some lagers for myself, a few won't hurt, besides we always have fun when we've had a drink.

My love is round one morning, working away as was I. She's laughing at the calls I have with my boss and colleagues, we're more mates than anything so the language is always choice. I hear her groan. What's wrong? She's just lost her other main client, having lost the other one just a few days before. She's upset, blaming herself saying how could she think she could run her own business.

I cuddle her, don't she tells me—I'll start crying. It's ok I tell her, you've lasted well over a year, most business if they're going to fail do so within that time, you'll be fine, there's plenty of work out there. She explains she has enough to last a few months so things will be ok, tight but ok. It's now just a month before I need to renew my contract, we go into the living room to talk. I suggest we move in together, we could find somewhere new and make a fresh start, together, forever I'm thinking.

She has to leave but we'll talk later, the child needs to be told of what we're potentially thinking and that's huge, I've already said the child would come first, I know what it's like being from a divorced family and I'm not going to come in their way, child always first. She tells me I'm amazing for this and so understanding.

She messages me later, the child wasn't surprised but ok with the decision. My love comes over to talk about it, to make sure we're doing it for the right reasons. My love tells me we can't be doing it for financial reasons, that would be a mistake. I tell her the money doesn't bother me, it never has, I can just afford it on my own so she can take her time and find the right client for her. I tell her I've been thinking about this for some time anyway, the coincidences I say just tell me it's the right thing to do, besides we spend most nights with each other, what real difference will it make? We're happy, this is the right thing to do, we're amazing together, share the same views on life, perfect together. We'll have been together 4 months by the time it happens anyway, besides if we're going to work, we'll move in eventually right, why not now?

MOVING AGAIN—ANOTHER YEAR, ANOTHER MOVE

It's arranged then, I tell me agent I'll not be continuing another year and begin to pack. My love coming over and helping me, her Dad helping with the big stuff, my mates with some of the other stuff. We get it done in a weekend. I set my computers up ready for work in the office. The child is having a bit of difficulty but give a bit of time and it'll be ok my love tells me.

Things are now perfect, I'm with my love, I remember my vows from before, I'm not going to screw this one up. I finish work on time, cook dinner and spend time with my love, showing her my affections all the time. She's having problems finding work though, it's not a problem I tell her, if needs be there's always a reserve I could possibly call on if things do get too rough. She spends some time looking for work, it's summer though so the child is off from school, they spend a lot of time watching TV, this is nice, they get along really well, have a special bond, it makes me smile to see them together.

We have our routine, I ensure we've always some wine in for my love, or her other favourite tipple and have a few beers on an evening, it's been my routine for years now. I've cut back though, keeping to sensible levels. Things are good, we're out 3 or 4 times a week, enjoying a quiz night, the racing, seeing parents. My loves family is very important to her, having suffered a terrible loss recently. It's all good though, I'm getting on with the child, very lovely, caring person, the parents like me, what more could I want? Nothing, I had it all now, a family, my beautiful, strong intelligent love with me.

All of my pain is now gone, or at least I was kidding myself it was. It was buried deep though, I could keep it there.

We decide it would be nice to eat outside, make the most of the sun, the fresh air. Out we go looking for furniture, she falls in love with a set, it looks expensive though, can we afford it? It's not as bad as we thought, I can stretch to it, it'll eat into almost the last of my reserves but it's ok, my love will find work soon, it won't matter.

We enjoy the summer months, taking it in turn cooking, me trying new dishes, not all work as well as they should but it's never that bad. The months are passing quickly, we've still not had an argument, we "get" each other. The one niggle I have is she sometimes refers to me by her ex's name, I'm half expecting her to call out his name during our passionate moments, she never does. I put this down to habit, she was with him many years so breaking that will take some time, it does, only a few months pass before this stops.

MY LOVES BIRTHDAY—HER BIRTHDAY NEARS

My loves birthday is fast approaching, I've noticed they share some things, so decide to get her own set, special edition, shipping has to wait though, my friend will bring it back but he's having difficulty with work so could be a while. My love understands this—still she can't be with nothing on the day, I can and pay for her hair to be done, she's been wanting to have it done for a while but we're a bit tight so hasn't bothered.

We go to the quiz with her parents, we did this every week. Always a fun night, we don't do particularly well most times but we're not that bad, besides, it gives us bonding time, we're all getting along well. We return and her Dad asks me to stay in the car, he has something he has to ask me. He's wanting to take my love out for her birthday, was that ok with me, we hadn't made other plans, he didn't want to step on my toes. That's awesome I say, was thinking of taking her out but with her family, it'll be even better. I have a question for him though, I ask permission to take his daughters hand in marriage, he's thrilled "yes of course you can, you're the best thing that's happened to her since sliced bread"! I'm thrilled, I plan to ask her on the anniversary of our first date, finding the money for a ring might be a problem but I'll find a way, I always do.

The next day I ask my love when she'd like her other gift, she can have it either today or tomorrow morning, she'll have it now, she's curious. She's thrilled, gives me a kiss and thanks. I'm told the following morning, the day she's having it done, that she's off limits, the child has a friend staying over and last time we were heard and my love was embarrassed—ok no problem but I'm left feeling a bit rejected, some of my pain starts to surface. Later on, I've had too much to drink again and we argue, our first argument. It was horrible. I wake the next day and realise I was being selfish, unreasonable and apologise, my love accepts it, I have to do the same to the child, saying how I'd made a promise to not argue but it's happened, I was stupid and not thinking straight, it won't happen again.

Everything is done, buried, water under the bridge, I vow to cut my drinking down further, things only get our of control when I've had a drink, I can't say my feelings though, so they bottle up, until they explode with alcohol, always venomous and nasty, this isn't me, that's not the person I am. I'll cut right back, just a few cans.

MONEY DRIES UP—THE CASH FINALLY STARTS TO DRY

My love still hasn't had any luck finding work, I'm now paying for everything, I don't mind though, it's only money afterall. My love tells me she doesn't like though, she's always paid her way. I remind her that I said in the beginning I didn't mind, the only thing I want is a few beers, they're cut down now so it doesn't matter. It niggles me that she's finding it hard to take, being supported the way I am doing.

She returns from the gym one night and I've done it again, had to many beers, I'm not going to explode though, this is nothing I can contain this. She senses something is bothering me, I tell her it's nothing, my stupid paranoia is getting the better of me, leave it. She tells me to explain what's wrong otherwise it's only going to bottle up. I ask her not to push, it's really nothing, she persists. I explain how it feels like she's taking the piss a bit, I'm working all day whilst she's spending most of it watching TV and not really seeking work. She doesn't take kindly to this, she's been trying to find work, there's just not much there, we have small argument about it, I apologise and tell her it was me and my stupid paranoia.

The following weeks though my love spends more time than me in the office trying to find work. Success, a nice contract, commission work that pays well, my love is excellent at what she does so I'm confident she'll do well. We go out to celebrate. Things are back on track, soon my love will have her own money and not feel like she's relying on me, we're back on track, nothing can break us. We've had a couple of fights but that's done with now, we're happy, in love.

We're less passionate now—that was to be expected, I was hoping it would have lasted a little longer than 3 months though, still we love each other, I have a family now, it's everything I wanted. We go to the fair with the neighbours children, we're happy, holding hands the whole time watching the children enjoy themselves. This is the life I was looking for, happy times at last, my love has work, we'll be ok soon, just a little longer.

THE MONTHS PASS—LIFE IS GOOD, TIME PASSES

Life continues, we have our routine, my love is working again, time passes quickly, it's not long now until Christmas. We've enjoyed our summer, lots of racing, even the child was enjoying that, something that was a surprise for my love. We've had BBQs with the neighbours, enjoyed ourselves but got a little too drunk, the evening was nice though, me being laughed at for being such the fool. I'd struggled to get up the stairs but managed in the end, had to take a sick day following though, I wasn't used to the hangovers anymore and couldn't cope.

I make sure my family is cared for, sometimes splashing out a bit too much on the shopping, I can't help myself. I treat my love to another hair do, it's time again, negating getting new trainers, they're starting to fall apart—it matters not though, I can wait, I have to ensure my love is taken care of first. I'm drinking a bit more again, thinking it won't do any harm, just a few to aid with the darkness, the insomnia is coming back a bit now, a few beers will cure that.

We spend our evenings watching series on the laptop in bed, something I know to be no good for my sleep but it was time with my love, she enjoyed them, I'll be ok. I'm trying to get back my routine of not using screens again in the evening, no TV or computers 2 hours before bed. I again read, getting back to where I was with my wizarding books. I'm feeling a bit like a 3rd wheel but why should my family have to suffer, it's my problem so I read, giving them some quality time together, to bond. I figure since I've had my two hour break from the screens, a quick show before sleep won't harm. It's not really working though, so I take a sleeping tablet, I'd not used them all from before so remembering the kick start it gave me almost a year ago that it would work again.

I wake the following morning and get to work, my love hasn't woken up yet, so I leave her, she's had migraines recently so thought she could use the sleep. I finally go to wake her, she looks at me puzzled, don't you remember she asks? Remember what? We'd gone to sleep after the series, I'd taken a tablet so knew I'd slept. Turns out I hadn't, I'd done my sleep walking routine again, taken another sleeping tablet and we'd had another argument. I have no recollection of any of it. She tells me the details, I'm disappointed in myself, apologise my heart out and we agree she'll keep control of my pills, since I'm apparently capable of possibly over dosing during my sleep walking episodes.

We visit her parents for a drink one afternoon, they have family around. My love recounts the story of my sleep walking, much to my embarrassment. Still it was amusing in a way, it doesn't bother me, so I explain how I'd done it before so knew I was capable of doing it, not anymore though, we've taken measures to prevent that.

CHRISTMAS APPROACHES—
CHRISTMAS IS LOOMING AHEAD

It's not long now till Christmas time. I've already bought my love a present, used my bonus from work to get a transformer tablet back in October. She'd mentioned in the summer she could really use one so that's what my love had!

I skip a payment to make sure we've enough for Christmas, I go on a shopping spree with the child, we're bonding well now I think, get along well, have a laugh. Spend far too much but we have lots of goodies.

Stocking fillers are bought, we're all set. Christmas tree is bought, everything ready.

It's the last race of the season, my love has a migraine again, so I go alone. My heart's not really in it today, my love isn't there but it won't take long. The racing finishes and I explain I need to get back, tend to my love. I drive as fast as I can to return, to tend for her, make her some green tea if she wants. I return and there's something on TV they're watching, oh it won't be long, you need to shower anyway and then you can do some gaming for a bit. I'm a little hurt now, I've just rushed back to tend to her and I'm told to go away, the program could be recorded and watched later I think, not to worry, it's keeping them happy.

I treat my love to another hair do, as she leaves the power goes out, not to worry, I'll have a little siesta, after having a chat with the child. My love returns and the power still isn't on, we'll go out for something to eat then, we've spend the afternoon doing nothing, so it would make a nice change. We have a nice meal, one of the cheaper places and return home, the power still isn't on but the men are there fixing it. My love says we can go to her parents, I suggest I wait and ring them once the power is back, no we'll all go. We have a nice night, few beers and watch some TV. The power should be back know, so we head home.

The power is back on, would I mind vanishing for a shower or something, they have TV to catch up on. Little annoyed at being told to vanish after spending the day doing nothing, I shower then game for a bit. Feeling a little rejected, this isn't the first time I've been asked to give them space. The TV was becoming a bit of an issue, the amount they recorded out weighed the free time we had together, often I'd be asked to have a lie in, or game, do anything to get out the way so they could catch up. I rarely watch things anyway so I try to ignore it, I get to watch a program I like whilst they get ready for the quiz, only takes me minutes anyway. This is fine, I tell myself, I knew they liked to watch things when I moved in, it's their time together, I'll give them their space, quality time together.

Christmas is coming though, it's not going to bother me, we're going to have a fantastic first Christmas together. The child was saving for something, my love and I had got it already, as a surprise!

We have an event with the race crowd, Christmas party if you like, at the end of the week. My love isn't well though, she's suffering with migraines and a cold. I go to get her some supplies, I return feeling pleased with myself having consulted with the pharmacist on what was best for her. No, I'm wrong, I should have done as my love asked and just got some lemons. Oh well not to worry, at least she's taking the meds. I do all the cooking for the week, making sure my love can rest and get better.

The quiz comes and my love decides she's well enough to go, we have our usual evening, it's always fun, my love has a few drinks, as do I, it's the routine we have. We get home and watch some more of our series before sleep. The following morning my love says she's not well, doesn't think she can come to the party. I'm disappointed it's only really our 3rd social event that we'd gone to, the second as a family, this one the whole family was coming along too. The rest of us all go, I have a few drinks, too many again. I explain to a friend how things are starting to feel like it's not right, I'm always asked to give them space, to catch up on TV, I've been working all the time yet I have no money, this doesn't really bother me, my love will have money soon, that should stop her from feeling like she does, relying on me for everything. I realise it's just adapting to a new life, it's only been 6 months, these things take a while. It feels like my love is oblivious to how this is making me feel though, the pains are coming back, I'm feeling rejected. I'd even been told to get off her one night of passion, being told "You're making love to me, I told you I only fuck".

Still Christmas was coming I wasn't going to ruin that, not our first Christmas, it was just teething difficulties. I'd promised the child would come first so if that meant giving them space, that's what I'd do.

We get back and I have another beer whilst watching one of the few programs I got to watch. Finally I go to bed, quite drunk. My love pretends to be asleep, I mutter "oblivious bitch" as I'm getting into bed, another event where I'd felt let down by her, everyone was expecting her there.

CHRISTMAS COMES—IT'S CHRISTMAS DAY AT LAST

I've done it, we've got to Christmas day and I've kept myself in check, hadn't caused an argument even though there were a few things that were bothering me, only the tiniest of things but they were building up, I've always had problems talking about things that could cause a problem so I bottle them up. Most of them are me being stupid anyway I convince myself, there nothing really, just small issues, I can let them go, not get upset by them.

The child opens the present, it's a dummy one, joy is faked until it's revealed it's a dummy, the proper is under the tree still. Joy is an understatement, never have a seen such of look of excitement and appreciation, big hugs are given.

I suggest my love gets her one from me. She's stunned, she knew I'd spent all my bonus but had no idea what it was. She gives me a big kiss, I ask for my game I know she's got me, there's nothing really I asked for so she had no idea what to get me, I have everything I need anyway, a family, my love. I've another present also, I thank her and give her a big hug.

I prepare breakfast whilst they get ready, ah I've made my mistake again of getting hard boiled eggs, not good for scrambled egg. Still there's just enough to make do. We've some bucks fizz on the go so I finish my glass. We eat then after I get ready go round her parents. A thoroughly enjoyable day, fantastic food and the company was good, we're all getting along well now, me being welcomed into their lives.

I've had a few too many beers by now though, nothing compared to what I used to drink but my love suggests I go sleep it off. I'll have to go home though, I like our bed. I thank them for everything and leave, having to return with a set of keys for my love. I get in and the beer gets the better of me, I finish installing my game and have another one. I can't be bothered to game though so go and watch TV. I pass out, my last thoughts being I won't ruin Christmas, let all those little niggles go, it's fine I get sent to pass some time whilst they watch TV, it's not their fault I can't stand the programs they enjoy.

My love returns 8 hours after I've left. She finds me asleep on the sofa, wakes me and takes me to bed. She puts me to bed and gives me a kiss, telling me she loves me. "I'll be up in a couple of hours" she tells me, "we have some catch up to do".

My monster erupts, I've spent 8 hours away from my love and now she doesn't even want to spend the last of Christmas day with me. I've had enough now, I can't take it, I'm feeling totally rejected, like I'm being used just to pay the bills and keep them in the lifestyle I was providing. I need air. I get dressed, I'm leaving, I need some space. My love returns upstairs and asks me why I'm dressed? "Cause I fucking I" I mutter at her, heading down stairs, how could she be so oblivious to the problems that were there for months. I'd spent the week cooking and looking after her and then get told to "get in that kitchen, I cooked last night" after my love had cooked the previous day. All these tiny little problems suddenly turning into a mountain, I'm screaming at myself to stop this, it's nothing you're just being stupid by my monster wasn't listening, intent on screwing things up.

I storm off and drive to a friends house, they're away but I have keys. I get there and help myself to some beers. They won't mind anyway. I drink myself to sleep, utterly frustrated, angry and annoyed at myself, what the hell had I just done, I've ruined our first Christmas, all through stupid little things that I couldn't talk about and let erupt, my monster finding a way out, bringing all the pains of my past with it.

NOW I'VE DONE IT—I'VE REALLY DONE IT THIS TIME

I wake the next day with a raging hangover, my monster feeding on it. My love rings me expecting an apology, one she most certainly deserved, my monster takes over, I attack on all the little things that were upsetting me.

She had a contract meaning she had the chance to go far abroad and do a presentation, we'd discussed it but hadn't agreed she would definitely be going. We were working before Christmas and I noticed her listed as a speaker, I'd ask her about it was told yes, definitely she's going. A decision like that I thought we'd have talked over and agreed on I tell her.

I know I'm doing damage to hang up, I can't talk to her at the moment, my monster is raging, I have to calm it. I ring a trusted friend, one I've known for years, asking if he has a shoulder to cry on that I can use. I head over, wish them a happy Christmas, apologise for having to be here like this. We enter the office to talk, he tells me not to worry, he's here for me now what's happened.

I recount my pains with him, explaining how it feels, like I'm always been told to make myself scarce, the TV seems to be more important than us, the trip away she decided on without really talking about it, obviously I was thrilled she was doing it, we'd talked and agreed we'd have a family out of it. I was upset though at not being consulted about the final decision. Our entire week was everything she wanted to do, with the exception of the racing but she was a big part of that now too. How I felt she'd let me down at the Christmas party, again after I had to face my ex, alone. My monster calming at releasing this. He tells me it's up to me, if I'm feeling like I'm saying then maybe I'm better out of it. I then tell him about the good times, the BBQs, how we spend a Sunday watching TV, films, just relaxed with each other. Another close friend rings me back, he'd lost his phone and didn't recognise the number. I thank my friend, suggesting that I might just go and collect my things.

I meet my other friend, we go for a beer, I tell him the same stories, how I've left all my other friends behind, didn't have enough money for petrol to visit them when they needed help. I knew I'd not be seeing them anyway, the life they had wasn't what my love would have liked, this was fine with me, I'd cleaned my act up, stopped being the party boy. I then recount the good times, my monster now buried again, the pains are here again but if I have my love back, I can bury them once more, bury them deep beneath the love I have for this woman. I don't ask him to help me move, instead we return and have a few more beers.

I try to sleep, the darkness refusing to come, my mind is now messed up, I love this woman, we can work this through, what have I done, you fool, on Christmas day too. I'm back smoking now, after having quit 7 months ago, it wasn't even an issue but now I'm stressed. I give up on sleep and go have a smoke. My thoughts not making sense to me.

The next day comes, I'm alone, I'd not even picked up my wallet as I stormed out. I have no money, no way of getting any, well I could have asked a friend but I don't like to do that. I decide to write a list of all the problems I have. They really are petty, there's not one thing that's really an issue, there's over two dozen of them though, they've all been building up feeding my monster, the pains I bury.

I hit the whiskey, I need some sleep, the darkness has been lacking recently. I try to sleep, little of it comes.

It's my birthday, I'm watching my messages (the only thing I did bring with me was my laptop) wishing for something from my love. My friend returns from holiday, she offers to take me to get some fresh clothes and toiletries, she speaks with my love and it's arranged. We collect minimal things, I've convinced myself we can make this work, my love and I. Head back and I have a few beers, hoping for the sleep to come, happy birthday me.

FIXING THINGS UP—A VISIT TO FIX THINGS UP

I wake from minimal sleep, I've waking up and reaching for my love, obviously not there and hitting the wall instead. I ring her and ask if we can talk, I've sent her my list of problems. We agree, she's not been at home either since I stormed out, my monster raging.

We meet and have a coffee, we discuss the list. One by one I realise how stupid the problems are, I was being stupid, it was all my fault. She agrees with me on some things, like spending time watching TV when it's our free time, agrees that she'll only do that whilst I'm working, she starts hours before me anyway so this is a good compromise. I tell her I don't mind that much but recently that's all she's been doing, leaving me feeling rejected. I explain I bottle things up and they erupt when I'm drunk, my monster raging out, making things a million times worse than they are.

I agree that I'll try my best to tell her if something is bothering me, not matter how small, we should be able to talk about these things, I trust her explicitly, trust her with my life, had done with the sleeping tablets, to make sure I didn't harm myself.

We talk for over an hour, addressing the issues, we both make compromises to try and make things work between us.

She then moves onto my real demon, my drinking, that which feeds my monster. She tells me I'm ok to have a few drinks when we're out but no more drinking at home, that has to go. If I don't agree to this then there's no moving forward. I tell her this is a big step, sure I can cut the drink out, hell I was drinking just a fraction of what I used to do when we first met, even less than a fraction of that during my dark years. It's an entire life style change I explain. She tells me it's probably best if I return from where I came to think about it—talk it over with my friend there.

I agree, as we leave the bar, paying for our drinks, she reaches out and grasps my hand! My heart leaps for joy, we can do this, I know this has to be done, I should have sorted this out years ago. We arrive at my car, talk a little more and we hug, small kiss and I tell her I think she knows what the answer is. She tells me she hopes so. I tell her I love her and get in my car, decision made. It's not all bad, it's not like I can't have a drink when we're out and if I'm not drinking at home, we'll be able to afford to go out more.

I head back and talk with my friend. It's agreed that I've needed to do this for a long time, 20+ years of almost constant drinking was all that had fuelled my life. I message her "Can I ask for a favour, remove the beer from the house and can I come home tomorrow, sorry that's 2 favours", "Of course, what time are you coming home?" We arrange for just after mid-day. I enjoy one final drink with my friend, not too many though, I can't cope with the hangovers now for a start but also, I don't want to return smelling of drink, my love will know I'll be having one but a start now is better than none, well a start by not drinking myself to the darkness.

The darkness comes, for a short period, I'm too excited, I get to see my love again tomorrow, it's been 5 nights alone now, my heart yearning for, just to know she's next to me.

THE RETURN—I RETURN HOME

I return home, what little things I'd taken with me in a bag. I enter, head in shame. My love comes and gives me a hug and a kiss, I mouth "I'm so sorry" to the child, the words not forming to come out as speech. They're playing a game, this is cool, I enjoy watching them and I'm certainly in no place to make demands, I sit cuddling into my love when it's not her turn to play. I keep on telling her how sorry I am.

My love asks me if it's ok to just stay in for new years, just our family, together. That sounds perfect to me I tell her. The dog is now on the floor, one of my problems being she didn't know her place and had bitten me several times when I'd moved her from my spot on the sofa. This is awesome, we're going to make this work, so long as I don't bottle things up and talk about everything—no matter how small we CAN make this work.

She makes dinner for us, I've not eaten since I left on Christmas day, I manage to force some down, not a lot but enough. We watch a DVD, one I'd just got from my friend, I'd watched it the night before but I didn't care, I wanted to watch it with my love then, I could do so now.

We're all exhausted so have a slightly earlier than normal bed time, I give the child a hug and we head up to bed. We get in and have a cuddle, she tells me it's going to take some time before we can be close again but we'll get there, she has confidence, so long as I stick to my deal. I promise her it's not a problem, hey I've quit smoking again so I can quit the drink. She tells me I smell of smoke still, I apologise, I'd not had anything clean to put on and I'd had a few before coming over, they're gone too though. She tells me if I want, I can continue, to help with cutting the drink out. Don't be silly, you wouldn't have had me to start with as a smoker so I'm not going to carry on.

This isn't a problem "Challenge Accepted" is one of my motos, from a TV series, before I moved in, my love had got me a mug with this phrase on it, how I'd accept this challenge and I would win!

FIRST NEW YEAR—OUR FIRST NEW YEARS

New years comes, we're having a quiet night in, it's been a hard few days, none of us have slept much, we're getting there though, we can make this.

We spend the day relaxing, not doing much, we're exhausted. The evening comes and we spend it watching TV together—our family. It's nice, the TV isn't what I'd select but it's bearable. We;re cuddling, getting close again, all of us enjoying the evening, a nice relaxed evening, just what's needed. I'm asked to open a bottle of champagne—ready for the fast approaching midnight. I'm allowed a glass to toast.

Midnight comes and we all toast and have a drink, fireworks going crazy everywhere. We head up to the roof to enjoy them, they're everywhere, it's quite awesome. Given we're tired we decide to head to bed, we head back downstairs, turn things off and head back to bed, giving the child a hug as was customary.

We're up early, I've almost had a good nights sleep, I've been next to my love, that's all I need, our family back in union. She wakes shortly after me, I've been watching her sleeping, she's so peaceful, so beautiful, I'd been a stupid idiot through the drink, that can go, this woman is everything to me, the drink, although it's been a large part of my life, it can go to hell. She smiles at me and gives me a kiss, passionate like they used to be, "We can play if you want" she whispers sexily in my ear. Awesome—we're almost fixed, we have an awesome passionate morning, even kissing allowed, that had been banned with morning passion a while ago. We finish and I ask her if the morning kissing is allowed again, yes, I still smell of smoke but it's a million times better than the beer, she can cope with it now.

The beer now gone in my mind, my pains and monster buried—we had our love, it's all I needed. Somewhere though my gut is telling me this is the last time we'll do so, having had to use protection since she'd not been well with all the stress. Part of my mind tells me "great, the last time you'll get to make love to this woman and there's a condom involved", well not "make love"—"fuck", I wasn't making that mistake again. I disregard my gut, it's upset still, we've been through a lot.

The child has forgiven me, I know I've a lot to make up but I'm grateful I've another chance. We decide to spend the day cleaning, it's been a while since we did so, we all pitch in, top to bottom. Fresh clean start to the year we tell each other, this is going to be an awesome year, I'm planning to propose in just over a month, still haven't found the money for the ring yet but I will, I've got a month, I have permission from her father, money won't stop me, it never has.

We watch some programs that I'd missed whilst gone, there were a few we all liked. Another early night. Off to bed, no fun tonight though, we're knackered from cleaning.

It's quiz night, I'm unsure if I can face her parents, she tells me it'll be fine, her parents don't carry grudges, just talk with her Dad as we get drinks and it'll be done with. I summon the courage to go, asking what I should drink, thinking it should be coke or fanta lemon. My love tells me it's fine, I can have a couple of beers, just don't go over the top.

I'm dreading them picking us up, I've made a huge mistake, will they hold that against me. We hear a horn, they're here. We head to the car, my love telling me don't worry. I climb in and immediately say "I'm so very sorry for Christmas, I was out of order and made a huge mistake". They ask if I've learned from my lesson, "Of course, I'll not be that stupid again". It's all ok.

We arrive at the quiz and I walk, holding hands with my love, we get the drinks in and do as good as ever, not badly but good enough, there's a few questions I manage to answer that I couldn't recall why I knew the answer, this was a frequent thing I did though, I was usually right too.

We've half an hour to go, at least. I've had my two pints, dare I have another half? I better check I tell myself, I ask my love if I can have another half, "Of course babe, that's no problem". I offer for the parents, they're good. One last half—there's no harm in that, 2 and a half pints over 2 hours, hell I'm only just over the limit to drive.

This is good, I've enjoyed myself and for once not had to have too many drinks. We finish and head home, the child didn't come with us tonight, too busy chatting with friends online. We get back and it's all good, the child has enjoyed her space for an evening, quick chat and off to bed my love and I head. We're both tired, I tell her I understand if she's not wanting to have any passion, I smell of beer and it must remind her of my monster coming out, she tells me no, just tired, night love you.

My love—it ends—The beginning of the demise of my love and I

The phone call—The phone call that started it all

We have a good nights sleep, I've had a few beers so that helps the darkness come, not for long though, just my 6 hours. I watch my love sleeping, so peaceful, beautiful—my heart is content. I try to get another hour, no good. She wakes, I give her a kiss on the forehead, telling her "morning beautiful". I said this to her every morning, always the first words from my mouth each day. She has to work, I'm on holiday still so stay in bed. I've nothing to do just yet, well nothing planned for the day, I might watch some more TV later, I can during the day, my love is busy and the child is busy with her online friends.

I hear my loves phone ringing, bit early for calls, hopefully it's business for her, she has a lot on now but it's never bad to have more clients in the pipeline. I hear her chatting, she sounds happy, flirtatious even. I assume it's her gym friend, they always had a joke around. The chatting continues, this is strange, it's never normally this long, it's almost an hour now.

My gut is screaming at me, something isn't right, I disregard it again, be quiet gut, we've not eaten properly and only just sorting ourselves out, give it some time. It's going to take a while to "dry out", having not really been off the beer for any longer than a month in over 20 years. It's just the reaction, my body not having what it's had constantly for years I tell myself. It'll be ok, just need time to adjust, I have my family back now, all I've ever wanted. My love, this amazing beautiful woman, so strong, knows what she wants, she's kept me in check for most the last year, ok I've made a huge mistake but we'll get through it. I want to get through it and when I want something, I rarely fail.

I hear my love coming up the stairs, odd, she should be going downstairs to the office I think, maybe it's good news, she's meeting her friend later or we've been invited out somewhere? It has to be something for her to come and talk to me again, she has work to do, her clients waiting for her.

The bedroom door opens and she's looking distant, she lies down on the bed, the back of her head resting on my stomach. "That was my ex" she tells me, my gut reaction, "shit this is us over with, she's going back with him", just from those four words. I ask what was up, she tells me; he was suicidal she tells me, asking if I still love him, I couldn't tell him no, that might push him over the edge, he's missing me and can't face his new baby, can't look him in the eye. I can't tell him I don't love him any longer, it's too risky, he sounded like he'd taken something already.

I ask her if she does still love him, I get the reply I fear, knowing she's just avoided answering a direct question with mis-direction "I'll always have feelings for him". Do you want to be back with him I ask? "No, I can't do that, the child wouldn't take him back anyway".

No mention of "us", suddenly I was gone, my gut's now screaming at me—it's all wrong, get out, you should have stuck do your decision you made boxing day—get your stuff and get out now.

I ignore it, my heart telling me this is my love, the one for me, it even now writing this is telling me so, I have my logic now and I'm ignoring my heart.

My love tells me she's late, her client has been waiting for too long now but she had to tell me, to be honest with me, we were afterall sharing everything now, nothing hidden, that was our arrangement.

I meditate for a few minutes, maybe an hour, trying to figure out what had just happened. She's been honest with me I reason, she could have not told me anything about it and said it was her gym friend, no she's wanting me, us to work, our new family. Don't be so silly. I tell my gut to be quiet, it's never been wrong before but it is this time. As I've said I can't lie, apart from to myself, yet again I break my promises to myself, not lying to myself.

I get a call from a very close friend, she's going to look at cars, she needs a new one, do I want to go and have a look at one with her? I tell her I'll let her know.

I get up and get dressed, heading to see my love, her working away, me still having the last of my holidays to use, not working. I ask if she can take a break to come and view the car, knowing the answer I'll be given. I know we'll be at least 2 hours and my love can't afford to take the time off work. No problem I tell her. She tells me it would be good for the child to speak with her ex, he was in a bad way. Well that'll give you the chance I tell her, thinking how awesome she is for being so compassionate, still caring enough to look after someone who broke her heart. It would be good for the child too, have a father figure in life again, he was called Dad by the child so the best thing that could come from it was the child having someone else who was loved back in their life, I understood this, I'd been there before, parents splitting, partners fighting, the pain, it's coming back now.

No I tell it, you're staying locked away, you're not coming back. We're working, patching up the last week or so, it was my mistake and mine to deal with. My pains aren't this battle, you're staying locked away, I'm through with you.

I text my close friend to say ok, let's go to look at this one. We'd previously gone with my love to look at a brand new car, me taking over the last portion of the driving. My friend never has luck with parking and was getting flustered, I'd seen the place as we passed it so decided to take over. As is my usual way, when I need a parking spot, one presents itself. It did again. She's annoyed at this, joking asking how it happens, mind over matter I tell her! We'd looked at the car, with my love, it was nice but a bit pricey, was it worth it?

With that in mind we head off to look at this second hand one, an ex hire, they're always well looked after, mechanically wise and it was considerably cheaper. Another mate is with us, friends to the two of us. The car is nice, we take it for a test drive. It's very similar to one my friend had before, she likes it.

I tell her about the ex ringing, the hour long call my love had just had with him. She asks me how I'm feeling about this. Not so good I respond, my gut's telling me it's the end but I can't face that. We'd joked many months before, after we'd toasted to at least 10 years that she was too old to do this again, me saying I couldn't face another breakup, not after the last one, it nearly killed me, I nearly killed me. There's no chance this is going to ruin us. It's just another little blimp, OK it's going to be hard thanks to my screw up—I shall remain in control though, I'm not going to let my monster take over this one.

AFTER THE PHONE CALL—THINGS ARE ALL A LITTLE UNHINGED.

I return from my car viewing, she's bought it, it's perfect for her, things are good. I head to my love, to tell her about the good news. She's pleased, she didn't think the other new ones were worth it. I ask if we're still going out for a Ruby, we'd had this planned a few days before. My love tells me yes, she has the gym first though, no problem. My love has to finish her day, I'm still not back at work so I go and catch up on some TV, the few programs I have recorded. I watch 127 hours, it's horrific, it breaks me into tears, some of my pain coming back.

I talk with the child, I'm now upset again thinking things are going to go wrong. My love comes up from the office, she's finished for the day, we talk. I tell her my gut's telling me she's leaving, she tells me don't be so stupid, we're a unit, a family. As to the meal, well you and the child decide that, I have to go now.

I talk with the child, in tears, telling her how frightened I am everything we've worked for is going to end. I'm told don't be silly, there's no chance, the ex won't be back in their lives, the child telling me they won't allow it. We decide that we'll not let this get us down, we'll keep our plans and go for our Ruby.

My love returns, I've already showered, shaved, tried my hardest to look my best for her. I've put on something I know she likes—putting my whole into making the best of a bad day. She asks jokingly if we're going out still then, I retort with no but go and shower anyway. She laughs and heads upstairs to get ready.

We've only been this Ruby once before, my memory just about recalling where it was, I hadn't driven, it was for the childs birthday, my loves Dad had driven so I wasn't really paying attention. Still it was somewhere I kind of knew, I could find it, my memory recalling the streets we'd passed, the buildings, the tobacconist, that which I'd not used for months.

I take a few turns, heading up roads that look familiar, it takes me just one correction and I've found it, I'm awesome—my brain can recall anything, it wasn't really even a correction, we couldn't have reached it without going the way I'd taken us. We enter and it's quiet, this is going to be nice, we can forget the events of earlier, our family, enjoying ourselves. I ask my love if she'd mind driving home, I fancy a glass of wine but I can't drink if I'm driving. "No problem baby" she tells me, awesome, we're good on our deal, I'm just having a small drink whilst we're out, I could do with something to dull the pain that's rising, not a lot but just a bit, it's more than I need.

The child is on her new Christmas present, my love takes it, saying it's rude, we're here as a family we should be talking. My love hands it to me and I place it in my coat pocket, the new coat my love had got me for Christmas, it wasn't exactly fitting for winter time but I love it, I'm wearing it, I can cope with the cold. It's from my love, the being, that which I've given my whole to, I can show her how much I love it.

The food comes, we laugh and joke about the waiter, whom had taken a shining to my loves friend a few months prior. The main course comes, we eat, the food is, as always good. My love passes me the rest of her wine, we've only had a glass each but where we are, the measures are always copious, "if I'm driving I can't drink this" she tells me, awesome, I can have a little more I think. We don't want desert, instead electing to drive home, my love doing the driving. First though we have to pay the bill, I ask for it, it comes eventually, they're not busy there but slow, we knew this anyway so not a problem.

As is customary we get a shot for each of us, I drink mine and my loves, she's told me she can't have it since she's driving so I'm welcome to it. Awesome, not a lot to drink but this should help with the darkness, the sleep I've lacked so much of late, my mind's still racing about the earlier events but I put it inside, bury it, beneath my monster. We pay and leave, my love telling me this was a good idea, it's helped out, let's go home and relax.

My love, as always has no idea where the car is, it's only 15m away but still, she's never been good at this, we joke as I direct us, here it is. We have a CD on the go, one of the tunes I'll mention later, maybe not talk about but it was something we both enjoyed. We get home, the child deciding to go and chat with her mates. My love and I decide to watch the second of the DVD set, her not remembering it.

She cuddles close to me, my love, feeling our connection again but my gut is still telling me this is wrong. The gas for the fire runs out, it's going to get cold very quickly. She calls the child, we're off to bed, early yes but we're finishing watching the DVD on the laptop. We have the usual hugs, make sure the dog's done her business and head upstairs, laptop at the ready.

We climb into bed and I place the laptop on my legs, as I always did when we watched things in bed. It's been a tough day, my loves ex, obviously stirring emotions in us both, her feelings for him, my monster being fed a little more. I decide to let it pass, we were strong, my love and I, we could get through this—it was nothing. We watch the last hour of the film, me constantly stroking her back, brushing her hair back, kissing her when I could, just a peck on the forehead or cheek. She's smiling, things are going to be good again, my gut's now relented and doing as I've told it, keeping quiet.

The film finishes, she remembers some of it but not all. We joke about that, how I myself have watched numerous films and never recalled, through my drinking. That which has now gone, I'm determined not to touch it again, well not at home, if I'm out, a few, only a few 3 at most is all I allow myself.

I turn and give her a kiss, one like I did on our first date, to remind her of our passion, that which she'd told me overwhelmed her, our first kiss. I've never thought of myself as a good kisser, with everything in life though, I try my best, it would seem I am.

These last few parts of my book are going to be hard for me to write, I'm again in tears recalling these memories, they have to come out though, I shall do this.

She break off the kiss and tells me good night. I lay there for a few moments, I was hoping we could have some passion, to bond again. I've made her a promise, I'll talk about things, I turn almost in tears, tell her I needed some re-assurance, to make us bond again.

My love tells me she still needs time, I've done damage and she still needs a bit of space. My gut now screaming go, leave she wants her ex back. We'd had passion new years day, this was only 2 nights later, we'd fix it, why didn't she want me? My pains, my fears of rejection come erupting through me, I won't ruin this though, she needs time I tell myself, be patient, you've done harm it needs time to heal.

That was a huge step for me though, I'd faced a problem—without drink, yet got rejected from it, she, my love dismissed it, I can let it lie, the darkness will come, things will be good soon.

The end of the love—It ends, all gone

We wake the next day, we have no plans till later, we're both off work, it's a Saturday. We both have plans, I have to go see a friend about some business, my love going to see her friend, outside of the gym for once.

We have no other plans apart from this, early evening plans, we spend the day together, enjoying our love for each other. We play a game, I get a bit cocky, realise my mistake and apologise, I love to win but I shouldn't be so cocky about it. I'd just cleared a level that she'd not managed to in over 2 years, me being stupid I tell myself. I try to walk her through it—it doesn't happen.

Oh well time to go out, my love gives me a lift to the top of the road, it's not far but she's headed that way, why bother walking? I get a glass of wine whilst awaiting my friend to arrive. He goes to the wrong place, I give him directions and he soon turns up. I get him a coffee, he asks how things are, it's been a while since we've seen each other, the last time him helping me put some fencing up, trying to stop the dog from barking at people walking past.

I explain how the ex has been in contact, my gut's telling me it's over. He tells me to stop being so stupid, it's just my paranoia. I get another glass of wine, continuing to talk, he needs my help so we discuss what I need to do, it's not much, won't take me long to sort this for him, a weekend at most. He has to leave, he's always busy. He reassures me I'm just been stupid, don't worry, he's seen my love and I and sees how happy we are.

I have one more glass of wine, realise I've a packet of smokes left over from Christmas so go and have one, my love did tell me I could if it would help cutting the drink out, I've only had 3 wines anyway, a drop in the ocean for me. I have a smoke and finish my drink, deciding to not have anymore, stick to the agreement and walk home.

The child sees me smoking, asks why. I explain I'm upset, my love will understand—get over it. We sit and talk, my love hasn't returned yet. I'm in tears explaining my fears. My love returns and instantly says I'm drunk. I tell her I'm not, I've only had 3 wines, I'm just terribly upset. She rings my friend to come and collect me, why I think? I'm not going nasty, my monster isn't coming out, I'm just afraid and upset. I recall the afternoon of us playing games, my love discussing things that were mine, what I came with, what was hers, what would happen if we split, she'd leave the racing, that was my hobby.

Why had she discussed this? We'd made up, things were going to be awesome, we'd toasted to the best year yet, my gut again screaming this is all wrong. My friend arrives, they talk for a while as if I'm not there, my rage now starting to build, I won't release it though, I'm strong, in control, well apart from being so upset. I mention about the electric bill, how my love had said we'd go halves, we're now going halves on everything, she's earning again. How was it fair to pay half of that when I've bought 3 other gas bottles, nearly a 3rd of the electric bill. I'd mentioned this before but it just got dismissed. We'll fix that tomorrow. I leave with my friend, my love giving me a kiss and hug, telling me she loves me and see you tomorrow, once you've slept it off.

I head back with my friend, where I'd only just come from. I explain the reasons for me being so upset, getting told I shouldn't have hit the drink, it was only 3 glasses of wine, that's nothing to me, I wasn't drunk, just terribly upset, fearing for the worst. It's ok though, I controlled my monster, kept my pains buried, just the fresh ones causing the upset.

I head to bed, anxious for the next day to arrive, to return to my love, my family. Little sleep comes but enough, soon I'll be back with my love, we can fix this, no matter what I won't drink unless I'm with my love and get her permission.

Dark years return?—The dark years, are they going to return?

Going home—I should go home

My friend asks if I want to go home yet, I suggest it might be prudent to check first, make sure it's still ok. My love is rang, she speaks with me.

She asks me how long I can stay with my friend, she needs some space to repair the damage, what damage? We'd not argued, I was just upset. I explain I can possibly take my last week as an emergency holiday but I can't work from here, my computer's too large and I can't impose on my friend like that. I'm told a week isn't long enough, something about her voice tells me something else is happening. Ok I tell her, I'm booking in to see a therapist, got a meeting arranged with AA, I'm obviously in need of help, I'll do what it takes to make me right for her, just let me come home, I need her there to help me through this.

She rejects my plea for help, she's not invested enough in us and needs this space. Not invested enough? I've literally given this woman everything I possibly could, space when she needed it with child, her gym, kept the house going leaving myself with nothing, I've not even had enough money to put petrol in my car to see mates when they've needed me to help them. I ask how long, she doesn't know, maybe a month, maybe two, she just doesn't know.

My world falls apart, everything I'd ever wanted in life was now gone, at least for a while. I can fix myself though, make it right, this is what I want I'll fix myself for my love, I'll have a few more nights on the beer, I'm heart broken then I'll sort it out. I've an AA meeting arranged, surely that will help, psychiatrist I'm waiting for a return call to arrange an appointment. I know I can't return to the dark years, I'd almost lost my job and if that goes I really am ruined, I'll seek the help I've obviously been needing for years but denying it, me lying to myself that I'm stronger than that, I don't need help, I was the dude, nothing bothered me, well the dude had died many years before.

When I met my love that cemented that death, I wasn't going to lead that life again, no matter how tempting it might be, I'd isolated myself away from any connections that could lead to that return, even though it meant I was missing close friends

Moving yet again—Less than 8 months pass

I ring work the following day and explain I need an emergency week, my stuff is still at my loves. I've kept my boss informed of the progression, for just this event, one I prayed would never arrive. He's not surprised and tells me no problem, is a week long enough? I can move in a week, I just have to find a house, I can't today everywhere is closed, tomorrow though, I'll find one.

I hit the beer again, I'm quitting soon, see what this AA is all about and I'll do this. I text my love, begging for her to take me back, she tells me no, it's better this way—too much needs to change.

There's only me that needs to change and I'm doing that, please I beg, I'll do anything. I'm asked to stop texting.

I head to bed, deeply depressed, I've lost the most amazing woman, my family, all gone over 3 glasses of wine, how stupid was I. The next day arrives, the darkness being brief. I find an apartment, from my old landlord, this is a touch of luck, he knows me, knows I'm a good tenant, least that's one worry that's not a worry.

I arrange my internet connection, it'll be done in a day or two, three most. I just have my laptop, not enough to work from, not that it matters, I have the week off. It's arranged to go and collect some of my things, my love having already put all my stuff in the office ready for collection.

I'm in tears collecting things, getting what I can to keep me going. Just the essentials to start, I've a mate helping me with the big things. To my temporary home I return, my new place doesn't have electric on yet, that's being sorted tomorrow.

I've given my love the dishwasher, she might as well have it, I'm having mine back and it's too much hassle to try and sell, besides my love was used to having one again now, she could have it, I'll have to buy a new one if I move again but that's no problem.

AA—THE AA MEETING

A close friend arrives to take me to an AA meeting, him being an alcoholic himself but sober for many years now. He tells me this is going to be hard, he's sorry he should have helped me but until I realised I have a problem, there was no helping me.

I explain the last 6 months of my life to him, how I've constantly been told to make myself scarce, how the TV has been the prime concern of my love, the ways I've tended to her, running her baths, taking her a glass of champagne to relax with. He tells me I'm probably better off without it, never see a woman who's only just come out of a relationship, give them at least 5 years.

The meeting starts and since it's my first time, the usual plans are cancelled and they instead recount their own stories.

I can't explain much of this, it's AA and there's a code to abide, that which I will. To be brief though I'm left wondering why the hell I'm there, I'm nothing like these people. I don't always have to have a drink, certainly not first thing in the morning, I don't hide my drinking, everyone knows me, that I'm always having a drink after work, always happy, too happy some say, nauseatingly nice one tells me.

Finally one member recounts a story I could connect with, this sounded more like me, maybe I do belong here? The ending though, it's not me, I've never hidden my drinking, not a single person I can connect with, well this was a waste of time then.

I'm grateful for my friends help though, I don't tell him how I didn't feel like I belonged there, not in the slightest. We talk at my friends for a while, having cups of tea, me faking that I'm willing to quit drinking.

The darkness doesn't come—again, I can cope though, I'm used to not sleeping, I'll manage for two or three months then crash out for a weekend, to recover.

NEW HOME AGAIN—I COLLECT MY THINGS

I've arranged with friends to collect my things, it takes the week but it's done in time. I turn up one time and my love is still there, I have to drive away, she doesn't want to see me, I can oblige. Tears roll upon seeing her walking away, from our house, that which is no longer.

Eventually I have all my things, our house now a barren shell, nothing compared to what it used to be. I'm deeply upset that I've had to take things away from my love, I'd left everything behind before, not this time though, I still have debts and can't afford to increase them, I've had to enough already to secure a house, I have no money, I've spent it all on my love, my family, making sure they had everything.

The house comes together nicely, I have my things, it's nice but it's not my home, it lacks my love, my family. My office is too small really but it'll do. I dig out an old router, the one I've been supplied with is faulty, doesn't take me more than a few minutes to fix that. The electric keeps tripping, I need to up the contract, it's not even enough to have my computers, heater and kettle on at the same time, I have to juggle around until they can come and upgrade it.

I've been texting my love still, trying to win her back, all whilst having a drink, it's the only thing I know I cry to her, I need her to help me come through this.

I now have my computer back though, I can send her an email explaining why I'm the way I am. I ask in it what's changed.

My love replies telling me that she just woke up after I'd left and decided enough was enough, she was obviously making me unhappy and she'd had enough of my drama, it was best we just moved on. This didn't fit, we'd left on good terms, her last words, I love you, see you tomorrow.

My head is destroyed, how did this suddenly happen, not a week before we were getting on track, we'd enjoyed a nice meal out and were making progress, OK I had 3 glasses of wine, didn't even touch the sides really, I knew my love was impulsive but this was out of character for her, something else was going on, I had to find out.

THE TRUTH—THE TRUTH IS REVEALED

My love had made the mistake of ringing her ex from my phone, that which I record all calls from. I'd warned her about this, telling her all my calls were recorded and I could listen to them at any time.

I'll leave it though, I lie to myself, I get upset and start to listen to the phone calls, starting with the first one. Her voice was so happy to hear her ex, she was so tender with him. How she used to be with me many months before, not so much recently but I'd messed up, I understood that. He was suicidal, obviously he'd taken something so she had to be kind, at one point telling him he's not doing bad, he has two women that love him. Did I hear that right? I rewind and listen again, yes she was telling him she still loved him.

I listen to the call my love made the morning of my supposed return. It doesn't take her long before she's asking if her ex meant what he said, she needed to hear him say that when we was better though, back on his meds. She's asked if she has a new partner, replying with yes but we're fragile, have been since Christmas. She almost says I'm an alcoholic but cuts herself short. "That has no bearing on me though" she says, explaining she just wants her ex well and if he tells her this when he's better, she'll be there for him. She's found out the one thing that she'd told me meant she couldn't return, that the ex's girlfriend would leave if it meant it would fix him, getting back with my love.

So this is why she needed more than a week, give herself some space in case her ex came back. She had her perfect excuse to get rid of me, I was a drunk, we'd only argued not even half a dozen times in a year, how could she just reject me like this? I'd given her everything, her ex refused to pay for her and she'd gotten in huge debt at his insistence she pays half for everything. He'd kicked her out on boxing day, the child was convinced he was seeing his current partner months before, cheating on my love, that which I could never do. How could she want to go back to that, after I'd supported her and child for the last 7 months without question, I cared not for the money, just their happiness, treating them as often as I could to everything and anything. I do at least have new trainers, finally a present for my birthday. My old ones are literally falling apart now, the sole on one almost completely free.

I listen to the other calls, it's obvious now, "it's always been him, always will be" she states about her ex. She never loved me, I was just a sugar daddy for her, giving me just enough passion to keep me happy, almost, that became less frequent shortly after moving in. I'm raging now, my monster ripping through me, showing it's full strength.

I send her another email, explaining I know what's happened now, she needed her week of space to wait for her ex to come out, waiting for him to tell her he'll take her back, the child having told me she'd not take him back, also, I'd heard wanted him back in their life. I'd never really felt like it was my home, sure I was the happiest I've ever been but something in my gut had told me months before, this wasn't to last. I'd ignored it. The signs had been there I'd just not seen them, well ignored them. The calling me by her ex's name, the rejection whilst "making love" everything.

I'd spoken with the child upset one night, my love was always a bit of a cold fish, the joke used to be it was warmer in the arttic than her. The child assured me my love wasn't always like that, she just needed time to bond

238

with me again, soon she'd be loving in return. She always cuddled me but kept on insisting that me telling her I love her so much would make it less. I cut that out for her, my only condition being that I tell her I love her before sleep. The thought that if something happened to me in the sleep, at least my last words would be that which I love her.

I email my therapist the recordings, trying to make sense of them. How could this happen? I'd done everything I'd promised, I didn't neglect her, my love would say I smothered her, well after my last failure I wasn't going to do that again, I needed to show my affections all the time. I'd gone without to make sure my family was looked after. That was all that mattered to me.

My monster raging I finish the email, it's nasty, how could I send this to my love, my heart is yearning for her yet I'm raging with her, the rejection, all my pains exploding all over me. I'm a wreck but she has to know I know, I'd always told her not to fuck with a geek online and the geek I am, it's all I'm called by friends now. I'd found out the truth.

I send the email, my heart telling me it's a mistake, my monster raging over it telling me I have to.

THE ONSLAUGHT—CONTINUED BARRAGE OF EMAILS

She replies to me saying she's not back with her ex, it was never about him, just me and my drama, what drama was that, a handful of arguments, I'd promised her I wasn't going to drink except with her permission, I keep to my promises, I hate breaking them.

I respond with more abuse, my monster now having fully taken over me. This continues for the week, she's threatened to go to the police if I don't stop. They're emails, she doesn't have to read them, I could ring her if I really wanted to pester her.

I've had enough, I can't take another failure, my love has gone, I'm empty, lost without her, my family, my love. She's told me she did love me but I'd chipped away at it with my dramas, less than 6 arguments. She tells me she no longer loves me, maybe give it a few months and we can see each other as friends. I'm begging her to help me through this, help wean me off the drink, I can't do it without her. I'm denied.

I head to the kitchen, bread knife being in my mind, these things are lethal, I've cut myself many times by accident, this will do the job.

I prepare a text to my therapist, tell him I'm sorry but it's the end. I send it. I then prepare another for my love, this one I will send once the knife has ripped through my wrists. I won't make a mess though, I prepare a few notes, putting them up on my website, for my loved ones to understand why I'm about to do this.

I ring my love, to tell her I'm sorry and goodbye, eventually she answers telling me to stop ringing her. I try to explain what I'm about to do, nothing, she's hung up. No hour consoling me, trying to talk me out of it—no this would make her happy, I'm gone, never to be seen again.

I'm all set, notes are there, they're brief but enough for the reasons to be clear. I head to my bathroom, phone in the hand of the arm I'm about to slice. I climb into the bath and pick up the bread knife. I hack at my wrists, damn it, I've just hit send, she'll ring and have someone come round and try and stop me. I hack furiously at my wrist, nothing is happening though, sure some scratches but it's not working, I try it on my finger, sure enough instantly cuts deep. Why isn't this working on my wrists then? I'm exhausted by now, I've not eaten in over a week, drinking heavily, this just isn't meant to happen.

Great I can't even kill myself properly now I think. I contemplate spending the night sleeping in the bath, hoping the knife will somehow impale me. It's not going to happen, my time hasn't arrived yet. I climb out the bath and into bed, not even bothering to undress.

The darkness comes for just 2 hours, I realise I've still my messages that need to be taken down, too late though, they've been read. Still no-one else can read them, I delete them.

BECOMING MY MONSTER—
MY MONSTER TAKES OVER

I can't cope with this, I've lost what I yearned for most in life, a family, my love, this beautiful, strong, compassionate intelligent woman gone. I see my therapist, I try to control my emotions, a few tears slip through. He tells me it's ok, let it out, no I reply, I'm stronger than this. As I've said, I can only lie to myself.

I've done so much damage by now, telling everyone things I shouldn't have, I know no better though, my Dad was always open with me about everything, when I'm hurting I just talk, talk I do—about everything. I've screwed this one up royally.

My love now won't respond to me, instead communicating through a friend, my very close friend. I decide enough is enough, I lost 4 years before to depression after my previous relationship failed, I wasn't going to do it again.

Calmness sets in, for the first time I relax and watch some TV, well I'd watched a few films but couldn't remember what, not through the drink but because my mind was consumed with my love. I've put her out my mind now, I'm going to move on, I've been vile to her, I'll apologise for that in a week or so, she needs some space from me, maybe a few months before I explain my actions, give my apologies. I know she'll accept, she's awesome, she has the compassion to forgive me. I wish we could be again but know that's never going to happen, she's seen my monster and it's hideous. I don't blame her, at least she doesn't hate me, she pities me for my pain, my monster.

I have the laptop next to me, it barks, I have a look. It's a friend of the childs, asking to be a contact. I ask her why, she enquires who I am. I tell her, "oooh it's you—fuck off bye then" she torts at me. I'm shocked, how could such a young child give me so much hate. I tell her to delete me and goodbye, you'll never see me again at your request.

I continue watching my film, having a few beers, my head's raging again, how could I be hated so badly, what have I done so wrong? I get hold of her on a popular website. I relentlessly try to find out what I've done so wrong, answers aren't coming, they're too good friends for this child to tell me. I hound her, my monster raging now, fuelled through drink. I've already asked the father why I've been added, he's not responded yet.

I send the recording, the one with my love saying she'll go back to her ex, asking if that's what was happening here. If this child can tell me no then I'll leave it, my boy in my needing assurance from someone the same age. I'm told that's not what was happening. Leave it now I tell myself, a child can see this, why can't I? I've been stupid.

I head to bed, darkness comes for just 4 hours.

I awake, realise I've made a huge mistake talking to this child, I didn't say anything out of line but still, I had to remove myself from this life. I message the father—apologising profusely, explaining I can't understand the hate I was getting from the child. He tells me there's nothing to worry about, I wish him a good life and delete him.

I delete everything I can think of, phone numbers, emails, face book posts, friends, everything that had any relation in the slightest to my love. I turn my phone off, I'm going into solitude, to find myself again. The only thing I retain is half a dozen photos of my love and I, she'd sent me them at my request, to remember the happy days we had, that would be enough for me to get through this.

I bury myself in work, re-vamping a few friends projects I'd done for them years before, they needed a bit of TLC anyway. I'm forgetting about everything now, all just a memory, only the good times but just a memory now.

The last message I'd sent was to the racing guy, I'd heard they didn't trust me anymore, I wanted to know why, he'd not responded in time so now I'd leave it all. Make myself a new life, hey I've done it 5 times before, I can do this again. I'll leave that life and start again, learn from these mistakes and not make them again.

Prison—What, I face prison?

I eventually turn my phone back on, I've had a week of solitude. This should be enough, I'm calm once more, back to me. I've told my therapist things are working out, I'm over my love, moving on.

I've lots of missed calls, word has got around now and all my old friends, those that I'd not seen for years were trying to get in touch with me. I ring the racing guy back, he explains it was never a case of not trusting me, they just needed all the details I held to do it themselves, he knows what I'm going through and only wants to help by taking pressure off me, getting others to do what I usually do.

My monster rages again, how did my love lie again, telling my close friend they didn't want me anymore, didn't trust me.

I fire up an email, I ask my love to do the right thing, step back from what was my hobby, leave me to it, if she won't step back gracefully I only have to ask and she's gone anyway. I wish her the best for her life, apologise for my behaviours of late, how it wasn't me, I was raging, my monster taking control over me. I don't have regrets in life but this is a regret I'll have to live with, I should have sorted my problems sooner, before meeting my love.

I finish with more kindness, wishing everything goes well for her, the child and business. Tell her she'll never see me again, I'll not email her again, text, ring nada, I promise I'll keep well clear of anywhere I know she frequents, goodbye my love, I'm gone.

I think that's the last of it, I've made it clear I'm not going to do anything else, keep clear—let her enjoy her life again, wishing she'll find someone to care and love for her as I do.

The Tuesday I get a phone call, it's from the police station, there's been allegations made and I need to go see them. I arrange a time, it's difficult though, my work can't suffer, the police seem accommodating though, I can't be in that much trouble? Can I?

POLICE—THE POLICE INTERVIEW

I've hit panic mode, taken an emergency day off work, I have to arrange things, I ring a lawyer, it's not his area so he gives me a friends number, he's a specialist in this area. I ring and see if he's free for the evening, the appointment time. He enquires as to what I've done, I explain I've sent some quite nasty emails, not my character but I've been hurting. He tells me it's almost certain I'm going to be locked up, if I've so much as called her "a fucking bitch" that's enough for a domestic violence charge.

I speak with another friend, he'd been locked up wrongly before, association is also enough to get you locked up here. I ask if I can have his lawyers number, he'd previously told me to just leave things, he's not surprised I didn't though, I have difficulty dropping things I care for, love with my whole being. It's not good, he's not in the area anymore, there is another one though, he gives me the address.

I go straight there, asking if they speak English, yes, this is good. I briefly explain the situation, I'm told he'll come with me, we arrange a meeting place. I can't remember where I need to go, my head's in tatters.

I've arranged for a translator, close friend again, I've been told it's almost certain I'm going to be locked up, by several sources. My friend takes me there, if I'm locked up at least they can have my car rather than it being stranded there I say. I'm petrified, I've not slept now for weeks, I know I can do stupid things when I'm in this state but I can't break it, break the endless staring the the ceiling.

We drive to the station, I'm shaking, I can't do prison, I'm not a criminal, I've only tried to do my best to be rejected, ok I've sent some nasty emails, they could have been deleted though, my love would know they'd not be nice but she'd read them all. My lawyer isn't at the meeting place, we have to go without him, this can't be good.

We arrive, my translator there to greet us, we head inside. I'm taken to the interview room and immediately break down in tears. The officer tells me it's ok, I'm not in trouble just have to answer a few questions. I reply with it's not that why I'm upset, I'm upset because I've driven my love to this, to get a restraining against me, all I wanted was to do the best for her, to love her and care for her.

The police have all the emails I've sent, I'm defending my actions. Thankfully my lawyer arrives, he has a quick talk, reads over the report and tells me it's not that bad. He'd found where I was even though I could only vaguely remember the town it was in, he was concerned since the time of the interview usually meant I'd be retained for the evening and have to face court the following morning.

I'm honest with the policeman, I can't lie, I explain how I was hurting, I've a problem with drink and I've acted stupid when I'm drunk. I'm working on this with my therapist, I'm getting some meds tomorrow I hope to help with the depression. I'm in tears the whole way through, my monster being spoken back to me, I'm hideous, this isn't me, I'm the loving caring drunk, I never do this. Well I have done and now I'm facing the consequences, I've pushed the one love of my life to take serious action against me.

I explain why I've gone to therapy, I've deleted all the emails, every bit of contact I have with my love, neglecting to mention the fact that my brain can't forget numbers, I still remember friends numbers from over 28 years ago. My loves number will remain in my memory, there's nothing I can do to stop that. I tell him about all I've done since leaving, giving her a dishwasher, I've transferred over £1000 to her to help her out, make sure my love and child don't struggle. I know I've been horrible and I'm deeply sorry, I've hurt my one love and family so very badly.

90 minutes later we're done. They talk, I can't understand. We leave the police station and my lawyer explains. He says it's obvious I'm a hopeless romantic, I just wanted my love back, there's nothing in the emails that suggest I'd be violent, I've never fought in my life, the worse that can happen is a restraining order and fine, most likely though nothing will come of it, my love had tried to pull out half way through but once you start, you have to continue or be charged for wasting police time.

I'm relieved, we head home after I've thanked everyone involved, I had quite a little task force with me. I'm taken home, asked if I'm coming up with my friend, no I need to go get some food, I've not eaten for over a month now, well the odd bit but nothing substantial. I can't eat, I never can when I'm hurting. I head to the shop and get myself a loaf of bread and half a dozen small beers, I can at least enjoy a small celebration, I've not been locked up at least!

THE AFTERMATH—WHAT HAPPENS NEXT

I write this now, still not knowing if there's going to be any further action taken against me. I've just had an email from my lawyer asking if I've heard from the courts. Nothing. My love has indirectly told me that if I leave her alone, she'll not continue, she doesn't want to cause me any more pain. She didn't want to do it but had to do something to get me to leave her alone.

I leave it for a while, I throw myself back into work, everyone telling me it's going to be OK, we're better off the way we are, things weren't good for a while. Well of course they'd think that, I only paint the bad side, I never painted how good things were with us. I'm still yearning for my love deeply, she was my world for almost a year. Pathetic I'm told by friends, it wasn't even a year. Well I gave it my whole, I don't do things by halves and she had it all, everything I could think she wanted or needed I tried my hardest to give her.

I continue to see my therapist, I've had to lock my father out my life, him having shown me the way I thought life should be lead. He of course thinks he's done nothing wrong, how can I still talk to my Mum but not him. Well he's respecting that at least and has vowed not to contact me until I'm ready.

I felt myself coming to a crash last week, so booked this week as a holiday, I can't screw up with my work, not again. I saw my therapist last Thursday, it's now the following Friday. I told him I was going to write this, my life. I've already sorted out a publishing deal, if I decide to continue.

So what have I learned? I love to learn and it's about time to conclude my life so far.

Conclusion—The conclusion

My life—The conclusion

Dark years—will they return?

So here I am, deeply depressed, on various drugs, including my old friend Valium, that which I was on at just 13, to try and aid me yet still doing the one thing I've realised destroyed me.

Drinking.

I've had to continue this though for these thoughts to be aired, many of them only return once I'm in the "steady state" that I've been in for 27 years. Keeping in control, remembering all I have, just enough Dutch courage in me to release the fears I've had about writing this, showing the world how truly nasty I've acted towards my love, not my intentions but my fears and my drink ripping me apart.

I'm now writing this after "The goodlife", conclusions in my mind. It has to be written now so I can continue.

Even after all the hatred I showed my most recent love, I'm still deeply in love with her. The family we had. That which I yearned for many years to have—I had, yet I destroyed it. I showed the child all that was bad about me, what made me bad, the life of constant drinking.

I've titled this book, The hopeless romantic, the life. It should really be called the Hopeless drunk, substance abuser, how he ruined himself. I am a hopeless romantic when not drunk, however it's clear that this a rarity, one that I just started to enjoy. It was too late though, the damage had already been caused, my monster coming out too often—only a few times but enough for her to realise it would take too much to fix me, she'd tried but the damage is too deep in me.

The problems that lead to our separating were created by me, I'm sure in my heart that we would have survived the ordeal with the ex. If only I had realised the mess that is me before and stopped the drinking. I immediately turned to this at the first sign of trouble, my only way of coping, it's all I've done for the last 24 years really.

My life hasn't been enjoyable, well it seems like it at the time but it's just one drunken blur, fuelled constantly by alcohol. I curb it for a while but then think why should I? I earn well, I have a good job that I'm pretty awesome at, what's the harm in me having a drink?

It starts with just a few but soon cascades. I think one more won't harm, something I learned from my father. The one person who I looked up to, he wasn't able to fulfil what I was looking for though, I never told him. He tried in his way and I love him dearly for everything he's done for me, this is my responsibility to find myself, I thought I had just over one year ago, things were under control, I then saw everything the way I wanted, to find my life back, the party life, that which almost ruined me. I took any small sign of drink, that it was ok to carry on, slowly building back up to levels that weren't good. Sure enjoy one or two, not the 12, 24 sometimes more than I know I'm capable of consuming.

Through my hurting, I hurt the one family that I could have called my own, complete with child, hurting that got amplified by the drink, turning into rage and anger, all the pains of my past mixing up, uncontrollably. I should have seen someone years ago, to work out a way to release this hurt, I'm too strong though I told myself, I'll get over this, pushing the control further.

Control which I seek but always push to the limits, driving, always on the speed limit, even when conditions say I shouldn't, I push the control further and further, seeing how far I can go. I do this with my drinking, pushing if I can manage just one more and keep that monster within me contained, I know I can, just one more. I failed miserably with the one person trying so hard to make me realise this.

I resented that, she was taking away my happiness, all my life the only good times I've had, a drink involved, seeing this from an early age, it seeded itself. Each time she was trying to protect herself from me but also me from myself, a bit more resentment grew.

You'll see this is quite a turn around from my earlier descriptions of events, well I've not written them yet, I know what they will contain though, I almost realised this in one of the emails I sent my love, only to screw my mind back up again.

"Dark years", they've not been written yet, dark years it seem return. The first time it took me almost 5 years to get over 10 years of relation, well almost 10.

I know I can stop the drinking if I want to—the question is do I want to? I can do anything when I want to, I quit smoking, stopped drinking for several largish periods of my life, large being anything more than a week! The happiness I always thought, was with the drink.

I have problems sleeping—yet for a very short period in my life, with my love, I was sleeping soundly, without drink, ok only 6 hours but that's all I need to function on. I was happy and content, just my vision clouded with my life, the party life, not being able to push myself to my limits. I couldn't sit back and be content, I had to push, push and push, to breaking point, not for me but for my love, she wasn't prepared to take it. I don't blame her, I couldn't see the happiness that was in clear sight. I use the drink to null the pain, leading to my monster coming out, lack of sleep, not eating, it's all returning.

So the question is, will I stop the drinking? Only I can answer that one and I have no idea at the moment, I need to finish my book first, then I most certainly will. I tried before for my love, it should have been for me, I can't lie to anyone except myself. I was lying it was for me but it wasn't, leading to my resentment building up, feeding the monster that I've buried deep inside me, until I'd fed him enough to come raging out and destroy something most beautiful. All because I couldn't face not being in control, not accepting I've been needing help for 22 years, I was stronger than that afterall.

Well no I wasn't. I've destroyed the most beautiful thing I ever had in my life, the most beautiful woman who I could have wished for, showing me her love in return, giving me a family.

Can I fend off another series of Dark Years? I don't know—I hate myself for what I've done. I know I won't get away with it at work again, we're too big to allow for that, so what must I do?

I need to free my fears, my pains, release them from myself, dig them all deep from where I've put them, face them and let them be free.

These are now my additional thoughts after completing this book . . .

I've spent the past week of my life doing nothing but writing this, it averages 30 words a minute if I've been working on it for 10 hours a day, there's no way I've been able to dedicate that much time to it, I am a geek though so I've reached the end in good time. I've done it within my weeks holiday, it had to be done.

I have my first race of the year tomorrow, it's going to be hard, my love was involved with that from the start almost, everyone will be expecting her by my side, this I know will never happen again.

I've not eaten for the past 3 months, I've only in the past two nights managed to get a decent nights sleep, too much, I can't cope with too much sleep, I'm better being deprived. My friends tell me what was the problem with my love, they all know I enjoy a drink, I'm always the foolish, happy loving drunk, what was the problem. Well the problem was me, I can't talk about problems, I can't face them, my fears come rushing back so I bury them, only for the drink to mix them all up to explode and I turn mole hills into mountains. My love knew I liked a drink but tried to help me come off it. I tried only to fail at the first sight of a problem. I didn't let my monster out until I'd hurt my love to no end, there's nothing I can ever do to repair the damage I've caused to her and my family. She was trying so very hard to help me become "normal". I've never had a normal life, it scared me. I resented her for the help she was trying to give me. My friends tell me I'm funny when drunk, yes but I don't spend my life living with them, the little things don't become a problem, only little things but they build, my love couldn't take my bullshit, it truly was bullshit, nothing that was a problem was a problem, mostly my paranoia fed by the drink, made them problems.

I've spent my nights and days listening to music that reminds me of her, crying myself to sleep, that which I've had so little of.

I pushed myself too far one night, I sent my love a text message, a link to my book, expressing how very, very sorry I was, I knew this could end up with my getting arrested, I had to see though if there was anything there with us, if she would press charges against me giving my final apology. Thankfully she didn't, she's relayed instead that it's very much not wanted, the seriousness of the position I'm in.

I know this, I miss her so very much though, even after everything, I'd take her back in a heart beat. To have my family back, this I know will never happen. It's not my place to have her back, it's hers to take me back, after all the harm I've done, she'd be a fool to do so, I know I've destroyed everything we had, all through my drinking and burying my past rather than facing it, dealing with it.

I ran out of my anti-depressants the day I saw the other doctor, not a problem, I could get more, well the chemist thought that one was a fake, instead giving me a full pack of Valium, a note on that prescription that I'm only allowed 10 at a time, I'm a suicide risk. They give me 40.

They've been sat next to me whilst I've been typing this, I know all of those is enough to finish me, for good. I took what was prescribed for the first two days, I've not touched them since.

I've not cried myself to sleep for the last two nights, I've shed a few tears recounting my love and the rejection I felt from her but no longer am I a total wreck. I've aired my demons, I know my problems.

Even if I publish this book I could end up in more trouble, if work figures out it's me, there's a good chance I'll be fired for my past life. I've always put work first though, never have I done anything but focus on my work, they own me for the time I'm paid for so that's the most important thing for me.

So what must I do, well the drink has to go, my love I have to let go, I've done untold damage to her, I really didn't mean to, my monster was fed though, my pains, my fears, now they're finally released, I can share my story with the world.

My life has been pretty good, as a child I had everything, so why all the pain? Well key points in my life, as you've read, events happened, events that my mind wasn't able to cope with. It's not been able to cope with those until now. I've released that pain now. To the world. It could be my demise to do so but I have to do this, I think.

All my friends tell me I need to leave my love and get on with it, my boss saying he'll get a flight to come and beat me round the head with a spiked bat, to knock some sense into me. Several others have told me they'll slap the shit out of me if I go near her again, I won't, I've done her enough damage and that pains me deeply. That pain is now the only pain I have but I've realised it was all my doing, well not entirely but my actions caused her reactions which fed my monster, I joked with her one night that it was a positive feedback loop, well it was. My love trying to help me but me not seeing it, fed into that loop of resentment. Then I destroyed it, utterly and thoroughly—I don't do things by halves!

So the love of my life is gone, where do I go from here? Well I'm not taking the pills, I've never done "drugs" in my life really, I smoked the weed, that's a plant, alcohol forms naturally in fruits, I keep to the natural things. I've realised my life has been a joke, the only time it wasn't, was with my love—her trying so hard to make me see this. I couldn't though, I had to lose it all, write this. I mentioned how she threw me off her one night, her telling me "I don't make love, I fuck", well we had made love many times before, when I was sober, why would she when I was "drunk"? Well not drunk, I'd cut back but I'd still had a beer, I always had a beer, how did that make her feel she asks me? Well looking back—I've acted hideously towards her, not intentionally, just living the life I've always known. I try not to be selfish but I was, incredibly so.

I gave her no consideration for going to have some passion without me having a drink in me, that was all I knew, have a drink, passion and sleep, how must that have felt for my love, me always having a beer inside me? I know exactly how that felt, she'd rejected me one night and it must have felt like for her almost every night, I only wanted her with a drink inside me. My shame is too great to put words to. To me though, I wanted her always, constantly, the drink, well that was just my routine, the more I had, the more I wanted her, not that it could really get much more wanting than the moment I awoke and laid my eyes over her sleeping, so peacefully, so beautiful, she never needed make-up, she's stunning just as she is!

I've had to speak with my previous ex, my first real love, get her approval, out of courtesy that she won't mind me publishing this, she's given me her full consent and is happy for me to do so, we never had hate, just we weren't right and our paths weren't right.

My love though, she's now lost from me, the damage has been done, all because I wanted my "party life", why wouldn't I? I'm always the happy one there, messing around, joking around, being the jester and making others laugh, it's the only way I've known for so many years, if I'm really honest, 27 of my 34 so far.

At last I feel content, happiness with myself, airing my issues to the world. My publishing deal is secure—if I decide to go ahead. I have just one thing to deal with now, my actions towards my love, how could I harm her the way I have, hurt her and our family so badly. Well that was me not seeing my life for the joke it was, how it needed to change, that which she was trying so hard to make me see.

There's a song "A fool for love" that's all I am, a fool for love. I desire so much to be loved, that which I was but I couldn't see my faults, face my fears, put my demons to rest. Not to bury them but face them and let them free.

I miss my lost ones deeply, this pain I've buried with drink for so many years. In writing this I've said my final good byes to them, tears flow now but out of relief, they know they're loved, always and I will never forget them, cherish my memories.

My love though, if I could turn back time, I'd have fixed myself years before meeting her, it's too late now though, I just hope one day she can forgive me, understand the reasons why I'm so thoroughly messed up, well was messed up. I've freed myself now, let my demons go, the only thing remaining is my hurt I've caused my love.

This I shall carry for a while, to remind myself of the actions I now need to take, to sort myself out at last, to not harm anyone else the way I've hurt my love.

So, shall I publish this? If you're reading this then that answer is obvious.

My thanks for your time, this is all I have, time to sort myself and my life out, for me.

FINAL NOTE—CLOSING THOUGHTS

Throughout my life music has always played a big part it in, I love house music, the lyrics are always so loving and caring, it's all I've tried to do in my life: give my love.

Well I've failed with that again. Here's a list of some of the music I've heard whilst writing this, the lyrics to most of these have some meaning with regards to my love and I, some the roles should be reversed, the guy for the woman and vice versa, others, it's just what I'm prepared to do for my love. That which I ruined.

A Great Big World & Christina Aguilera - Say Something
Adele - Set Fire To The Rain
American Authors - Best Day Of My Life
Angel Haze - Battle Cry (feat. Sia)
Avicii - Addicted To You

Avicii - Hey Brother
Bastille - Flaws
> My love always said I wore my heart on my sleeve, that and my flaws, just I hid so many of them
Bombay Bicycle Club - Luna
Calvin Harris - Summer
Calvin Harris & Alesso - Under Control (feat. Hurts)
Childish Gambino - I.Crawl
Christina Perri - Human
Chvrches - Recover
Clean Bandit - Rather Be (feat. Jess Glynne)
Coldplay - Magic
Disclosure - F For You (feat. Mary J Blige)
Disclosure - Latch (feat. Sam Smith)
Duke Dumont - I Got U (feat. Jax Jones)
DVBBS & Borgeous - Tsunami (Jump) (feat. Tinie Tempah)
Ellie Goulding - Goodness Gracious
Example - Kids Again
Faul & Wad Ad - Changes
Foxes - Let Go For Tonight
Frankie Knuckles - Your Love
> The god father of house music, RIP 1955-01-18 2014-03-31, this is an awesome song that always fills me up, "I need your love" is all I ever want!
Gorgon City - Ready For Your Love (feat. MNEK)
HAIM - If I Could Change Your Mind
Half Moon Run - Full Circle
Imagine Dragons - Demons
Jakwob - Somebody New (feat. Tiffani Juno)
John Martin - Anywhere For You
Katy B - Crying For No Reason
Katy Perry - Dark Horse
Kiesza - Hideaway
Klaxons - There Is No Other Time
London Grammar - Hey Now
Martin Garrix & Jay Hardway - Wizard
Naughty Boy - La La La
> The child looked this one up, explained the reasons for it, it was awesome!

OneRepublic - Counting Stars
Pitbull - Timber (feat. Ke$ha)
Route 94 - My Love (feat. Jess Glynne)
Rudimental - Waiting All Night (feat. Ella Eyre)
Sam Smith - Money On My Mind
Sigma - Nobody To Love
Taylor Swift - I Knew You Were Trouble
The Neighbourhood - Sweater Weather
Tiësto - Red Lights
Tove Lo - Habits
> How can I do another day alone, it kills me without my love, miss her with my whole.

Tove Lo - Stay High (Habits Remix) (feat. Hippie Sab . . .
Trey Songz - Na Na
Zedd - Stay The Night (feat. Hayley Williams)